AFRO-PERUVIAN *MESTIZOS*

AFRO-PERUVIAN *MESTIZOS*

THE INVISIBILITY OF BLACKNESS IN POST-ABOLITION PERU

DANIEL S. COZART

THE UNIVERSITY OF ALABAMA PRESS
Tuscaloosa

The University of Alabama Press
Tuscaloosa, Alabama 35487–0380
uapress.ua.edu

A portion of chapter 4 originally appeared in *Latin American and Caribbean Ethnic Studies.*

Typeface: Arno Pro

Cover image: *Cuadrilla de negros festejando el 28 de Julio de 1821,* by Pancho Fiero
Cover design: Sandy Turner Jr.

Cataloging-in-Publication data is available from the Library of Congress.
ISBN: 978-0-8173-2248-9 (cloth)
ISBN: 978-0-8173-6220-1 (paper)
E-ISBN: 978-0-8173-9576-6

To my family

Contents

Preface

Historic Invisibility and Contemporary Afro-Peruvian Activism

During my first research trip to Peru in 2013, I had the honor of presenting early stages of this work at the Pontificia Universidad Católica del Perú (PUCP) in Lima alongside Afro-Peruvian poet and musician Octavio Santa Cruz. After our presentations, Santa Cruz emphasized that Afro-Peruvian culture was distinct from *criollo* (Creole) culture. I had referenced the phrase "Criollo Nostalgia" used by ethnomusicologist Heidi Carolyn Feldman to refer to how white culture bearers in Lima enacted "a selective type of remembering" through *música criolla* (Creole music) in the 1950s. Santa Cruz took the time to make sure I noted that Afro-Peruvians did not intend to express "nostalgia" through the performance of music and dance, much of which expresses collective memories of abuse by and exclusion from white-dominated *criollo* culture in Lima.[1]

In June 2015, I met the director of the Afro-Peruvian Museum of Yapatera, Abelardo Alzamora. Alzamora has worked with activist organizations since the 1980s to demand social services from the state to improve his community's living conditions, and he had recently begun an educational reform program to promote positive images of blackness and better knowledge of Afro-Peruvian history. I asked him for more information on the town's history, and if yapateranos ever identified as *criollo* or with *criollo* culture. His response was revealing: "Thirty years ago," he said, the town "didn't know its own ethnicity, [nor] the history of Afro-Peruvian contributions to the history of the country." Asked whether he ever identified as *criollo*, Alzamora responded, "No. Before there was an affirmation we identified as *mestizo*. But we've since learned to identify as Afro." He went on to explain that Afro-Peruvian poetry had always been a source of pride prior to the arrival of activists, yet nobody wanted to call themselves "Black" due the "negative associations" of the term before the 1980s.

The complexities and contradictions of the term *criollo* and its oversimplified translation to English-language scholarship as Creole struck me as uniquely important to the African-descended population of Peru, prompting my extended analysis of the etymology of the term and its fluid meanings from the colonial period through the twentieth century in chapter 5 of this book. My conversations with Alzamora and Santa Cruz also heightened my awareness of my subject position. As a white man from the United States, producing historical knowledge of a marginalized population in South America must be done with great care. Of course, it is the historian's duty to imagine and analyze contexts far from their own, but self-reflection seems especially necessary in a work that dialogues with anthropologists as much as historians.

I was drawn to the topic of Afro-Peruvian history my first week as a graduate student, when I was assigned *The Autobiography of María Elena Moyano: The Life and Death of a Peruvian Activist*. The tragic account during Peru's Dirty War (1980–2000) noted her Afro-Peruvian identity—an identity that seemed novel and underrepresented in an Andean nation typically framed as predominantly indigenous with a white elite population in coastal cities. I quickly noticed a dearth of literature on the topic of Afro-Peruvian history, in contrast to an abundance of antiracist activist writing easily accessible online. The history of Afro-Peruvian activism since the 1950s has increased the visibility of this population, and various organizations have emphasized the importance of recognizing the historical contributions of African-descended Peruvians as a central component of fighting racial discrimination and exclusion in the present. This book's analysis of the historical process of Afro-Peruvian invisibility therefore serves larger objectives consistent with those of today's Afro-Peruvian activists.

Afro-Peruvian activists began organizing to fight racism in the same era of the Afro-Peruvian "rediscovery" of the 1950s. The first such organization, named after the leader of an eighteenth-century slave revolt, was the Movimiento Negro Francisco Congo ("Francisco Congo Black Movement," MNFC). It was formed in the 1950s to promote Afro-Peruvian solidarity and collective interests. This organization recognized that "it was necessary for the Afro-Peruvian community to become conscious about their condition in order to become agents of their own liberation."[2] In a further effort to promote inclusion, The MNFC reorganized in the 1980s to become the MNAFC, adding Afro-Peruvian to its name. The objectives of the movement became more specific: to gain "respect for the human rights and the vindication of the identity of our Afro-descendent peoples." Several MNAFC activists also left to establish other organizations to promote Afro-Peruvian interests, such as the LUNDÚ Center for Afro-Peruvian Studies and Empowerment, which challenges homogenizing historic discourses that deny racism and racial difference in Peru in favor of a singular nationalist cohesiveness.[3]

Other activists involved with the MNAFC went on to establish the Centro de Desarrollo Étnico (Center of Ethnic Development, CEDET) in 1999, which has joined political activism with scholarship on Afro-Peruvian history. This organization became the leading publisher on the topic and prompted greater recognition of Afro-Peruvians in Congressional publications and in national politics. Their works of anthropology and history guided my research agenda and exposed areas in need of further investigation. The CEDET demonstrates how historical research on Afro-Peruvians contributes to a greater recognition of this population's contributions to the nation and thus, their well-earned belonging.

When I arrived in Lima on my first research trip in 2013, Lilia Mayorga Balcazar, a director of CEDET, graciously welcomed me in her office. After discussing her work and the successes of the organization that has combined grassroots activism with scholarly research, I explained my research plans and how they aligned with the goals of her organization. Mayorga encouraged me to extend my research from Lima to Chiclayo and Piura. She assured me that my research questions were appropriate and that I would find answers in the museums and archives of Yapatera and Zaña, two Afro-Peruvian communities in the north that have maintained unique cultural traditions despite a dominant narrative that presumed their disappearance. Challenging an official narrative of invisibility that persists in archival records would require a wider array of sources from a wider geographical scope, it seemed, and Afro-Peruvian activism guided the path of my research between 2013 and 2015. Naturally, such organizations have the expertise to guide an outsider through the hidden (yet visible) history of Afro-descended people along Peru's Pacific coast, as well as the persistent racism that has resulted from centuries of abuse and neglect. As I pored over a wide array of archival records in Lima, Trujillo, and Piura, however, I was struck by the absences more than the contents of the documents. They revealed little of the historical agency of Afro-Peruvian populations, and my research came to focus on what was missing: the absences and silences in the archival records were a product of their context and led to the narratives I analyze in this book. These narratives of mestizaje and Peruvian national identity (*peruanidad*) asserted the erasure of blackness in Peru, contributing to the invisibility of African-descendants from the early twentieth century through the present day.

In contrast to my interactions with activists and culture-bearers, one Lima archivist dismissed my research questions, assuring me that racism doesn't really exist in Peru. Unlike the United States, he pointed out, Peruvians don't discriminate against each other on the basis of racial difference. Only a small white population, who look like me (he emphasized), held racist beliefs that benefitted them. Our conversation revealed a narrative of *mestizaje* (racial mixing) analyzed throughout this book. This view presumes the history of racial mixing in Peru has resulted in a "raceless" nation, which renders race irrelevant while denying a long history of suffering and exclusion specific to Afro-Peruvians. It also served as an example of the very narrative Afro-Peruvian activists have worked against since the 1950s, prompting me to examine narratives of invisibility in addition to the history of Afro-Peruvians since the abolition of slavery.

The need for such activist groups exhibits the enduring power of ideologies of *peruanidad, mestizaje,* and "silent racism" examined in this book. At the same time, they demonstrate the resilience of Afro-Peruvians to demand recognition of their centrality to the nation's history and the promises of equality they have been denied. My hope is that this book contributes to the valiant efforts of such activists to demand legal protections against racial discrimination by scrutinizing the process by which elite intellectuals erased blackness from the Peruvian nation.

Acknowledgments

Completing this book would not have been possible without the interminable support of scholars, family, and friends in the United States and in Peru. The scholarly community at the University of New Mexico provided a nurturing and encouraging environment for me to pursue my interests in Latin American history, and in particular I appreciate the patient guidance of Judy Bieber, Tiffany Florvil, Kimberly Gauderman, the late Linda Hall, and Liz Hutchison. I also appreciate Carlos Aguirre's helpful feedback and guidance on the topic of Afro-Peruvian history. I hope this work meets their high standards of quality.

My research in Lima, Trujillo, and Piura, Peru was made possible by a Field Research Grant from the Latin American and Iberian Institute and Tinker Foundation at the University of New Mexico. I am also grateful to the Conference on Latin American History for providing funding through the James R. Scobie Award.

Lilia Mayorga Balcazar of Centro de Desarrollo Étnico (CEDET) generously took the time to meet with me to discuss my research agenda and provide local contacts in Yapatera. I also appreciate the help of the hardworking archivists at the Archivo General de la Nación, the Instituto Nacional de Estadística e Informática (INEI) as well as those of the Biblioteca Nacional del Perú and the Municipal Archives of Lima. The director of the Casa/Museo Ricardo Palma in Miraflores, Lima, Alberto Varillas Montenegro, helped me navigate the collection of archival materials throughout this historic building. Nearby, Dina Cardenas Boyasbek and her husband, Klaus Lynge, welcomed me like family, and I appreciate their hospitality including an unforgettable trip to Pachacamac to celebrate the Inti Raymi festival. Lima activist Guillermo Orrego Pacheco also remains a good friend and was a helpful guide to the vibrant civic-cultural life throughout the capital city, for which I am grateful. I acknowledge reuse of some text from my article, "*Peruanidad* and blackness in national and local perspectives: popular literature and racial science," published in *Latin American and Caribbean Ethnic Studies* 14, no. 2, (January 2019): 194–213, www.tandfonline.com, courtesy of Taylor and Francis, in chapter 4 of this book.

I owe my gratitude to the archivists of the Archivo Regional de Piura, who generously accommodated my tight schedule and allowed me to access more documents than seemed reasonable in the sweltering heat. My local contacts in Piura were also generous with their time and interest in my research: a special thanks to John Charles Ramos Arechaga and Martin Berendson for helping me understand the local culture and history in which they were raised. John directed me to the Centro de Investigación y Promoción del Campesinado (CIPCA), which was an invaluable source of records and accounts of Afro-Peruvian history in northern haciendas. For his part, Martin generously drove me several hours north of Piura to reach Yapatera, at no small cost to his car. After meeting directors of the Afro-Peruvian Museum in Lima, José Portilla Carrasco met me in Chiclayo and introduced me to the mayor of the nearby town of Zaña, Hildebrando Briones Vela, and I appreciate the time they spent to discuss the town's history with me.

The community of Latin Americanist scholars in the Southeastern Council of Latin American Studies (SECOLAS) and in Charlotte, North Carolina, has been incredibly supportive. I appreciate the friendship and encouragement of Thomas Genova and Margott Paucar Espinoza, who helped me find my way around Lima on my first research trip there. At the University of North Carolina at Charlotte (UNCC), Jürgen Buchenau continues to be a sage mentor, and I appreciate the time he took to read and comment on this manuscript. A special thanks to Greg Weeks, who remains a charitable mentor and whose work continues to remind me how political science informs history. Vanessa Castañeda organized a Latin Americanist writing group at a fortuitous moment in my writing process, and I appreciate her comments and the feedback from members of the group including Oscar de la Torre, Maria Labbato, and Andrea Pitts. I also appreciate the encouragement and support of Erika Edwards, Carmen Soliz, Gregory Mixon, and Benny Andrés. I owe much gratitude to friend and former UNCC colleague Carol Higham for her comments on a previous version of this manuscript. My former colleagues at Utica University provided support, guidance, and encouragement during my two years there, and I'm deeply grateful to

Clemmie Harris, Sherri Cash, Peter DeSimone, and David Wittner. I appreciate the feedback from peer reviewers and the support of acquisitions editor Wendi Schnaufer at the University of Alabama Press. And finally, a special thank you to my family: to my parents, for supporting my education and taking an interest in my work, and especially to my wife, Julia, for her patience and love, even in the most difficult times.

Abbreviations

ABML	Archivo y Biblioteca Municipal de Lima
AHML	Archivo Histórico Municipal de Lima
ARP	Archivo Regional de Piura
BINEI	Biblioteca del Instituto Nacional de Estadística e Informática, Lima
BNP	Biblioteca Nacional Del Perú, Lima
CEDET	Centro de Desarrollo Étnico, Lima
CIPCA	Centro de Investigación y Promoción del Campesinado, Piura
CMMG	Casa Museo Miguel Grau, Piura
CMRP	Casa Museo Ricardo Palma, Lima
MNA	Museo Nacional Afroperuano

AFRO-PERUVIAN *MESTIZOS*

Introduction

Afro-Peruvian Invisibility and *Mestizaje* as National Identity

"Who told you / that you have no history to tell us? Who told you that you have no / traditions that speak to us/of what the men/ and women of Piura were?"

—Carlota Ramos, "Sangre Mangache"

This is a book about history and power. It deals with the many ways in which the production of historical narratives involves the uneven contribution of competing groups and individuals who have unequal access to the means for such production. The forces I will expose are less visible than gunfire, class property, or political crusades. I want to argue that they are no less powerful.

—Michel Rolph-Trouillot, *Silencing the Past: Power and the Production of History*

In 1943 Peruvian intellectual and politician Victor Andrés Belaúnde (1883–1966) defined *peruanidad* ("Peruvianness," or a sense of what it means to be Peruvian) as a synthesis of Hispanic and Indigenous heritage. Building on a long tradition of analyzing a shared history to characterize the Peruvian national identity, Belaúnde defined the "nation as a collection of men united by the memory of the deeds carried out in the past and the will to accomplish them in the future."[1] The mid-twentieth-century intellectual emphasized that the "cultural physiognomy resulting from the community of traditions must be combined with the factor of a collective will oriented towards the same ideals to build nationality."[2] Belaúnde's construction of Peruvian national identity in 1943 built on the work of generations of Marxist scholars who preceded him, yet his work brought renewed attention to the role of spirituality and religion, rejecting the Eurocentric approach of his predecessors. The scholar therefore argued that Marxism and anarchism were "repugnant to the national idea" and thus not a part of the "cultural physiognomy."[3]

Belaúnde's construction of peruanidad relied on a selective reading of Peruvian history, which, in fact, echoed a common theme used by many Peruvian scholars before this 1943 collection of essays: The opening essay in the volume celebrated the historic Inca Empire and subsequent cultural "amalgamations" of the Indigenous descendants of the Inca and the Spanish-descended *criollos* (Creoles). As in the works analyzed in the pages that follow, Belaúnde's most glaring omission in his interpretation of the past and his understanding of Peruvian *mestizaje* (racial mixing) was the population of African descent. After all, Africans were among the first outsiders to arrive to the Pacific coast of South America, and their forced labor laid the foundations of Peru's capital of Lima, quite literally. Unlike his predecessors, however, Belaúnde may have had newfound demographic justification for this erasure, as the collection of essays was printed just three years after the national census reported that the African-descended population of Peru had all but disappeared.

The other obvious omission from this analysis is the role of women, whom Belaúnde preferred to discuss in terms of the family unit as a metaphor for the nation and its future.[4] In his view, family was the primary element that facilitated the "integration" of distinct social institutions into the "Nation." And much like the literature, social science, and official representations of Peruvian culture produced in Peru between 1854 and 1940, Belaúnde celebrated the outcome of mestizaje without celebrating each of its constituent parts. Using the family as a metaphor for the nation confined women to the role of mothers who birthed peruanidad by erasing racial differences. Intellectuals, social engineers, and governing elites celebrated women's roles in mestizaje while denying the possibility of their individual agency and assuming that their reproductive roles erased racial, cultural, and even class differences. In the process, Peruvian elites assumed that even Afro-Peruvian women contributed to a bright future for the nation by erasing blackness through mestizaje. As Belaúnde's celebrated work suggests, understanding the process by which elites erased Afro-Peruvians from the nation's history and future requires a close reading of popular literature, with particular focus on social constructions of race, gender, class, and national identity. This book contends that the same assumptions that created a selective recording of events in the archives also persisted in the narratives, consolidating an exclusive sense of peruanidad in nation-making narratives like Belaúnde's.

MESTIZOS, CRIOLLOS, AND *BLANQUEAMIENTO*

Colonial records show that Africans and African descendants composed the majority of Lima's population and were the primary laborers on *haciendas* (plantations) along the Pacific coast. Yet the 1940 census identified less than one half of 1 percent of the nation's population as Afro-Peruvian or *negro/a* (Black). This book interrogates the process by which national elites rendered the Afro-Peruvian population invisible between the abolition decree of 1854 and the national census of 1940. Following abolition, recordkeepers from national census takers and local notaries and judges saw no reason to note African ancestry or "race," limiting the visibility of Afro-Peruvians in the archives. This archival absence produced a dominant narrative of erasure and invisibility, which culminated in the 1940 census.

As in other Latin American countries, scholars have attributed this invisibility to mestizaje, the process of racial mixing primarily between white and Indigenous populations. However, this book analyzes mestizaje as a narrative process constructed by intellectual elites in the nineteenth and twentieth centuries, which shaped a public image of Peruvian national identity that occluded the Afro-Peruvian population and denied the existence of racism. According to this narrative, African descendants in Peru underwent a process of *blanqueamiento* (whitening) by claiming white and *mestizo* ("mixed," typically referring to children of white and Indigenous parentage) identities and denying any African heritage. Mestizaje as an ideology therefore equated mestizos with modernism and cast Blackness and indigeneity in the colonial past. As an extension of the historical record in this period, much secondary work has assumed that mestizaje universally entailed whitening. However, this work shows that Afro-Peruvians did not uniformly seek to "marry up" to improve their social status and deny any African ancestry. To the contrary, census records at the local and national levels reveal increased intermingling between Afro-Peruvian and Indigenous populations in this period, and the recordkeepers interpreted this process as destined to erase Afro-Peruvians as a distinct identity.

Since the conquest of the Inca Empire in the 1530s, the majority of

Peru's population settled in urban centers along the coast, while the Andean and Amazonian interior remained predominantly Indigenous. White criollos (Creoles, white Spaniards born in the Americas) imported enslaved Africans to work on sugar-producing haciendas along the coast and for a wide array of forced labor in the cities of Lima and Trujillo. These Creoles laid claim to an emerging patriotic nationalism in the late eighteenth century that expressed anxieties about Peru's African and Indigenous populations, seeing them as unfit for citizenship in an "enlightened" democratic republic.

When slavery finally met its demise on December 3, 1854, the descendants of white colonial elites associated slavery and Afro-Peruvians with the colonial past while championing liberal ideals of citizenship and equality as natural products of the modern nation-state. For state and ecclesiastical officials, citizenship rights were now equally available to all Peruvians regardless of race, so racial differences no longer mattered. While allowing former enslavers as well as liberal elites to deny any accusations of racism, this nineteenth-century myth of racial harmony obscured the historic roles of African descendants in shaping Peruvian national culture and identity. Believing that racism against Afro-Peruvians ended with abolition, elite intellectuals and social reformers assumed the African-descended population would disappear through mestizaje. This is evident in the omission of racial categories in quotidian records as well as the diminution of categories indicating African ancestry in census records, showing that Afro-Peruvian invisibility in the sources was directly connected to the erasure of Blackness in nation-making narratives, a process doubtlessly influenced by the dominant global discourse of scientific racism.

While some Afro-Peruvians may indeed have striven to claim white and mestizo identities, this work interrogates the narrative of Afro-Peruvian invisibility from a wide array of sources and perspectives. Together, the archival records, popular literature, and local accounts consulted highlight the paradoxical and complex construction of Afro-Peruvian identities within the dominant ideology of mestizaje. These sources reveal elite anxieties regarding the African-descended population that shaped the historical record and contributed to Afro-Peruvian invisibility following the abolition of slavery. As a product of the same power dynamics that gave rise to the ideology of mestizaje as a contested, reciprocal, and open-ended process, this book locates Afro-Peruvians through an ethnographic approach to the archives.

Several twenty-first-century works have argued for an ethnographic approach to archival records and criticized the "fetishization" of documentary records. Whereas historians Ann Laura Stoler and Antoinette Burton have interrogated archival records to recover what was neglected by those making the records, this work provides the broader context that shaped the motives and subject positions of those in positions of power who recorded the daily lives of Peruvian citizens and observed major events between 1854 and 1940.[5] Although landholding elites created and maintained the category "*negro/a*" (Black), which they associated with slavery and inferiority, the label served them no purpose following abolition. Instead, those who constructed the archival record between abolition and the census of 1940 marked the end of Afro-Peruvian history in 1855. It no longer served elite interests to record this group as a distinct ethnoracial category following abolition. Thus, this work does not take archival records at face value but locates them in a broader context of transnational literature on race, modernity, and nationalism to explain how elites eliminated Afro-Peruvians as a subject of historical analysis.

A HISTORIOGRAPHY OF RACE, *MESTIZAJE*, NATION-MAKING, AND THE AFRICAN DIASPORA IN LATIN AMERICA

Early US scholarship on Latin American history was rooted in racial determinism. For nineteenth-century historians, the former Spanish, French, and Portuguese colonies were composed of "inferior," "mixed" races, which explained the region's "underdevelopment." In their racist worldview, Latin America was predetermined to remain "backward" and "beneath" the United States due to the region's large Indigenous and African-descended populations. The racial mixing between the Spanish-, African-, and Indigenous populations worked in tandem with the so-called Black Legend, which blamed Spanish violence and Catholicism for the demographic decline of the Indigenous populations and subsequent economic underdevelopment.[6] Until the mid-twentieth century, US scholars had little to say that was meaningful about the history of the transatlantic slave trade and the African diaspora in Latin America. Simultaneously, historians in Peru constructed historical narratives of national identity that celebrated generations of mestizaje and the unique cultural products of this process. As the work of celebrated Peruvian historians such as Jorge Basadre and Alberto

Flores Galindo demonstrates, the hegemonic narrative of the nation's history elided discussions of racial differences while emphasizing national cohesion. When race, ethnicity, or mestizaje has been discussed in the dominant discourse, most Peruvian scholars have focused on the Indigenous populations and the celebrated, if not mythologized, history of the Inca Empire.

US scholars shifted from environmentally and racially deterministic interpretations of Latin American history to cultural explanations of the region's underdevelopment in the mid-twentieth century. Although many scholars emphasized the region's shortcomings due to the lack of a "Protestant work ethic," one early postwar publication brought comparative race relations in the Americas to the center of comparative historical analysis of the Americas. Historian Frank Tannenbaum's 1946 book, *Slave and Citizen*, was a groundbreaking work on comparative race relations that uncritically analyzed the work of Brazilian anthropologist Gilberto Freyre. Freyre had posited that the historic genetic and cultural mixing between Portuguese and African populations facilitated racial and cultural mixing in Brazil. For Tannenbaum, racial mixing resulted from a more benevolent form of slavery in Brazil compared with the United States. According to these scholars, racial mixing in Brazil led to harmonious race relations, solidifying the myth of "racial democracy." They contrasted Brazilian racial democracy with the United States, where they believed a harsher form of slavery had led to more restrictive laws enforcing racial segregation and hostile race relations.[7] Tannenbaum's analysis revealed new perspectives and possibilities for analyzing the African diaspora and the legacies of slavery as a hemispheric phenomenon with distinct trajectories in terms of national identities and subsequent race relations. The "Tannenbaum thesis" held particular appeal for those in the United States interested in the ongoing civil rights movement and growing discontent over Jim Crow laws and segregationist policies. But for all of its appeal, Tannenbaum's work lacked the historical rigor and critical analysis required of such an important line of inquiry, assuming that different "slave systems" explained the apparent differences in race relations in the United States and Latin America.[8] Moreover, its assumption that racial mixing had ended perceived racial differences in Brazil meant that racism was impossible in Brazil. The impossibility of racism also denied the lived experiences of many Afro-Brazilians who continued to encounter racism in the form of colorism and social exclusion, sparking robust intellectual debate and organizing among Afro-Brazilians.[9] Nonetheless, the "Tannenbaum thesis" led historians of Latin America to investigate similar nation-making myths founded on racial mixing in other parts of the region, with a focus on African-descended populations.

Influenced by a wave of cultural politics and social upheaval, scholars in the United States turned to Marxist interpretations of Latin American history in the 1960s. However, Dependency Theory, which posited that Latin America stood in a permanently dependent position relative to the United States, applied a Eurocentric structural interpretation of the region's past that treated Latin American popular classes as passive actors in national politics and global interactions.[10] Dependency theory blamed the United States for Latin American underdevelopment but presented the region's racialized masses as a uniformly oppressed underclass without historical agency.

The cultural politics and growing interest in comparative race relations of the 1960s led to growing scholarship on social histories of Latin America. Historical analysis of colonial Latin America moved beyond the institutional perspectives in the mid-twentieth century, leading to new understandings of race relations, mestizaje, and the African diaspora in this decade of social change. Shortly after the US Congress passed the Civil Rights Act in 1964, historian Magnus Mörner published a detailed study of the process of racial mixing in Latin America, and James Lockhart published an influential study of the social history of early colonial Peru.[11] These works set the stage for subsequent historians to move beyond the institutional histories, whose historical perspectives were limited to those of colonial and ecclesiastical authorities, sparking interest in understanding the lived experiences of distinct ethnoracial groups.

For US scholars interested in comparative race relations in the Americas, the most obvious difference between the United States and Latin America was the legal prohibition of racial mixing in the form of anti-miscegenation laws.[12] Scholars in Latin American tended to agree with this distinction and pointed to mestizaje to contrast race relations in their own countries to those in the United States. Although the colonial-era *sistema de castas* (caste system) in Latin America sought to categorize and control the process of mestizaje, Latin American republics notably had not erected or enforced such barriers to mestizaje.

Mörner declared in 1967 that "the development of race relations and the mestizaje forms the main theme in Latin America's entire history."[13] This early study of mestizaje conceived of race as biological difference but recognized that "basic biological differences have yet been found among contemporary races, all of which represent a parallel evolution from man's humble beginnings."[14] Criticizing the "stupidity" of racists who "seem to be convinced that their own race is innately superior," Mörner noted the historic difference in barriers to interracial marriage in the United States and mestizaje in Latin America without romanticizing it. In contrast with the "Tannenbaum thesis," Mörner pointed out that the Spanish crown sought to limit mestizaje due to racial prejudice. Beyond the well-documented *real pragmática* (Royal Pragmatic) of 1776 that empowered parents to restrict the marriage choices of their children,[15] Mörner pointed to a royal decree of 1805 that "declared that persons of 'pure blood' had to ask permission of the viceroy or the *audiencia* [a colonial governing body with royal authority] in order to marry 'elements of Negro and Mulatto origin.'"[16] Additionally, Mörner drew attention to revolutionary leader Simón Bolívar's "mixed disdain and envy" toward "men of more or less dark skin," showing that the elimination of *casta* categories did not eliminate racial anxieties among such Creole elites.[17] As Creole elites in Latin America came to emphasize the power of mestizaje to erase racial differences and, by extension, racism, they erased Blackness from the process and ended up perpetuating anti-Black racism in more subtle ways.

Simultaneously, historians in Peru constructed historical narratives of national identity that celebrated generations of mestizaje and the unique cultural products of this process. The hegemonic narrative of the nation's history elided discussions of racial differences while emphasizing national cohesion. Such narratives implicitly rejected the US- and European-centered discourses on race and nation, which equated Latin American underdevelopment with racial inferiority, yet they did not celebrate or recognize the unique contributions of Afro-Peruvians.

Mörner edited a volume on race and class in Latin America that was published in 1970 and included an anthropological study of mestizaje in Peru. Peruvian anthropologist Mario C. Vásquez emphasized the ubiquity of mestizaje in both urban centers and rural regions in Peru. Noting that mestizaje between Afro-Peruvian men and Indigenous women "in the Andes was greater than usually is believed," Vásquez pointed out that in most coastal towns where such interactions occurred "the Negroes have been disappearing as an ethnic group through fusion with the local population."[18]

Vásquez concluded that Peru "today is genetically and culturally mestizo" and racial prejudice against mestizos has "practically disappeared," although "discrimination against the Indian, Negro, and Asian have persisted."[19] Even as Vásquez drew attention to racism that remained under the guise of mestizaje, he positioned Afro-Peruvians as outsiders who would disappear through mixing with the "local" population. As these studies produced in the late 1960s revealed the persistence of racist attitudes in mestizaje and its role in erasing Afro-Peruvian representation, scholarship on Brazil began to critique the "Tannenbaum thesis."

Beginning in the 1970s and continuing through the early twenty-first century, a large body of scholarship has incorporated a wider array of sources to refute the "Tannenbaum thesis." The transition from institutional history to social history helped historians uncover the racism and the legacies of slavery that have marginalized Afro-Brazilians.[20] These studies also led to historical analysis of Afro-Brazilian intellectualism, agency, and activism obscured by the myth of "racial democracy."[21]

In contrast with the historiography on racial democracy in Brazil, scholarship on mestizaje in Peru has generally continued to focus on cultural and racial mixing between Indigenous Peruvians and coastal "Creoles." When contrasted with the history of US racism and segregation, mestizaje has been a source of national pride in Peru because it precluded racial segregation even if racial prejudice remained.[22] This book takes cues from the historiography of race and racial democracy in Brazil by challenging a similar myth of racial harmony that developed into the ideology of mestizaje in Peru, which similarly denied the possibility of racism and erased the roles of Afro-Peruvians from the nation's history.

The historiography of the African diaspora and race relations in Peru is not as robust as that of Brazil. Historian Frederick Bowser provided the first detailed study of the history of Afro-Peruvians, which focused on the early colonial period. The most widely accepted works about African slavery in Peru posit that Afro-Peruvians had positive incentives to adopt whitening strategies in their quest for social mobility. For example, Bowser concludes that due to the "utter foreignness" of Africans in Peru, the majority originating from Senegambia and Guinea-Bissau, they often "identified with everything Spanish more rapidly than did the Indian," in turn making them loyal servants.[23] A more recent historiography of colonial Brazil, Mexico, and Peru suggests more complex processes of interethnic relations and identity formation, and this book contributes to and extends the growing body of knowledge on Black-native relations into the national era.[24] Moreover, while Bowser documents the occupational diversity of Afro-Peruvians and forms of resistance they utilized, he concludes that "free Afro-Peruvians who came to acquire modest fortunes were quick to see that racial solidarity was all very well, but that 'whitening' and 'passing,' culturally if not racially, was the key to socioeconomic advancement."[25] Documentary evidence supports Bowser's claim regarding assimilation in colonial Peru. His book is a landmark study in the social history of African slavery that expanded on James Lockhart's significant 1968 intervention on the topic.[26] Bowser agrees that "free persons of color exhibited a high degree of solidarity" in early colonial Latin America, but "splintering was inevitable, in large part as a result of pressures from the larger Spanish society."[27] In contrast, the present study shows that while mestizaje obscured distinct Afro-Peruvian histories and identities following abolition, the process was not universal, nor did it always entail a denial of Blackness by Afro-Peruvians themselves.

Several historians built on the pioneering work of Bowser by focusing on Afro-Peruvian agency in dismantling slavery and gaining legal equality through the abolition decree of 1854. Historian Christine Hünefeldt has shown that the process of abolition began in the wars for independence, first proclaimed by revolutionary general and Creole elite José de San Martín on July 28, 1821. San Martín enacted a "free womb" law on this date, promising that henceforth no children would be born into slavery. Although this declaration stated that enslaved Afro-Peruvians who had fled the country as well as those who fought for independence would be free, "no slave was freed by the decrees passed under San Martín. At very best a slave might achieve the status of *liberto* [literally "freed," typically translated as "free Black"], which in the majority of cases was synonymous with slave conditions of life until a certain age, yet might mean the payment of a minimal wage."[28] Such details were conveniently silenced in the making of narratives that celebrate mestizaje as peruanidad.

Although scholars have revealed Afro-Peruvian roles in the wars for independence and their success in attaining abolition in 1854, the post-abolition period has drawn less historical scrutiny. As the historical records in the archives occlude Afro-Peruvian roles after abolition, several scholars have assumed that this population's denial of any association with their African ancestry is the best explanation for Afro-Peruvian invisibility. Historian Peter Blanchard reaffirms Bowser's analysis of whitening in his 1992 book, attributing the demographic decline of Afro-Peruvians to "whitening" through self-classification in pursuit of social ascendance.[29] The development of this official narrative coincided with elite intellectual discourses on mestizaje that denied racial distinctions and disparities while asserting the disappearance of Afro-Peruvians. Despite this manipulation of the nation's public image, Afro-Peruvians preserved valued cultural traditions that contributed to a collective identity while also seeking social mobility. This book asserts that these were not mutually exclusive pursuits.

Historian Carlos Aguirre has since qualified previous claims of Afro-Peruvian whitening by analyzing distinct Afro-Peruvian cultural forms that have become intertwined with the performance of a collective Peruvian identity. For Aguirre, the apparent demographic decline misses the point. Afro-Peruvians carved out spaces to express economic and cultural autonomy, and in the process they contributed to the formation of "Peruvian culture." Still, their contributions have generally been unappreciated by the "official culture and the dominant classes."[30] Aguirre's analysis does not explain the dramatic decrease in Afro-Peruvians in the national censuses, but it does demonstrate Afro-Peruvian agency obscured by the narrative of disappearance. Aguirre's work also points to a more general problem with claims of "whitening," a structural interpretation that ignores culture and denies individual agency. Aguirre, Hünefeldt, and Blanchard effectively revise prior explanations of abolition as resulting from the opportunistic philanthropy of "*El Libertador*" ("The Liberator") Ramón Castilla or as an inevitable consequence of the development of global capitalism. Such dated analyses have rendered Afro-Peruvians passive actors in the abolition of slavery, just as "single-track" assimilation, creolization, and whitening limit agency and creativity in the process of identity formation.[31]

By the late 1990s, scholarship on race and nation-making in Latin America began to see mestizaje as an ideology used by elites to foster social cohesion while maintaining their social status and denying the relevance of race or racism. Like the body of literature that had unraveled Brazil's myth of "racial democracy," anthropological approaches proved essential to dismantling the historical narratives that equated mestizaje with the end of racial discrimination. With a few notable exceptions, however, scholars examined mestizaje in terms of racial mixing between white and Indigenous populations.

Research on "peasant politics" and lower-class roles in shaping national identities in nineteenth- and twentieth-century Latin America tended to focus on Indigenous populations through the 1990s.[32] Historian Jeffrey Gould has argued that in Nicaragua the myth of racial harmony, as a product of mestizaje, has led to the invisibility of "the Indian."[33] Just as the construction of the "Ladino" identity led to Indigenous invisibility in Nicaragua, the construction of the Peruvian mestizo erased the Afro-Peruvian population.

Recent scholarship has connected the casta system in colonial Spanish America to the development of mestizaje as an ideology in the national era. Ben Vinson III's recent book explores the origins of the nineteenth-century ideology of mestizaje that were central to a nation-building process with its roots in *castizaje* (mixing between castas, requiring the creation of "extreme castes") in the late colonial period.[34] Similarly, historian Milagros Denis-Rosario's recent book shows how the pseudoscience of race combined with US imperialism to perpetuate colonial-era racial hierarchies and erase Afro-Puerto Rican's from the island's social and political history.[35] In Peru as in Puerto Rico, this process entailed circumscribing women's contributions to their reproductive capacity out of a concern for the future of the nation.

Anthropologist Mary Weismantel's research on gender and race in the Peruvian Andes reflects Gould's analysis of the Ladino identity in Nicaragua, bringing an intersectional approach to the narrative of dualism separating Indigenous populations of the interior from the Creole populations of the Pacific coast. Weismantel challenges the traditional understanding of Andean racial dynamics as composed of a minority white elite, a mestizo middle, and Blacks and Indians at the bottom. Instead, "in actual practice within specific social contexts, there is no intermediate or 'mixed' racial category: race operates as a vicious binary that discriminates superiors from inferiors." Her research helps explain Afro-Peruvian invisibility in the twentieth century as a product of power dynamics in mestizaje. As the myth of racial harmony denied ethnoracial distinctions between Afro-Peruvians and Indigenous Andeans, these groups fell into a singular category that elites deemed inferior. As one anthropologist has concluded about Peru, "Race, then is fundamentally binary: white and nonwhite, superior and inferior."[36] By comparing the so-called Indian problem of Andean countries to the so-called Negro problem of the United States, and by incorporating Indigenous perspectives on Afro-Andeans, Weismantel ultimately contributes a great deal to disrupting the traditional narrative of Peruvian dualism, which tends to ignore the African diaspora altogether.

Weismantel's analysis included African-descendants in the process of mestizaje, but anthropologist Marisol de la Cadena's 2001 book provided crucial insights on the hegemonic nature of the ideology of mestizaje in twentieth-century Peru. Citing Antonio Gramsci's theory on the role of culture in shaping dominant discourses of race and identity, de la Cadena defines hegemony as "an ambiguously defined dialogic field shared by elites and subordinates" that ultimately "produces a conflict-laden consensus." For "indigenous mestizos," the narrow consensus asserts that education legitimizes ethnoracial social hierarchies.[37] This book locates Afro-Peruvians in the process and ideology of mestizaje, however, revealing a narrow consensus between this population and narratives of nationalism, patriotism, and a preference for class-based rhetoric as opposed to race. My analysis of Creole literature on mestizaje, Peruvian national identity, and Blackness reveals a persistent strain of gendered anti-Black racism even as intellectual elites promoted myths of racial harmony, which became the ideology of mestizaje.

In contrast with the culture loss implied in the process of mestizaje for Indigenous Peruvians, the process contributed to both the invisibility of the Afro-Peruvian population and the white appropriation of their culture. The result of this invisibility was a unique form of anti-Black racism that denied this population's roles in the nation's history. Trapping Afro-Peruvians in racist stereotypes associated with the past is more "acceptable" when this population is perceived as fully integrated. The ideology of mestizaje has presented Afro-Peruvians in a paradoxical manner: they were both trapped in the past and yet celebrated as emblems of national culture in the present in literature and visual arts. They were fully assimilated as mestizos yet are viewed as the Other, as relics of an inferior element in the national identity. Visible yet invisible. Central yet peripheral. Equal yet inferior. Analyzing the narrative of mestizaje as national identity underscores the paradox of the ideology itself: while promising to eliminate the strictures of the colonial-era casta system and thereby produce an identity based on racial mixing and equality, mestizaje simultaneously perpetuated and reified ethnoracial hierarchies from the eighteenth and nineteenth centuries. The paradox allowed national elites to deny the existence of Afro-Peruvians while denying their own racism. According to this dominant discourse, the

African-descended population had acquired legal equality with the abolition of slavery, so racism could not be the cause of modern social inequalities. Denying the relevance of race or ethnicity in the official records, however, only hid the problem from view. Between 1854 and 1940, mestizaje produced silences in the archival records and in narratives of national identity that rendered the Afro-Peruvian population invisible.

This invisibility had detrimental consequences for African-descended people in Peru. As a marginalized and hidden population, Afro-Peruvians suffered from state neglect, lacking access to adequate health care and education and being subjected to harmful stereotypes. Contradictorily, then, abolition led to an "incomplete freedom," as Afro-Peruvian invisibility contributed to the perpetuation of living conditions and social relations under slavery.[38] Clearly, Afro-Peruvian invisibility came at a major cost, and the narrative of invisibility continues to affect Afro-Peruvians negatively in the present day.

This book builds on the scholarship on mestizaje and nation-building in nineteenth- and twentieth-century Latin America, bringing this work into conversation with twenty-first-century studies on Afro-Latin American history and critical studies that reconceptualize the historical archive. Assessing an overlooked and erased history requires an innovative approach to reading the historical record. Between 1855 and 1940, few historical records included taxonomies for race. As Michel-Rolph Trouillot argues in his now-classic study of power and the production of history, "any historical narrative is a particular bundle of silences, the result of a unique process, and the operation required to deconstruct these silences will vary accordingly." Taking cues from Trouillot's analysis of silences in historic accounts of the Haitian Revolution, this book scrutinizes four crucial moments of historical production that resulted in silences regarding Afro-Peruvian history: "The moment of fact creation (the making of sources); the moment of fact assembly (the making of archives); the moment of fact retrieval (the making of narratives); and the moment of retrospective significance (the making of history in the final instance)."[39] Although landholding elites created and maintained the category "*negro/a*" as a label associated with slavery and inferiority, the identity served no purpose following abolition. Instead, those who constructed the archival record between abolition and the census of 1940 marked the end of Afro-Peruvian history in 1855. It no longer served elite interests to record this group as a distinct ethnoracial category.

Creole literature in the form of novels, essays, and newspaper articles became the ideology of mestizaje as national identity in ways that cannot be separated from law or official census records, as the reports that accompanied the censuses echo the writings on mestizaje by Creole elites. The "official" reports that accompanied census data interpreted their findings through the lens of mestizaje, in a reciprocal process that shaped the assembly of facts in the archives and then shaped the making of narratives of national identity.

This book uncovers the understandings of race and nation that shaped the nature of Peruvian archives regarding the nation's African-descended population. Reading popular and elite literature as archival sources themselves reveals elements of the ideology of mestizaje that were widely accepted and others that Peruvians generally rejected. Yet the Peruvian case also demonstrates the "epistemic uncertainties" that led to contradictory representations of Afro-Peruvians in the archives and in national literature: free in the present yet confined to representations of the past as enslaved people, politically active yet denied representation, historically significant yet without a history, present yet invisible. The contradictions of the dominant discourse eventually prompted Afro-Peruvians to construct counter-hegemonic narratives of their equal place in the nation and positive associations with Blackness.[40]

Silences in the archives often reflect and perpetuate violence by dehumanizing African- descended people. As historian Marisa Fuentes has argued, historians have the responsibility of subverting and illuminating biases in archival records that constructed the lives of enslaved people from positions of white domination.[41] The continuities and legacies of slavery evident in the archives of northern Peru help to "illuminate the terror of the mundane and quotidian,"[42] which are easy to overlook in a convenient narrative of racial mixing and harmony.

Recent work by the political scientist Juliet Hooker provides a strong framework for juxtaposing, rather than comparing, hemispheric writings on race between the 1850s and the 1950s. Hooker identifies three claims in Latin American "ideologies of mestizaje" that coalesced in the early twentieth century: "(1) That Latin American identity has been defined by long-standing and widespread practices of cultural and biological mixture; (2) that the principal result of a process of mixing that began in the colonial era has been a national population that is homogenous in its mixed-ness, to the point that the various groups that contributed to the mixing process (Spaniards, Indians, and Africans) disappeared as separate racio-cultural groups per se; and (3) that as a result of a racial system that blurred the boundaries between races and did not include legally encoded racial segregation, Latin America avoided the problems with racial stratification and discrimination that plagued other countries, particularly the United States."[43] The present work historicizes the development of this ideology in Peru with a focus on the interplay between the archival record and narratives of mestizaje that came together to erase Blackness. Building on Trouillot's approach to the archive and Hooker's transnational approach to racial theories traditionally examined through a narrow national lens, this book seeks to contribute to the explosion in scholarship focused on Afro-Latin American histories. Much of this work has focused on the central roles of African-descended populations of Cuba and Brazil,[44] and historian George Reid Andrews brought Afro-Latin American history to its rightful place at the center of the region's nation-making processes.[45] Indeed, scholarly production over the last three decades has done much to correct the invisibility of Afro-Latin Americans in the historiography that preceded it.

Uncovering the histories of Afro-Latin American roles in wars of independence and nation-making has shed light on how national myths of racial harmony developed into ideologies of mestizaje, which erased these contributions from the historical record. Historian Marixa Lasso has distinguished the nineteenth-century "myth of racial harmony" from twentieth-century "racial democracy" while noting that "the linkage between nationalism and racial harmony and equality did not change."[46] Lasso's work marked a significant development in the historiography of race and nation-making in nineteenth-century Latin America. The present study builds on Lasso's insights by showing how the nation-building myth of racial harmony in nineteenth-century Peru obscured Afro-Peruvian history. By locating African descendants in these narratives and in the twentieth-century ideology of mestizaje, this book reveals how Creole elites fashioned a narrative of mestizaje that shaped the archival records by eliminating Blackness as a category of analysis.

Despite the fact that far more enslaved Africans arrived in Latin America than in the United States, Afro–Latin American invisibility remains a common problem in the region. Historian Erika Denise Edwards, for example, traces the history of the Afro-Argentine invisibility to the late colonial period, describing the process of whitening "both as a series of choices made by [African descendants] and as an institutionalized project constructed by governing and ecclesiastical authorities" in the late eighteenth century through the passage of the Free Womb Act of 1813.[47] In contrast with Edwards's analysis, however, this book focuses on the post-abolition period in Peru. The present work necessarily relies on institutional sources in addition to popular literature, elite positivist writing, and local records to examine the state project of "whitening" in Peru. However, in contrast with the ambitions of Black women in eighteenth-century Argentina, Afro-Peruvian men and women in post-abolition Peru were subjected to a modernizing discourse of mestizaje, displaying a process of "institutional whitening" more than "individual whitening."[48] This dominant discourse combined elements of gendered nationalism and a raceless national identity that absorbed Afro-Peruvians initially as "criollos" and later as "mestizos" and "*blancos*" (whites). The primary and secondary sources analyzed in this work point to the power of elites to construct this public image of a "modernized" Peru, while Afro-Peruvians maintained cultural traditions rooted in African ancestry that maintained connections with the African diaspora rather than distancing themselves from it.

Most scholarship directly addressing Afro-Peruvians as a category of historical analysis since abolition has been conducted by anthropologists and focuses on the period from the beginning of the Afro-Peruvian "rediscovery" in 1945, gaining greater national attention through the 1950s and 1960s. The mere existence of an extensive body of anthropological research on Afro-Peruvian identities and local histories challenges the narrative of disappearance and "social whitening," prompting this work to examine how elites wrote out Afro-Peruvians from the nation and rendered this population invisible despite their obvious historical and contemporary presence.

The 1950s "rediscovery" analyzed by ethnomusicologist Heidi Carolyn Feldman was also the reclamation of a long history of Afro-Peruvian cultural and political contributions that had been appropriated by white Creole culture and denied by a hegemonic narrative of mestizaje.[49] Feldman's book built on anthropological research on Afro-Peruvian culture and identities since the 1980s, and together these works inspired subsequent research that began to examine the historical records of Afro-Peruvian communities from Chincha in the south to Piura in the north.[50] More recently, scholars have noted the importance of the rediscovery in inspiring Afro-Peruvian activist movements that empowered women and made transnational connections from the 1980s through to the present day.[51]

Despite the invisibility of Afro-Peruvians in the historical records following abolition, ethnographic research shows that this population maintained cultural traditions and collective identities rooted in Blackness, which operated in dialogue with national narratives of mestizaje. Such work makes the significant yet generally overlooked point that Afro-Peruvians did not emerge from a vacuum in the 1950s, implicitly challenging previous historical assumptions of Black disappearance through mestizaje and whitening. Anthropologist Tanya Maria Golash-Boza, for instance, points out that "there is remarkably little historical research on the African-descended population or on slavery in Piura."[52] Citing the limited documentation, Golash-Boza shows that the enslaved Afro-Peruvian population of this region began to decline in the late eighteenth and early nineteenth centuries. Furthermore, her subject population of the town of Ingenio de Buenos Aires in the department of Piura underscores "how regional particularities must be taken into consideration to understand fully the meanings of blackness in Peru."[53] This book builds on Golash-Boza's findings in northern Peru by analyzing a variety of sources in this understudied region. Afro-Peruvians had different experiences in small communities along the north coast and in Lima and constructed Black and mestizo identities in different ways, but they also share common historic origins as African descendants.

AFRO-PERUVIAN INVISIBILITY IN THE ARCHIVES

Throughout the colonial period, ecclesiastical and colonial recordkeepers used several terms to denote African ancestry. These included *zambo/a* (a child of Indigenous and African parentage), *mulato/a* (a child of African and Spanish/Creole parentage), *pardo/a* (brown), and *cuarterón/cuarterona* (one-fourth African), among others. Following the abolition of slavery, however, authorities reduced these terms indicating African ancestry to *negro/a* (Black), effectively erasing the African ancestry of Peruvians whose ancestors had mixed with other ethnoracial groups. This erasure is evident in the regional archives of Piura and in the national archives of Lima.

As in most of Latin America, the gradual process of abolition began during the wars of independence when San Martín enacted the law of the free womb, and full abolition came after decades of rebellion and resistance. Revolutionaries educated in classical liberal ideals, like José de San Martín and Simón Bolívar, sought the support of Afro-Latin populations with the promise of freedom. However, Peruvian white elites were particularly resistant to ideas of popular sovereignty and its implications of social equality. As in the rest of the Americas, the African-descended population of Peru continued to struggle against the legacies of slavery following abolition.

Documentation in the regional archives of northern Peru reveals that local practices of enslavement did not immediately change following Castilla's decree of abolition. The historical record of Piura casts light on the lived experiences of Afro-Peruvians, which have been overshadowed by the traditional narrative that posited that abolition meant the full assimilation of Afro-Peruvians as citizens in 1855 and their subsequent "disappearance." A dominant narrative has emerged that celebrates Castilla as the "Great Liberator," but local records following abolition show that both abolition and integration were incomplete.

Ramón Castilla's December 3 decree declaring the end of slavery was implemented in several stages. The *caudillo* (landholding elites who used their resources for patronage and maintained private armies in nineteenth-century Latin America) revolutionary leader defeated his rival Rufino Echenique through a military uprising, although Echenique had defeated Castilla in the presidential election of 1851. By promising complete abolition of slavery in 1854, Castilla gained the critical support of Afro-Peruvian militants to defeat Echenique's troops. News of Castilla's decree was initially dispersed through unofficial printed flyers. Lima newspaper *El Comercio* first mentioned the decree on December 18, and finally published the official decree in more detailed form on January 23, 1855. As a law, it included specific instructions on how the abolition process would be carried out in enslaved communities. The first step was the creation of "registration boards," *juntas de inscripción*, consisting of the governor, a priest, and a neighbor as witness. The purpose of these boards was to collect information on enslaved people and servants to submit to the national registry, making them officially free. However, Castilla supported the enslaving aristocracy by guaranteeing indemnification for their losses and severe punishments for any crimes committed by formerly enslaved people or servants. Most significantly, the law made a special provision for enslaved people who were newly free and servants who still worked in domestic service, requiring them to remain in their current homes until they could find alternative employment.[54] Given this provision, Afro-Peruvian women were likely to remain in the same conditions, with meager pay and no freedom of movement, indefinitely.

The notarial records of post-abolition Piura reveal little change in the customary practices of *hacendados* (plantation owners, or owners of haciendas) and other enslavers between the 1850s and the 1880s. Whereas *libertos* (freed people) in Lima participated directly in the democratic process just after abolition, many Afro-Peruvians in Piura saw little changes to their daily lives. The word liberto itself had vastly different meanings in Lima and Piura. While wealthy landholders expressed concern over the participation of libertos in the National Assembly in 1856, hacendados in Piura continued to treat libertos as property.[55]

Piura is an important department in northern Peru, which stretches from the coast to a long border with Ecuador. Its urban center shared some similarities with Lima, but its port of Paita never rivaled the major port of Callao near Lima. The city of Piura boasted few factories, aside from the legendary soap and leather factory known as "La Tina." Between Piura and Lima, enslavers imported fewer enslaved Africans to meet the demands of haciendas scattered along rivers near the coast. Like Trujillo, a larger city and capital of the department of La Libertad just south of Piura, the northern urban center was a commercial center thanks to the sugar-producing haciendas worked by enslaved Africans. Although Lima was a rapidly modernizing city that offered greater economic opportunities to Afro-Peruvians in the period under study, sugar-producing haciendas connected the formerly enslaved people on such plantations with those in the capital city. The economic networks that delivered sugar to urban centers for commercial export, in other words, also fostered cultural and political connections between rural and urban Afro-Peruvians.

Piura's distance from Lima, however, isolated it from the national policies that would benefit its Afro-Peruvian population. For example, on March 7, 1884, Doña María de Nieves Armestar remunerated her daughter and son-in-law for their services during an emergency. Nieves Armestar dictated to the notary that her "donation" consisted of a home worth 450 pesos and a liberto named José María, "ten years of age, born in my home of a slave named Candelaria Seminario," whom she valued at 100 pesos.[56] The liberto José María, it appears, was born into slavery twenty years after Castilla had abolished slavery. The same notary recorded the sale of a liberto a few days later, on March 11, for 300 pesos, as well as the manumission of a "slave named Juana" on March 17, who purchased her freedom for 150 pesos, and a curious criminal case of an Afro-Peruvian woman labeled "liberta" who was "sold" by one local elite to another the year after abolition.[57]

These records reveal the "incomplete liberty" of Peruvian abolition beyond Lima, which several Peruvian historians have noted, as scholarship on Afro-Peruvian history has developed in the twenty-first century in coordination with activist work.[58] These records confirm the futility of the abolition decree without the presence or will of national or local authorities to enforce the law, underscoring how Afro-Peruvian invisibility meant their continued oppression. Therefore, this book utilizes new sources to contribute to a growing body of literature on the elite's maintenance of white supremacy and anti-Black racism between 1855 and 1940, directly challenging the narrative that equates mestizaje with racial equality.

ORGANIZATION OF THE BOOK

This book is organized in five chronological chapters from the immediate post-abolition period to the *indigenismo* movement of the 1920s and 1930s, jumping back in time at points to demonstrate continuities in pre- and post-abolition writings on race and national identity. Reflecting the hemispheric discourses of race, this book follows the contradictions of liberalism that became the contradictions of positivism, both of which laid the foundations for the ideology of mestizaje as a central component of indigenismo in the 1920s and 1930s. The first two chapters examine print media and legal records in the immediate post-abolition period, from 1855 to 1866. The first chapter shows how white Creole elites expressed their anxieties regarding Afro-Peruvian citizenship in "raceless" terms, which occluded their own racism while simultaneously erasing Blackness from the sources they produced. The archival records between 1855 and 1862 demonstrate how Creole elites saw the benefits of associating slavery with colonialism to consolidate a gendered and racial hierarchy through the notion of honor as military service. The second chapter shows how elite conceptions of race, mestizaje, and gender shaped census records and the official analyses of these records in the working-class neighborhoods of Lima in 1860 and 1866. This chapter argues that unequal access to the means of production of knowledge reduced Afro-Peruvian visibility in the censuses, as Creole elites erased Blackness from their vision of mestizaje.

Expanding on this microhistorical approach, the third chapter examines censuses of Lima and of the nation in the early twentieth century, which documented the most dramatic decline in the Afro-Peruvian population. I argue that these censuses and the official analyses that accompanied them are the products of their context: they reflect Creole elite fears of being associated with Blackness, which they associated with backwardness, as they sought to modernize the nation through social engineering in tacit agreement with the influence of positivism and the contemporary pseudoscience of race. Thus the first three chapters show the selective recording of Peruvian daily life in the making of sources, which rendered Afro-Peruvians invisible by omission, in what Trouillot calls "the moment of fact assembly (the making of *archives*)."[59] The selective account served the interests of Creole elites by producing a narrative that equated abolition with the end of racism, which meant that Afro-Peruvians could no longer claim a common experience of oppression in the present. Denied as full citizens in raceless terms, Afro-Peruvians would disappear through mestizaje.

The maintenance of racist stereotypes and racial hierarchies even in narratives of mestizaje created problems for mestiza families with African ancestry. The racial anxieties associated with Blackness in mestizaje and national identity are illustrated by the writings of Ricardo Palma and his son, Clemente Palma, whose works I analyze in chapter 4. Bringing their writings into conversation with each other and with romantic literature on race, slavery, and mestizaje in northern Peru shows the complex process by which intellectual elites constructed the ideology of mestizaje from the selective recording of events in the early post-abolition period. The case of the Palmas shows that elite mestizos with African ancestry had to tread carefully to avoid public attacks against them, suggesting that Blackness had to be jettisoned to ascend socially as an Afro-Peruvian mestizo. Contextualized in the discourses of scientific racism and romantic novels about mestizaje under enslaving regimes, the literature ultimately shows how the discourse of mestizaje as Peruvian national identity (peruanidad) held Afro-Peruvians in the past and presumed the erasure of Blackness.

The erasure of Blackness from the historical record denied the possibility of Afro-Peruvian political agency, despite rare glimpses that suggest Afro-Peruvian enthusiasm for civic engagement and military service. This paradox is evident in the contemporary accounts of major events such as the War of the Pacific (1879–1883), the rise of populist politics under the "democratic caudillo" Nicolás de Piérola, and ultimately in the indigenismo movement of the 1920s and early 1930s.[60] Championed by populist politicians and bolstered by liberal white elite intellectuals, indigenismo rejected biological racism as a foreign phenomenon and constructed a national identity rooted in Peru's Indigenous past. The movement reified Peruvian "dualism" while claiming to promote "indigenous interests" and denying the existence of Afro-Peruvians. While elites turned their attention to the "Indian problem" in the late nineteenth and early twentieth centuries, they ascribed the African-descended population to the past and denied their presence in the modern state.

Like their contemporaries in Mexico and Brazil, many Peruvian elites embraced the French philosophy of positivism at the turn of the twentieth century as a way to improve the nation's well-being through public education and through European immigration to "whiten" the nation through mestizaje.[61] Peruvian eugenicists did not apply sterilization policies aimed at reducing the African-descended populations, but the nation's intellectual elites did accept Eurocentric assumptions about race, which influenced the state's construction of race labels in censuses and their analyses of their findings. This belief was enough for some to promote European immigration, contradicting celebratory narratives of mestizaje that denied racial difference.[62]

Between the abolition of slavery in December 1854 and the national census of 1940, Afro-Peruvians as a category of analysis disappeared from the historical record in Peru. The disappearance of Afro-Peruvians from civil, criminal, notarial, and census records of this period corresponded with a complex body of literature that associated Blackness with an immoral past, which posited that Afro-Peruvians would disappear through the process of mestizaje. My comparative analysis of the making of archives in Lima and Piura shows how these distinct processes led to different regional narratives regarding Afro-Peruvians in mestizaje. Finally, the conclusion reflects on the retrospective significance of erasure for Afro-Peruvians in the twentieth and twenty-first centuries as a collective identity that has demanded to be seen. Uncovering the complex process by which Creole elites erased

Blackness through mestizaje offers significant lessons for historians interested in hidden histories of the African diaspora in the Americas and reveals areas where further research is needed to provide a more comprehensive account of Afro-Peruvian historical agency, which has been obscured by the ideology of mestizaje.

PART I

"The Making of Sources" and "The Assembly of Facts"

Chapter 1

La Patria Peruana

Race, Honor, and Citizenship in Post-Abolition Discourse and Law

The 1854 Liberal Revolution abolished slavery and granted civil rights to Afro-Peruvians, but former enslavers and the wealthy elite refused to see their newly equal compatriots as fellow citizens. Obfuscating their racial anxieties in a rhetoric of culture, Lima elites continued to associate Blackness with the recent past of slavery. The opening lines of Lima newspaper *Zamacueca Política,* an ephemeral biweekly publication in print from January to July of 1859, read,

> The world is a great fandango, and he who doesn't dance is dumb. This vulgar saying encapsulates much philosophy, like almost all Spanish proverbs, and applied to our politics, is a hard-hitting truth. Effectively, in this country, it is not the fandango but the zamacueca that the dumb one who doesn't dance will necessarily die sadly, so that his cadaver will be buried unshrouded and on charity.
>
> Look, as the country is purely zamacueca, it is not something we need to force ourselves to try, as it is visible to all. Who does not dance the zamacueca in Lima? The *libertos* whom slavery had reduced to the state of ignorance, by the fault of the police

> have become a plague of uneducated vagrants, they do nothing other than dance day and night in the *callejones* of Montserrat, Cocharcas, Barbones, etc., at the expense of the poor storeowners who are looted at night.[1]

The authors used culture as a euphemism for race in ways that highlight elite fears of Afro-Peruvian citizenship. Aside from its initial issue, little of the newspaper survives. The opening issue or "Prospecto" satirized the Afro-Peruvian population and blamed Castilla for Lima's moral degradation. The newspaper cast Afro-Peruvians as the Other and criticized their patriotism as overly exuberant and immoral, associating their citizenship with the Afro-Peruvian dance form called *zamacueca*.

These opening lines exemplify white racist attitudes toward the Afro-Peruvian population, highlighting their perceived lack of civility and morality and thereby constructing an image of Afro-Peruvians as unfit to participate in politics. The opening issue of *Zamacueca Política* went on to directly criticize Ramón Castilla and his government, asking, "And what is a Congress that always lives on a diet because it does not work well . . . and always works poorly?—Zamacueca. And the government of General Castilla that asks for money to order the production of laws, and afterwards asks for more money to destroy those same laws by gunshots?—Zamacueca. And the so-called popular elections, when in reality they are military elections?—Zamacueca."[2] The authors thus equated what they considered uncivilized Afro-Peruvian cultural manifestations with Castilla's ineffective government, emphasizing that the government was incapable of establishing order and progress in Lima due to its association with Blackness. Even when writing about the Afro-Peruvian population specifically, this paper avoided the terms "Black" and "African," instead referencing "libertos" and cultural forms with well-known African origins. Similar to the "silent racism" directed toward Indigenous Peruvians, intellectuals maintained negative attitudes toward Afro-Peruvians in cultural terms. This criticism of Afro-Peruvian culture exemplifies the paradoxical invisibility of Afro-Peruvians in the archives and simultaneous visibility of Afro-Peruvian culture, showing the power of mestizaje to erase Blackness by addressing it only in terms of culture and not in terms of race. The *Zamacueca Política* highlights white elite anxieties of Afro-Peruvian citizenship, which they presumed would be resolved through mestizaje. Focusing on external threats and the promise of mestizaje to erase racial differences became crucial elements of denying and avoiding the topic of racism.

Elite intellectuals codified the negative connotations of Blackness in the early post-abolition years, relegating them to the bygone days of slavery and excluding Afro-Peruvians from contemporary national politics. The stigmatization would be central to erasing Afro-Peruvians from the historical record, as elites and African descendants alike elided the question of race as a foundational principle of the dominant discourse of mestizaje in the making of sources. These elite anxieties regarding Afro-Peruvian citizenship were central to the development of the ideology of mestizaje, leading to a narrative construction of nationalism that cast out the new citizens who had attained legal equality. Post-abolition print culture in Lima shows how Creole intellectual elites erected rigid conditions for Afro-Peruvian citizenship: the acceptance of a national identity in terms of "raceless" patriotism that required masculine honor through military service.

RAMÓN CASTILLA'S LIBERAL REVOLUTION AND ITS CONTRADICTIONS

Enslaved Afro-Peruvians struggled against slavery since their arrival in the Conquest era, and Creole elites made concessions to gain their support in the wars for independence. The erasure of their contributions began in influential accounts of the nation's culture and its early republican history during and after Castilla's Liberal Revolution that abolished slavery. A Spanish immigrant and influential advisor to Ramón Castilla, Sebastián Lorente fought alongside Afro-Peruvian *montoneros* (soldiers/militiamen) in support of Ramón Castilla's Liberal Revolution in 1854, and his writings in *La Voz del Pueblo* expressed his support for the revolution and the abolition of Indian tribute as well as the abolition of African slavery. In fact, while serving as Castilla's advisor during the Liberal Revolution in 1854, Lorente pushed Castilla to end these exploitative institutions. The December 3, 1854, emancipation decree certainly helped gain Afro-Peruvian support to facilitate Castilla's defeat of his rival, Rufino Echenique, on January 5, 1855, and Lorente was named inspector of public instruction in April of that year. Despite witnessing Afro-Peruvian men fighting for their freedom in favor of the Liberal Revolution, Lorente excluded them completely from his accounts of the revolution and from the nation. Considering the white elite anxieties of Afro-Peruvian citizenship in this context, Lorente's selective accounts of the Peruvian past and present must be seen as a conscious decision to avoid any association with Blackness. The fifth chapter examines his writings in detail to demonstrate his role in silencing Afro-Peruvian history, showing the interplay between the making of sources and the making of narratives that erased Afro-Peruvians as a category of historical analysis.

Ramón Castilla is remembered as the "Great Liberator" of Peru, whose domestic policies mark the true beginning of the republican era. Historians have noted that Castilla's centralizing government during his second term as president (1855–1862) succeeded due to the nation's economic boom in guano exportation, funding advances such as gas lighting in Lima, a reorganized postal system, and modernization of the military and navy. Most importantly for non-elites, his Liberal Revolution of 1854 abolished slavery and Indigenous tribute. His 1856 constitution granted universal male suffrage, broke away from colonial models of education, and established the freedom of the press.[3] These praiseworthy accomplishments dominate the historical memory, and less attention is given to his "openly conservative positions" during his second government.[4] As historian Carlos Aguirre has shown, Castilla's modernizing programs engendered a larger conservative backlash. This backlash pushed Castilla and his political allies to less progressive positions and limited their ability to resist sweeping changes to the legal codes they had established. These changes are evident in the public and elite discourse on nationalism and citizenship, which corresponded with significant changes in the 1860 constitution. Elite intellectuals expressed their concerns over Afro-Peruvian citizenship through the rhetoric of mestizaje, masculinity, and patriotism. This dominant discourse did not articulate a clear vision of Afro-Peruvian citizenship after abolition or a distinction between the Indigenous and African-descended populations, implying that mestizaje would resolve these distinctions by leaving their different histories in the past.

POST-ABOLITION ANTI-MONARCHISM AND "RACELESS" NATIONALISM

In the 1860s, Peruvian nationalists grappled with notions of racial difference in response to European economic and military intervention in the region. Historian Paul Gootenberg has analyzed the paradox of Peru's nineteenth-century commercial elite, whose reliance on foreign goods and credit fomented antipathy to foreign interests and "came to form the wellspring of nationalist ideas among the Peruvian elite."[5] Although intellectual elites developed a mestizo national identity in opposition to perceived European and Anglo races, they struggled to incorporate their newly integrated "masses" into an inclusive vision of national democracy. Creole elites established the paradox of Peruvian nationalism in the 1860s, a decade in which the "society was dramatically shaped by exclusionary practices along social, cultural, gender, and racial lines."[6] The Liberal Revolution delivered the legal promise of freedom and citizenship, but on limited and unequal terms. An analysis of the narrative process in print media in the post-abolition years reveals how elites shaped gendered and racialized understandings of the nation, particularly in relation to notions of honor, patriotism, and pan-Americanism.[7]

The Lima-centered political debates between 1854 and 1860 focused on citizenship rights, military recruitment, and criminal justice in ways that reveal elite anxieties about the freed Afro-Peruvian population without explicit reference to race. These debates shaped changes to the national constitution between 1856 and 1860, showing how elites expressed racial anxieties in "raceless" terms to preclude accusations of racism while seeking to maintain the status quo. Afro-Peruvians had fought in support of Ramón Castilla's Liberal Revolution, in support of his national abolition decree, and they rightfully expected full citizenship rights as a result of this effort.

This chapter builds on work that has expanded the pioneering approach of Benedict Anderson in his book *Imagined Communities*.[8] Historians of Latin America have criticized Anderson's suggestion that print culture defined "national space" just before independence by invoking evidence that such contested spaces were still debated later in the nineteenth century. Furthermore, as John Charles Chasteen has argued, analyses of newspapers from later in the century allow historians to see how elites sought to draw their majority nonwhite populations to their political causes through the "nativist formula." The idea of "America for Americans" carried "tremendous political utility" to unify republican forces to defend against the threat of European invasion.[9] Peruvian elites began to see Latin America as a regional identity in opposition to North America based on cultural and racial affinities in the 1860s. Peruvian intellectuals located racism in the United States and saw it as a relic of colonial Spanish America that had been rejected through abolition in the national era. Yet while anti-imperialism helped to tie Latin America together politically in the 1860s, intellectuals in the early twentieth century highlighted the region's common Indigenous roots. Approaching this narrative process as "open-ended process of articulation," Afro-Peruvians found themselves in an ambiguous place in the contested construction of Peruvian nationalism.[10] Although Afro-Peruvians were included in nationalist discourses intended to unite Latin America against European intervention, they were simultaneously cast as the Other, requiring their sacrifice to prove their place in the nation.

Discourses on race and national identity converged with the rhetoric of patriotism in the decades following the abolition of slavery. However, frequent calls for nonwhite men to pursue military service were grounded in an ideological complex of race, class, and honor that contradicted the inclusive language of democratic participation and social equality. The legal restrictions to full citizenship that emerged in 1860s Lima were consistent with contradictory elite discourses and reveal "a constant relation of reciprocal determination between nationalism and racism" not limited to Peru.[11]

LIBERAL PATRIOTISM IN 1860S LIMA: AN EXCLUSIONARY CITIZENSHIP

Following Castilla's 1854 Liberal Revolution, his 1856 constitution represented the platform of his "Government of Liberty." Conservative politician and priest Bartolomé Herrera Vélez became Castilla's main political adversary during his second presidency, as Herrera promoted an "ultra-reactionary project" in response to the Liberal Revolution. Herrera pushed to reverse many of the liberal laws of the 1856 constitution such as freedom of religion and other individual freedoms, but only succeeded in "making a few touches to the text." Historian Jorge Basadre has concluded that debates raged over the fourth article of the constitution, in which Herrera convinced the drafters to include "the prohibition of any religious practice other than Catholicism."[12] If the state's authority over religious practice became the center of congressional debates in the 1850s, the changes to citizenship laws in the 1860 constitution reveal just how far Castilla and his allies had retreated. Universal male suffrage was exposed as a temporary measure to gain popular support, because the "masses" were considered not yet worthy of enlightened citizenship.

The debates in Congress surrounding the constitution of 1856 were a continuation of arguments between abolitionists and defenders of slavery. As Carlos Aguirre and others have shown, the abolition of slavery contributed to the criminalization of Afro-Peruvians, as conservatives were concerned with "the disorder and danger that supposedly characterized the *libertos*."[13]

Such criticisms of Afro-Peruvian libertos echoed newspaper accounts decrying their comportment just after abolition. As Blanchard has documented, reports of clashes between Afro-Peruvian and white Limeños increased in the years following abolition, in particular accusations of Afro-Peruvian men harassing upper-class white women. One such account claimed that in an 1857 confrontation with police, libertos shouted, "Death to the police, long live Castilla, death to the whites."[14] Such reports heightened white fear of the formerly enslaved population and influenced political debates on criminology.

At the time of abolition, the Castilla administration agreed to remunerate enslavers for the loss of 25,505 enslaved Afro-Peruvians. As many as 6,000 of these "slaves" were in fact libertos, as hacendados defrauded the revolutionary government to maximize compensation. Excluding the free Afro-Peruvian population at the time of abolition, the enslaved population was less than one percent of Peru's population of 2,000,000 in 1854. In this perspective, the hysteria surrounding Black criminality following abolition was clearly exaggerated.[15] This exaggeration underscores elite anxieties regarding Afro-Peruvian citizenship and equality.

A congressional law passed in 1860 that would appear in the new constitution specified who could and could not vote in Peru. The law granted suffrage to citizens who were "married or at least twenty-one years old, who know how to read and write, or who are the masters of a trade, or who own real estate, or who pay a contribution to the public Treasury." The second article of the law specifically forbade suffrage for "*mendigos* [beggars] and domestic servants."[16] This law did not forbid all Afro-Peruvians from the right to vote, but it determined suffrage along class and gender lines, denying full citizenship to the poorest Peruvians and those working in occupations that carried over from slavery. Peruvian women would not gain the right to vote until 1956. The *Ley Orgánica de Elecciones* (Organic Election Law) of 1861 did not expressly prohibit domestic servants from voting, but it required the payment of a "contribution," proof of literacy, or a position as head of a workshop in order to vote. This precluded a large portion of the Afro-Peruvian population from participating in electoral politics until the law was reformed in 1919, demonstrating the exclusion of Afro-Peruvians as a legacy of slavery.[17] The law thus reveals a social hierarchy of race, occupation, and ultimately honor, and the law echoed Creole elite political discourses expressed in 1860s Peruvian newspapers.

The third article of the law granted suffrage to military authorities and officers, even if they did not exercise the authority to command. Despite these significant restrictions, the constitution of 1860 upheld the illegality of military recruitment, a law enforced by European and Brazilian monarchies. Patriotic newspapers of the 1860s represented Peruvian military practices as superior.[18] Because Peru's military was less authoritarian in nature, intellectuals' associating forced military service or impressment with monarchies allowed them to champion their recruitment policies as more progressive, egalitarian, and patriotic.

ELITE NOTIONS OF HONOR AND BELONGING

The ideological objectives of Peruvian newspaper publications in the 1860s also mirror the Society of the Founders of the Independence of Peru, an elite republican society established in Lima in 1861. The society's constitution began with statements explaining who could and could not become members, first inviting the "sons and relatives of the founders," then "citizens, notable for their talent and republican virtues, or for their positive service that in some form has contributed to the *patria* and the cause of liberty." They further specified that this would include "the partners who . . . will decide for the suffrage for the two thirds of the present members."[19] Beyond those directly related to the revolutionary leaders whose membership and citizenship would be immediate, the society reserved the right to judge the honor of those interested in joining. The society thus claimed the authority to decide who would attain full Peruvian citizenship based on the history they constructed of the nation's independence struggle. In their selective account of Peruvian independence, these elites omitted the fact that African descendants made up 53 percent of Lima's independence troops. The silencing of this fact also allowed these elites to elide the fact that no enslaved Afro-Peruvians actually attained freedom through military service in the independence war, despite serving because they were promised gradual emancipation.[20]

This group of national elites asserted their influence on the lawmakers in Congress, and their influence went beyond patriotic rhetoric to reveal class and racial disparities. The society's constitution, unsurprisingly, barred from membership anyone who had fought against the cause of independence or combated the "republican principles sanctioned by the national institutions." However, it went on to equate Spanish loyalism to lesser offenses, precluding the "honor of admission" from "those who have dishonorable flaws or judicially proven crimes," "those sentenced by the courts to a defamatory penalty," and "those who carry an independent position, or who lack an honorable means of subsistence."[21] The language of honor and citizenship ran parallel in post-abolition newspapers, elite society, and law. Without using the language of race, elite society excluded those Afro-Peruvians from membership who had served with royalist forces for the promise of pay and self-manumission. It also excluded Afro-Peruvians who continued to struggle against the legacies of slavery that barred them from "an honorable means of subsistence." Elite intellectuals constructed social expectations of honor and citizenship in "raceless" terms in order to homogenize Peruvian society, rendering ethnoracial differences obsolete in their analysis of the nation's past and present. As these elites elided the history of race-based slavery and Indigenous tribute while maintaining a social hierarchy rooted in that recent past, they preserved a tacit socioracial hierarchy beneath the surface of republican rhetoric and laid the foundations for the ideology of mestizaje.

Elites connected their concerns over honor and citizenship to social class, which was implicitly tied to race. The constitution stated that its principle objective was to "inspire the sons of the founders and the rest of the associates, just as the rising generation, love for the *patria* and her institutions; respect for the law and its defenders; the cult of democracy; the sincere and constant desire to introduce it to the public; enlightening the popular masses."[22] The elites planned to enlighten the masses through public instruction at its "core." In contrast with the schools that would educate the children of the wealthy, a free school would focus on "technical, moral, and social teachings, to the benefit of the working classes."[23] Elites would reap the benefits of the codes of honor and morality they constructed, keeping their own children in elite schools while educating the working classes enough to be informed citizens but remain manual laborers.

The discursive parallels between elite patriotic societies, newspapers, and the 1860 constitution suggest closer ties between Lima elites and government policy than previously assumed. Lima elites compared their national development with the struggles experienced by other emerging Latin American republics. Napoleon III attempted to create a French client state in Mexico shortly after the young nation's civil war, but he was driven out in 1867. Spain's attempts to claim the guano-rich Chincha Islands just south of Lima similarly followed Peru's civil war between rival caudillos. The European powers likely saw political disunity as an opportunity to take back their former colonial strongholds, but their interventions fostered a sense of unity within and between Latin American republics. As the narrative process demonstrates, intellectual and political elites of Peru and Mexico, unlike the Dominican Republic and Brazil, used the interventions as an opportunity to foster nationalist patriotism while codifying ideologies of honor and citizenship. Brazil was still a monarchy in the 1860s, of course, and Dominican president Pedro Santana exchanged his country's independence to Spain for a royal title in 1861. Requiring the support of "the masses" to protect their independence from Spanish ambitions, Peruvian elites sought to integrate the Afro-Peruvian population on their terms.

The exigencies of European intervention led to the construction of national patriotism that invoked slavery as a rhetorical device now feasible in the post-abolition years. Nationalist elites in the Americas tended to see the Indigenous masses as the core of their national identities, whose deplorable condition would be improved by their civic engagement in the democratic republics and through the education systems. In this schema, "degeneration" best described the downfall of the once-great Indigenous civilizations. Degeneration took on a distinct meaning among Brazilian racial theorists, who were concerned that African racial mixture caused social regression.[24]

Nonetheless, elite perspectives on Afro-Peruvian political participation underscore the paradox of Peruvian nationalism: the same elites who called for equality and freedom lamented that "Black citizens . . . are capable of discrediting every democratic institution [and] degrading it to the point that Whites renounce to their rights as citizens."[25] While distancing the republic from slavery and calling for Afro-Peruvian political and military support, the Peruvian state limited their citizenship rights, wrote them out of the nation's history, and demanded their continual military sacrifice as proof of their patriotism and place in the nation. In response to intellectual discourses that denied them a political voice and called for their military service, Afro-Peruvians fought for patriotic causes to improve their social conditions and sacrificed their lives to gain honor, conforming to elite expectations. In other cases, they fought alongside caudillos like Ramón Castilla and Nicolás de Piérola to demand such improvements.[26] As elites fomented a sense of nationalism in the context of European invasion in the 1860s, they erased ethnoracial distinctions while maintaining implicit racial and gender mores established in the colonial period. Such contradictions were fundamental to the shaping of Peruvian mestizaje.

LA AMÉRICA AND *EL PERUANO*: A POST-ABOLITION PUSH FOR PAN-AMERICAN SOLIDARITY

Newspapers that sought the military support of Afro-Peruvians and the mestizo working class utilized a more ambiguous rhetoric when describing this population. The white elite rhetorical construction of Peruvian nationalism expressed their anxieties about Afro-Peruvian citizenship by casting out African descendants as an insignificant element of mestizaje. The city's intellectual elite likely recognized the important roles Afro-Peruvian men played in the wars of independence and in caudillo rivalries leading to the abolition of slavery. Fresh from military success in the Liberal Revolution of 1854, such Afro-Peruvian men had the experience necessary for success in critical battles. Presumably, they also had newfound reasons to defend the "Government of Liberty." Lima elites established newspapers that expressed a more inclusive national identity seeking the political support of the nation's newest citizens following Castilla's Liberal Revolution. Patriotic newspapers were not a new phenomenon in 1860s Peru. The proto-nationalist newspaper *Mercurio Peruano* first constructed an exclusionary vision of the nation in the late eighteenth century (which I discuss in the context of Peruvian "dualism" in chapter 5), and Simón Bolívar founded the patriotic *Diario Oficial el Peruano* shortly after independence. These newspapers revised historical narratives and constructed new visions of national and regional identity in ways that reflect the nation's more exclusionary citizenship policies during the decade following abolition in Peru.

La América was the first of a new generation of newspapers in which elites envisioned a more expansive national and regional identity, although it likely took cues from the longstanding official daily *El Peruano*. This short-lived newspaper was published almost every week for an eight-month period in 1862, during a period of heightened fears of European imperialism. The paper's stories mainly covered diplomatic relations between Peru and Mexico while also keeping a close eye on European actions toward Latin America. This included concern over a Spanish naval fleet headed for Buenos Aires as well as the Spanish press's reaction to a speech by Prince Napoleon in which he defended the virtues of democracy. The irony of such rhetoric was not missed by the Lima elites, who associated Europe with colonialism and the Latin American republics with freedom and democracy. Appearing in Lima on April 5, 1862, the newspaper's first line read, "The independence of America is currently threatened by those who seek their power and force through the enslavement of her peoples."[27] Beyond the contradictory language of liberty and equality that buttressed the frequent calls for military sacrifice in *La América,* the newspaper sidestepped the constitutional limits of post-abolition political participation. While the directive junta of the Central Liberal Society acknowledged the distinct entities of "peoples" (*pueblos*) of Latin America, the central argument of their inaugural article sought to bind Peruvian interests with those of Mexico, condemning the "unjustifiable invasion" of the "sister nation" by France. The article went on to call for the peoples of Latin America to defend their liberty and sovereignty from the triumvirate of European power: France, England, and Spain. This political cause was the express reason for this newspaper's establishment, as its immediate objectives were "to put to action all of the defensive elements, to combine the forces that we can make available, to bring into contact all of those whose cause is democracy—and to defend beginning today American interests, highly shared—we have begun by founding this newspaper—exempt from any internal political intervention—in this we do not propose any other end than that of serving the interests of America and the cause of liberty."[28]

The call to arms saw inclusion as the best policy, and the article even pointed to the common "love of *la patria*" between liberals and conservatives in the Americas as a unifying force. Nevertheless, the language that these intellectuals chose appears designed to associate slavery with colonial rule and freedom and abolition with the nation, similar to concurrent discourses in Brazil.[29]

The newspaper recognized Brazil's exceptionalism, crediting Dom Pedro II for his moderation, while still seeing republicanism as the superior form of government. On June 4, 1862, an article by Francisco de P. G. Vigil offered a "comparative look" at the Brazilian Empire of Prince Pedro II. The issue began with words of praise for this "honored man," who "works arduously to stay informed of the latest publications in Europe, always maintaining his intelligence at the level of all scientific discoveries."[30] His success as emperor, however, was due to his work educating the people of Brazil: "So it was not the emperor who saved Brazil; it was the [Brazilian] man."[31] The article cautioned that the peaceful transfer of power between the Brazilian monarchs was uncommon, and "the pages of history show us a long list of monarchs whose grandiosity and opulence did not consist in the wellbeing of the governed, but in that of the kings and their aristocrats."[32] For this reason, the Brazilian monarch could not offer everything he should have to the social life of his subjects/citizens beyond science. Brazilians particularly lacked individual rights and "ample liberty." Therefore, Vigil argued, "our humble court presents better guarantees to the citizen-man of the republic than the monarchy."[33] Don Vigil preferred the theoretical language of political philosophy to empirical realities—his comparison with Brazil failed to mention the "imperial republic's" maintenance of slavery, which would continue until 1888. Eliding this comparison allowed the authors to avoid addressing the Afro-Peruvian population, demonstrating their selective criticisms of monarchism, which was in keeping with the unifying rhetoric of mestizaje. Rather than point to the abolition of slavery in Peru and the continuation of the institution in Brazil as obvious evidence that republicanism facilitated liberty for African descendants, Vigil's analysis presumed that the question of Afro-Latin American rights was irrelevant. His praise for Pedro II therefore suggests he saw monarchy as somewhat rational in the context of a country with a much larger African and African-descended population.

The authors of *La América* had good reason to be concerned about Spanish maneuverings in the Americas, especially in light of Peru's reliance on guano exportation as the basis of its economy under Castilla's administration. The young nation's weak military, in comparison with Spain and Chile, risked damaging a national sense of honor in a global context. This fear and resentment came to a head on August 4, 1863, in the northern hacienda of Talambó in the Chiclayo Valley of the department of Lambayeque. A Spanish naval squadron had paid a diplomatic visit to Chile before docking in Callao and moving north along the Peruvian coast. While the squadron visited the hacienda Talambó, a fight broke out between the Spaniards and locals, leading to the deaths of one Peruvian and one Spaniard. Spain demanded indemnification for the acts of aggression and invaded and occupied the guano-rich Chincha islands when Peru refused.

In March of 1865, the *New York Times* reported on the Spanish-Peruvian war in a manner that criticized both parties. The newspaper noted the punitive conditions for Spain to agree to end the hostilities. In order to "receive back" the islands, Peru had to "allow an investigation of the Tambó case, to indemnify all Spaniards for the losses and confiscations caused by them during the struggle for independence, and to pay Spain the $3,000,000 which this expedition into the Pacific is said to have cost her." The article went on to explain that "these terms were equally hard and humiliating, and by assenting to them the Lima Government has evinced an utter disregard of its own dignity and national honor." According to this report, a party of Spanish sailors had landed in Callao after the Vivanco-Pareja Treaty ended the war in January. An angry mob confronted the crew and killed several before the rest fled. The *New York Times* attacked Peru's honor further, calling President Juan Antonio Pezet a "pusillanimous," "imbecile executive." The event and the media coverage of it only reinforced the hardening narratives of honor as military service and strength.[34] Spain had yet to recognize Peruvian independence, and the stipulation that Peru compensate Spain for damages in the wars of independence was insulting to the young republic. The resolution ended Spanish occupation but heightened the anxieties of patriotic elites working to consolidate national and regional identities based on popular sovereignty and anti-monarchism.

Other Lima newspapers were forging pan-American connections by comparing Latin American relationships with former colonial powers in the 1860s. While *La América* focused on Mexico's tribulations, *El Peruano*, the official daily newspaper of Peru, monitored the young republics of the Caribbean. On August 24, 1861, *El Peruano* reported that the "democratic institutions and continental security" had suffered an attack at the Republic of Santo Domingo.[35] The article went on to assert that the attempt to reincorporate this republic into the Spanish monarchy obligated the Peruvian government to join with the rest of the American republics to defend against this "common danger." The Peruvian newspaper criticized Dominican president general Santa Anna's treasonous act of accepting a contract that benefitted him at the expense of his people's liberty and autonomy. The captain general of Cuba, it stated, responded to news of this contract with a show of force, remitting a naval battalion to the shores of Hispaniola. As Spain sought to declare Santo Domingo part of its monarchy without any political representation, the article argued, "Spain is devoted to its retrograde system of colonization, letting it be known that it has not abolished slavery in principle, but as a circumstantial measure that can be reestablished."[36] As the article called for Latin American solidarity to defend itself from European imperialism, it appealed to Afro-Peruvians by associating slavery with European monarchism, which could return if Spain recolonized Peru.

Like many articles in *La América*, the article in *El Peruano* used the rhetoric of slavery to criticize European imperialism. This rhetoric, however, coexisted uneasily with contradictory language about Indigenous and Afro-Peruvians. The European powers were exploiting the divisions between liberal and conservative *americanos*, the article argued, and these "true oppressors" and "speculators of human flesh . . . try to change our sovereignty, our liberty, our riches by the luck of the slave."[37] The patriot Creole elites had benefited economically from enslaved labor in the Americas, but they placed primary responsibility for such exploitation squarely on the European powers. Thus by invoking slavery rhetorically to condemn imperialism, intellectuals elided their own positions on abolition and racism.

In the opening lines of *La América*, the authors declared the newspaper's columns open to any who supported their cause, "whatever their political color." They went on to contrast the problems of the French monarchy with the benefits of American democracy: "The powers aligned against Mexico recognize as possible and still attainable their *intervention* in Mexico's internal affairs, to make them change their form of Government and substitute the just and rational system of democracy for the Monarchy, with all of its inconveniences, its injustices, its inequalities, and its character essentially contrary to the dignity of man, to his rights and guarantees."[38]

The contrast between European monarchism and Latin American democratic republicanism continued with a critique of the latter's depiction in European newspapers, which presented "exaggerated and false descriptions of our situation: they suppose that we find ourselves in a situation of constant anarchy: they paint us as little more than savages."[39] This statement encapsulates a common predicament among patriotic elites in Peru. Even as they saw Europe as a model of civilization toward which they aspired, the elite intellectuals struggled to "civilize" their masses whom they too considered inferior. Their goals of "enlightening" the racialized underclass to make them honorable citizens while simultaneously asserting a hard-earned sovereignty from Europe exposed the contradictions of Peruvian nationalism. Yet like most of Spanish America in the nineteenth century, such unifying rhetoric helped Peruvian elites to elide these contradictions during what historian Hilda Sabato has called "the revolutionary political experiment."[40]

Sabato's significant intervention on this period forces historians to recognize the impact of large sectors of non-elites in shaping Latin American republics in the nineteenth century. The interplay between print media and the law in post-abolition Peru demonstrates "the relationship between people and government that developed after the adoption of popular sovereignty as a founding principle of power." The hegemonic narratives of this period also highlight "the common traits and shared tendencies in the relationships *between* 'the many and the few.'"[41] By refusing to address Afro-Peruvian's place in post-abolition society in direct terms, these elites cast out Blackness in their rhetoric of nationalism, honor, and citizenship, erasing Blackness from the making of sources and subsequent archives. This erasure by omission was the easiest way to assuage elite anxieties and became a central component of Peruvian mestizaje.

Despite the inclusive tone of pan-American democracy these intellectuals sought to convey, their assumptions regarding race excluded those deemed inferior or "regressive." Toward the article's end, the authors proclaim their racial proximity to the Europeans, stating "the race of our parents [read fathers] has still not degenerated; the remains of the heroes of Junín and Ayacucho, and the recent memory of their acts, will temper the spirit of the current generation, which certainly does not need foreign examples to achieve great, noble, and elevated actions."[42] Drawing from the emergent language of racial degeneration to proclaim their civilized and "elevated" status, the authors reveal their own concerns for the very nation and region they love. Their praises for the revolutionary heroes who fought for Peruvian independence implicitly dismissed the many Indigenous and African-descended patriots who also took up arms against Spain. This rare but transparent racial language suggests the authors omitted the roles of Indigenous and Afro-Peruvians intentionally, thereby erasing them from the nation's history and identity.

The opening article of *La América* was signed by Francisco Javier Mariátegui (president), José Casimiro Ulloa (secretary), and José Celedonio Urrea (secretary), and it set the tone for the remainder of the short-lived newspaper. These elite intellectuals had graduated from the prestigious

University of San Marcos and held influential government positions. Francisco Javier Mariátegui was the ancestor of Peru's most famous leftist intellectual, José Carlos Mariátegui (whose *indigenista* writings I analyze in chapter 5). The authors also argued that freedom was part of their natural environment, lamenting the colonial "brutalization of the indigenous races that [for] three centuries has not been able to bring true civilization."[43] Latin American republics, the article concluded, would never treat their native peoples with such brutality. In this instance, the enslavement of Africans and their descendants was not seen as relevant. The ideology of mestizaje not yet cemented, these authors established a tacit socioracial hierarchy below the surface of republican rhetoric.

An article by one of *El Peruano*'s correspondents in Madrid sheds further light on convoluted elite perspectives on race and national interests in 1860s Peru. On December 1, 1861, Señor Don Hector Varela described the Mexican situation in contrast with a Spanish "expedition" to Africa. This expedition had the support of the Spanish populace and was much discussed in the newspapers, unlike the "indifference" and hopelessness surrounding the expedition to Mexico. "The African War," Hector Varela wrote, "which the people applauded, was a necessary war, a civilizing war, a just war."[44] The author thus used sixteenth-century logic of conquest to justify Spain's actions in the 1859–1860 Spanish-Moroccan war and ignored Spain's colonial ambitions in Africa, which shared similarities to Spanish actions in the Americas.[45] Varela's historical analysis reveals assumptions relating to race that were common among Peruvian elites in 1860s Lima, who saw Indigenous Peruvians as victims of colonial brutality but Afro-Peruvians as descendants of a barbarous continent. Thus, decades before the early twentieth-century pseudoscientific race theory and Vasconcelos's notion of the "cosmic race," Peruvian intellectuals envisioned a racial hierarchy that held whites at the top, Indigenous a level below, and Africans at the bottom.[46] The groups they considered inferior could be improved or erased through mestizaje, a facile resolution to a complex problem. Varela's analysis also reflects Iberian debates of the mid-sixteenth century that argued for papal authorization of the trade in enslaved people and maintained that Indigenous people of the New World were rational and therefore able to accept Catholicism. Although these nineteenth-century intellectuals perceived neither group as "civilized," they sympathized and identified more with the Indigenous populations of the Americas based on pre-Enlightenment debates.

Despite such contradictions, the authors continually addressed and instructed the historically oppressed peoples of the Americas. Their enlightened worldview, they assumed, would guide Indigenous and Afro-Peruvian men to a more civilized and politically active status: "To you all, men of the people, we write these pages—to you all it is dedicated, hard-working agronomists, honored artisans, all members of the society that lived with the work of your hands and ate bread dampened with the sweat of your brows. In all the nations you comprise the immense majority, and yet you are deprecated and scorned, enslaved and oppressed. . . . And what cause? Your ignorance and nothing other than your ignorance. . . . You [must] stop deprecating yourselves, scorning, enslaving, and oppressing yourselves; because you do not know what you are because your lack of knowledge has degenerated the noble race from which you all descend."[47]

As the Indigenous populations composed the "immense majority" of the Peruvian population, these lines appear to be directed to them. The lines therefore reflect the common narrative of Indigenous degeneration from a once-civilized status, resulting from the Conquest, in contrast with Africans, who would be raised out of savagery by Europeans. The lines also demonstrate a complete lack of awareness of African kingdoms and their imperial interactions with Europeans. Furthermore, the intentional vagueness of the "men of the people" suggested a mestizo working class in which African ancestry had been subsumed under a process of mestizaje rooted in an Indigenous past.

The paper blamed exogenous forces for Indigenous and Afro-Peruvian inferiority and believed that they could be enlightened, civilized, and educated into equality. These intellectuals blamed the colonial powers for the ignorance of the masses but assumed their liberal political philosophy could restore the equality that God granted all men. Furthermore, they argued that although individuals were born with equal political rights, some were born with more abilities than others. Such differences in aptitudes, they resolved, could be overcome by hard work, a raceless, meritocratic approach that would be echoed by late-nineteenth-century caudillo populist Nicolás de Piérola.[48] The inherent contradictions of liberalism were better clothed in the rhetoric of freedom and equality, and this meant discussing Afro-Peruvians only in the context of slavery, which was in the past. Although a "divine birthright," the experience of equality had been and continued to be "diverse": "From the beginning until today the world is divided into servants and lords. There are countries that call themselves free yet they conserve slavery as an institution. What an error!"[49] Instead, they argued, Latin American republics should be ruled by "the majority." Exhibiting the highly coded anxieties of Afro-Peruvian civic engagement, they added, "Public opinion . . . is not comprised of everyone's opinion, but only of those who are capable of having one. In order to have an opinion, one needs sufficient intelligence, some knowledge, and freedom. With the exception of the demented and idiots, all have sufficient intelligence. Not all have the necessary knowledge, but all can and should acquire it through instruction."[50] This was the only article that linked education to citizenship. The article intended to celebrate Peruvian democracy in contrast with European monarchism ultimately reveals the same anxieties seen in *Zamacueca Política*, but expressed in raceless terms that would not alienate Afro-Peruvian, Indigenous, and mestizo working classes. After all, these "masses" were still needed to defend the nation's fragile sovereignty.

Rather than focus on education as a path to social equality, however, the authors of *La América* advocated for military service as a path to honorable citizenship. They laid out a contradictory system of voluntary recruitment that disproportionately affected the poor and people of color while moving toward creating a national guard for the privileged, which would enable elites to be credited with patriotism with little risk of having to make the sacrifice of blood. The issue published on April 16, 1862, ended with a direct call for youth military action: "Young Americans!" the article began, "Alert! Be prepared, danger nears." The article described European naval battalions en route to America to "monarchize" her, admitting that they were a reputable force but insisting that their weaponry could be defeated by sheer numbers.[51] The concerns over Spanish attempts to reclaim possessions of her former colonies were not ungrounded, as evinced by the war that Chile and Peru fought together against Spain's seizure of the Chincha Islands from 1864 to 1866. This experience contributed to a nascent "Latin American" identity, building on the solidarity expressed during the Franco-Austrian occupation of Mexico.

However, there was an ulterior motive found within the newspaper's florid language of democracy, equality, and brotherhood and its call to arms. This nascent identity drew attention to racial animosity in the United States to contrast it with Latin American exceptionalism in race mixing, exalting mestizaje as evidence of progress toward a racially inclusive democracy and Latin American progress toward popular sovereignty. This concluding address directly followed a poem that neatly illustrates the paradox of the newspaper itself. Dated September 16, 1861, the poem was signed by M. M. de S. in Santiago. The initials do not match any of the newspaper's directors or correspondents, so his identity is a mystery. Titled "To Washington," the poem begins with short phrases praising this "Genius of liberty" who "received the power from God himself to create Eden on earth." Moving to the US Civil War, the poem continues, "And what do I see? Your shadow concerned, / Upon news of the fratricidal war, / Throws a look upon *la patria,*/And with a powerful and passionate voice: / Union (he says), men are brothers, / Here in heaven there are Africans too."[52] The Chilean poet's imagined posthumous words of George Washington effectively revised US history in the same manner that the newspaper's writers reimagined Peru's national history. Both whitewashed the national histories of slavery and patriot leaders' implicit relationship with the institution. This poem followed a similar ode to Simón Bolívar, which did not mention the role of African-descendants in the independence struggles. Having witnessed slavery's abolition just six years prior, Lima intellectuals began to use US racism as a foil for Latin American mestizaje. In the process, it became easier to avoid questions of race and racism at home.

The post-abolition newspaper's rhetoric continually distanced patriot leaders from slavery, but the poem to Washington also reveals a Peruvian perspective on race relations in the United States during the civil war. While the European interventions in the region had contributed to a common political affinity, Latin America also identified itself in opposition to the "Anglo-Saxon race" of the United States. These "damn heretics, *of such a strange race,* act less arrogant in these circumstances, less demanding of us, and more humane and considerate than those of *our race,* who come asking us for reparations for grievances and payment for debts, fixing their bayonets and pointing their fanatical cannons at us."[53] The authors thus equated the racial differences between the United States and Latin America with the differing responses to European intervention, and further likened European and white North American identities and politics. Emphasizing that the Spanish invaders were of "our race" subtly positioned the authors as Creole white elites while separating Latin America racially from Anglo-America. This framework facilitated a policy of unifying the masses of the Americas to a common cause: the defense of *la patria*. The perceived racial differences further solidified a month later when the authors called for a "Union of the American Republics," which did not include the United States.[54]

Just a few weeks following this racial analysis, however, members of the newspaper's elite liberal *junta* attended a "patriotic banquet" in Milan, the purpose of which "free men of all countries will know how to appreciate." The banquet was held at the beginning of April in honor of revolutionary general Giuseppe Garibaldi and included speeches by representatives of France, Hungary, and Venice, where Garibaldi had just accomplished a major military victory over the Papal army to advance his national unification project. The representatives lauded Garibaldi's achievements and the "civilizing" project of bringing the people together in a republic based on science and reason. They showed clear support for Garibaldi's ultimate goal of "liberating" Rome, and the Peruvian delegates connected this struggle to President Lincoln's war with the Confederacy.[55] The mid-nineteenth-century elite discourses on Peruvian national identity made clear connections to nation-making projects throughout the Americas and in Europe.

These intellectuals admired the French Revolution and Enlightenment, continually using its rhetoric as a foundation for their vision for modern Peru. This rhetoric, however, consistently coincided with calls for patriotic military participation. One article criticized the practice of forced military "recruitment" for "dispensing of men just as of things," which they saw as a "barbaric" practice that "directly attacks their sacred right of individuality, in which the right of *honor* is found."[56] The authors went on to lament the class differences of becoming an honorable citizen while simultaneously constructing this social reality. The poor, unlike noble families, "do not have titles in order to be respected," whereas the wealthy had the title of "Don," making "them sacred to the recruiters."[57] Once again directly addressing the "honored artisan," the authors criticized the fact that the lower classes of all nations made up the majority of their military conscripts. This status quo disrupted families and made the lives of struggling mothers and hungry children even more difficult, they argued. Nevertheless, the practice of paying soldiers for their patriotic service was also a mistake. Instead, they proposed the solution of "national guards." This system of voluntary military service would generate more patriotism, and "upon seeing the actions of the more enlightened, [men] will successively experience their own development and in the end we will obtain true citizens and not automatons."[58] Ironically, of course, all of the newspaper's contributors held the title of "Don," so none of them would find it necessary to serve in the national guard to gain honorable status. Nevertheless, voluntary service would be dominated by elite men, who had the time and resources to gain even more honor and serve as the "model" citizens the working class should aspire to be. Despite acknowledging the difficulties and consequences of working-class men leaving their struggling families to fend for themselves while serving in the military, the authors suggested the sacrifice would bring their families greater honor and improve their social status.

The implicit racial and social hierarchy undermined the rhetoric of equality and patriotism in the newspaper even as the authors distinguished their national identity from the United States'. Because this was particularly evident in the discussion of military service and conscription, this model of progress and citizenship had striking similarities to the construction of civil society in postcolonial Brazil. These intellectuals sought to differentiate their "national guard" policies with those of recruitment and impressment in Brazil, but in both nations military service "offered narrow avenues of social mobility or at least temporary shelter."[59]

The patriot intellectuals explicitly contrasted their national guard policy of military encouragement with the recruitment and impressment policies of the Brazilian monarchy, but the language of military service as an honorable sacrifice ran parallel in the neighboring nations. Some issues of *La América* resemble Brazilian recruitment strategies of the 1860s that sought to "win over" the working classes to "the nationalist cause."[60] The June 4 issue of the Peruvian newspaper encouraged military participation as part of one's civic duty, stipulating, "As all men form part of the political association, they are civilly and morally obligated to the defense of their *patria*." Although this service would not be forced, "all should work in harmony so that they contribute what is due: from this comes the contribution called 'of blood' and has no other end."[61]The post-abolition newspaper thus equated political participation with military service and utilized existing racial hierarchies to qualify the Afro-Peruvian sense of belonging. Their role in national independence and culture written out, the oppressed would have to continually prove their loyalty to the *patria* by sacrificing their blood.

The patriot intellectuals who authored *La América* also sought to justify the conservative victory in establishing Catholicism as the national religion in the 1860 constitution, similar to the reaction of Mexican conservatives to that nation's liberal constitution of 1857. Mixing Christian doctrine with language of the Enlightenment, the newspaper described the resurrection of Christ as a triumph of the downtrodden over their oppressors. "The consequence of this triumph of liberty and equality, was the triumph of Christian brotherhood that destroyed the castes once and for all," argued the republican journalist and historian Emilio Castelar.[62] His emphasis on Catholicism and the elimination of casta categories exhibits the conservative influence on and consensus around erasing Blackness in the early shaping of Peruvian mestizaje as an ideology. Castelar's revisionist theology ignored the contradictions of the Church in the Americas, preferring to point out that Christ was born in a stable and not on a throne. Castelar emphasized that Christ sought out the humble and the enslaved people, not the powerful, and was the son of an artisan. Although the journalist did not acknowledge the role of Christianity in the Atlantic slave trade or in the Conquest of the Americas, his analysis of religious doctrine argued that the post-abolition republic would reflect more accurately Christ's teachings: "We swear to work ceaselessly for liberty, for equality, for the brotherhood of man, and being democratic, we will be more Christian. . . ."[63] Castelar's analysis inherently denied that the primary debate surrounding the 1860 constitution was a struggle between liberal and conservative principles, effectively justifying Bartolomé Herrera's ideological victory two years earlier.

A military song titled "Colombia's Hymn" followed Castelar's theological piece on June 7. The song was unsurprisingly an ode to Simón Bolívar, and it pledged the patriotic sacrifice of blood to protect the freedom for which he fought. The song's third stanza highlighted the assumed connections between liberty, military bravery, and masculinity that undergirded the newspaper's political philosophy: "Liberty is the life of the soul; / Servitude makes the male vile; / Defending a tyrant is opprobrious; / Perishing for the *patria* is honor."[64] Although the song did not address race or national identity directly, it suggests that Afro-Peruvians had no honor under the institution of slavery but could gain it through military service. Slavery, it suggested, had emasculated and feminized Afro-Peruvian men. They would have to recover their masculine honor through military sacrifice.

CONCLUSIONS

While religious freedom may have been the focus of debates leading up to the 1860 constitution, the exclusion of other religions was less consequential to non-elites than other revisions to the liberal constitution of 1856. The intellectuals who shaped hegemonic narratives of patriotism, honor, and liberalism stoked nationalist and pan-American sentiments to defeat the most urgent threat of their time: European invasion. These liberal nationalists addressed their readers directly, and the consistent evocations of slavery and liberation suggest that they expected Afro-Peruvian men to embrace the publications. However, the rhetoric never specifically addressed the formerly enslaved African-descended people of Peru, instead appealing to a generalized fear of recolonization, which, they suggested, may even subject them to a similarly subservient position. Fearful of European imperial drives, then, Lima elites in the 1860s could now point to the abolition of slavery as an advancement of *la patria* while clumsily equating slavery with monarchism. They also excluded women from their "brotherhood of man," preferring to ignore gender disparities altogether.

Consistent with these oblique appeals to Afro-Peruvians for their military and political support, the men of *La América* slowly developed a general foreign policy agenda based on their analyses of Latin American independence and the region's troubles with European intervention. These newspapers notably omitted the Monroe Doctrine despite its stated promise of US defense of Latin American autonomy, as it had already become clear that such intervention would arrive only if the northern nation would benefit from the effort. The contributors described the Latin American wars for independence as a singular struggle, noting the intracontinental support among revolutionary leaders against Spanish rule. Once again, Brazil was an outlier in this schema, but the authors hoped that the "arbitrary and scandalous intervention of Napoleon III" in Mexico would trigger an enthusiasm for patriotism and the republican form of government there as well. Their optimism led them to further develop the earlier notion of the Union of the American Republics. The "spirit" of all of the Hispanic American republics, the authors concluded, would naturally result in an "extended union—the American Federation."[65] The naïve optimism of Latin American unification through mestizaje presaged the rise of *arielismo* and *neo-arielismo* in twentieth-century anti-imperialist movements and was a presumed panacea for historic conflict and contemporary racial tensions.[66]

This early call for a politically unified Latin America, however, was only briefly discussed. Instead, the newspaper's final issues focused on nationalism. The final pages of the newspaper in December 1862 turned the focus to national industry and revealed concerns over the political participation of the same citizens who were encouraged to serve in the national guard. The authors discussed the need for a national bank and the standardization of currency while pointing out Chile's success in monopolizing the tobacco industry through state-supported free trade. One author, M. Palma, pointed to the singular importance of agricultural production, concentrated on the fertile land along the coast, but he cautioned that the application of the military to agricultural work would present "grave inconveniences." Returning to the notion of honor, Palma asserted that the "soldier would see his career denigrated, the government dangerously scattering her troops to different places, exposing them to the seductions of men who live in political revolt, and the lover of liberal principles would see this as an attack on public liberties."[67] Such Lima elites thus recognized that subjecting soldiers to agricultural work would smack of slavery, which would contradict any association with honor and likely incite rebellion.

As Afro-Peruvians had taken up arms against the Spanish in the wars of independence and fought for the abolition of slavery in the Liberal Revolution of 1854, elites likely saw them as useful combatants to defend *la patria* from European invasion and yet refused to say this explicitly. Spain's aggression in taking the Chincha Islands only reinforced the messaging of Lima's post-abolition newspapers, including race and gender ideologies tied to narratives of national identity. Yet the promise of gaining honor in the process was largely disingenuous, as Afro-Peruvians had to continue to push back against the legacies of slavery and dominant discourses that denied them their rightful place in the republic.

Contrasting the inclusive and democratic republic of Peru with the authoritarian systems of Europe required Lima's intellectuals to address the Afro-Peruvian population that had recently attained freedom from slavery in the mid-nineteenth century. The inherent contradictions of criticizing monarchies for their oppressive practices while minimizing the recent struggles and contributions of significant portions of their own population epitomize the paradox of liberalism in the nineteenth century. These intellectuals used the rhetoric of popular sovereignty and freedom while simultaneously constructing a hegemonic discourse of exclusionary citizenship along race, class, and gender lines. While these intellectuals had to address the question of freed Afro-Peruvians in this context, they did so in oblique terms and preferred to equate abolition with social equality. They relegated

Afro-Peruvians to the past as well, implying that this population had joined the indistinguishable "masses" through mestizaje. The raceless rhetoric of mestizaje served two elite purposes in 1860s Peru: it denied the possibility of racism, and it promoted a shared national identity to gain the support of the mestizo working classes.

The nearly weekly issues of *La América* concluded in December of 1862, part of a flurry of publications that Basadre has contextualized as "the antimonarchic agitation."[68] The final issues of *La América* began to address the central concern for post-abolition Peruvian society of economic and industrial growth without enslaved labor. They framed the principles of global trade and economic development as a national challenge that could be overcome only by increased production. M. Palma reiterated that "there cannot be income without production, and the only way to increase the treasury is by trying to develop the country's industry."[69] Palma identified the central problem; the solution, however, would emerge later.

National elites eventually saw Chinese laborers as the best solution to the labor shortage along the coast, but the authors of *La América* avoided discussion of such solutions in favor of a paternalistic discourse of romantic patriotism. The December 13 issue concluded with a poem by Ricardo Rossel titled "Song of the *Patria*." Similar to prior odes to liberty and patriotism, the poem repeated previous calls to arms to defend "Divine Liberty." Rossel identified Peruvians as "sons of the Andes," rooting the nation's history in its Indigenous past, and he carried on the theme of nationalism as antithetical to slavery. One stanza states, "You would know again, fighting bravely, / To die free to no longer live a slave."[70] The implicit hierarchies of race in such romantic prose would become more clearly pronounced as the century neared its end and positivism provided "scientific" legitimacy to elite notions of race and nation. Before turning to the rise of positivism, however, the following chapter shows how the contradictions of liberalism in terms of race and gender shaped the making of archives through an analysis of census records of working-class neighborhoods in Lima.

Chapter 2

Callejones of Lima

Race, Class, and Gender in Post-Abolition Peru

As the Afro-Peruvian population gained equal legal status in the mid-nineteenth century, racial pseudoscience emanated from Europe and dominated elite perceptions of social hierarchies around the world. The faulty science served to reinforce and justify social hierarchies established during Spanish and Portuguese colonialism, and elites in these former colonies sought to project national identities based on European standards. In short, "race" was inseparable from national identity, heightening the anxieties of Latin American elites seeking to modernize their young republics. In 1856, Austrian world traveler and writer Ida Pfeiffer wrote,

> The inhabitants of Lima, like those of Acapulco, Callao, and, I believe, all the Spanish American states, are of such mixed Indian, European, and African blood, and proceed from such an inter-ramification of races, as can be found in no other corner of the world. Among the higher classes of Creoles and Old Spaniards there are some very beautiful girls and women, and the Lima ladies have the reputation of knowing how to increase their attractions by their rich and tasteful toilet . . . I never in my life saw women of the lower classes so richly and extravagantly dressed as here. You meet milk and fruit women riding their asses to market, and with their goods before them, in silk

> dresses, Chinese shawls, silk stockings, and embroidered shoes, all of staring colors, but most of the finery more or less ragged, and hanging half off. I do not think it all became their yellow or dark-brown faces; and they often reminded me of Sancho Panza's remark concerning his lady, who, as queen of the "undiscovered islands," he says, will look like "a pig with a gold necklace."

Pfeiffer continued, "All whose complexions approach at all to white call themselves 'Old Spaniards'—a race to with which they are eager to claim kindred. Creoles are those who have been born here, but of genuine European parents."[1] Such negative European descriptions of Lima's racial mixtures troubled its white elites, and Pfeiffer's commentary about the term "Creole" suggests that lighter-skinned Peruvian mestizos were eager to claim a category that connoted whiteness.[2] Her perspective may have been influenced by North American understandings of race and reflects the common tropes of Latin America among nineteenth-century English travelogues.[3] The city's "Old Spaniards" and "white" Creoles sought to counter such racial aspersions of Lima's population by regulating traditional practices associated with its African and Indigenous ancestry and by highlighting its European customs and roots.

This project of improving Peru's public image to the "modern world" imposed Eurocentric understandings of race, which are particularly visible in censuses of the mid-nineteenth century. Just five years after the abolition of slavery went into effect, Lima's census officials surveyed the city's inhabitants. This census sought to understand Lima's racial demography as the population grew and some Afro-Peruvians migrated to the capital while others remained in the homes of former enslavers.[4] In the process the census officials wielded significant power in categorizing people and would begin the steady course of erasing African ancestry in the making of *archives.*

Castilla's defeat of rival caudillo José Rufino Echenique was largely due to the military support of Indigenous and Afro-Peruvians fighting for their own freedom, and his reforms included the abolition of Indigenous "tribute" and the end of ethnic-fiscal categories of *indíjenas* and castas.[5] The 1854 decree did not mark a clean break from slavery, as Afro-Peruvians had undermined the system for decades prior, and the formal dismantling of slavery in Lima after abolition took at least two more decades.[6] Castilla's proposed replacement for the Indigenous tribute, a universal poll tax, however, was not implemented until the dictator Manuel Ignacio Prado established it in 1866. Although the end of tribute meant that Indigenous Peruvians had less economic incentive to claim a Black or mestizo identity, the abolition of ethnic-fiscal categories (like the poll tax) did not mean that the state was no longer concerned about the racial demography of its citizens. As historian Mark Thurner has revealed the contradictions in Castilla's treatment of Peru's Indigenous population, the liberal state's conflicted relationship with Afro-Peruvians warrants closer analysis.[7]

During this institutional, fiscal, and legal shift for these marginalized groups, census records of Lima neighborhoods in the mid-nineteenth century show continued concern over the racial demography of the emerging "liberal" state. Although the casta categories that "did the work of race" in the seventeenth century no longer applied, the nineteenth century witnessed the rise of fixed racial categories based on the "standardization of physical characteristics, the imposition of uniform expectations of behavior, and the obsessive definitions of phenotype."[8]

LOCAL CENSUSES, *MESTIZAJE*, AND DIMINISHING RACE LABELS

This chapter examines census records of Lima *callejones* in 1860 and 1866 to reconstruct patterns of racial mixing among Afro-Peruvians and other populations, keeping in mind that these documents reveal as much about the officials who recorded them as do the subjects under observation. Callejones were shared living spaces with a common entryway and a central patio surrounded by small living quarters, which typically housed several families. These simple communal homes were constructed with adobe and thatched roofs. Scholars have asserted that 70 percent of the entire Afro-Peruvian population resided in Lima by the twentieth century, and many were *callejoneros*, residents of these abodes.[9] These windows into plebian lives in mid-nineteenth-century Lima show increasing racial mixing between Indigenous and African-descended Peruvians, which complicates previous understandings of mestizaje. Mestizaje could lead to upward or downward mobility for the children of Indigenous peoples depending on whether they mixed with African descendants or white Creoles, and the censuses suggest a higher degree of mixing between Indigenous and Afro-Peruvians in working-class Lima neighborhoods than was previously assumed. The evidence of mestizaje in these records does not reveal a uniform aspiration among Afro-Peruvians to "marry up" in pursuit of whitening, but the process of mestizaje produced specific gendered and racial elite expectations of behavior in terms of education, social mobility, and work among those categorized as zambo/a (the offspring of Indigenous and African parentage). While Indigenous and African-descended Peruvians dominated numerically, white elites distanced themselves from the racialized majority. The censuses thus provide a perspective on mestizaje that challenges previous arguments that have assumed "whitening" was the universal outcome of mestizaje, through which Afro-Peruvians shed a collective identity for individual social and economic improvement. However, the records may also reveal a reluctance among census officials to document mixing between working-class whites and Afro-Peruvians, even though these ethnoracial groups were closer culturally to one another than they were to Peru's Indigenous population.[10]

Historian Iñigo García-Bryce has shown that 43 percent of Lima's artisans identified as African-descended (negro, zambo, or pardo) in the city's 1866 census although the Afro-Peruvian population in Lima as a whole was much lower, approximately 10 percent.[11] His research on Lima's nineteenth-century censuses reveals an important aspect of Afro-Peruvian social history, as they were disproportionately represented among the city's artisans. Other research using Lima's censuses has shown that the state reduced categories indicating African ancestry between 1790 and 1860 (i.e., mulato/a and pardo/a to negro/a or zambo/a). These new categories were applied to 90 percent of the Afro-Peruvian population by the 1860s.[12] Reducing the categories indicating African ancestry to "Black/negro/a" and "zambo/a" diminished the perceived Afro-Peruvian population by eliminating Blackness from Afro-Peruvians who had mixed with groups other than Indigenous. Thus, the percentage of Afro-Peruvian mestizo/a artisans in 1860s Lima may have been even higher than the census records indicate.

Censuses were subjective records, especially with regard to racial categories. The ascribed categories depended on both the social position of the person surveyed and the perspective of the census official. Although the boundaries between categories connoting African ancestry were unclear, comparative analysis of the Lima censuses of 1700 and 1790 is revealing: the population categorized as Spanish (i.e., "white") decreased from 56.5 to 38.1 percent over this period. No intermediary categories connoting African ancestry other than mulatos appeared before the 1790 census, and the most common new category was zambo/a, who were said to compose 6.8 percent of the city's population that year (the percentage of Lima's mulato population had risen from 3.37 in 1700 to 12.1 in 1790).[13]

What remains less clear in analyses of such censuses, however, is the process by which census officials determined and documented racial categories in post-abolition Lima. The enumerated percentage of Afro-Peruvian residents in Lima declined precipitously from the colonial period through the nineteenth century, a result of the process of mestizaje and official recordings of racial categories in the censuses.[14]

RACE, LITERACY, AND GENDER IN LIMA CENSUSES

Censuses recorded for the city of Lima in 1860 and 1866 reveal the typical living conditions of the city's working class, as well as relationships between literacy, occupation, and social mobility. They also show correspondences between racial categories, occupation, literacy rates, and regional origins for Afro-Peruvian women and men living in Lima during the decade after abolition. The censuses provide further insight into how domestic labor and "servitude" brought together, in Aguirre's words, "the triple oppression of class, race, and gender."[15]

The records reveal more about state officials' conceptions of race, gender, and citizenship, details that complicate prior understandings of Ramón Castilla's "government of liberty." Castilla's desire to quantify the nation's demography followed a "boom" in international conferences on statistics in Europe.[16] Historian Jesús Cosamalón Aguilar has analyzed the 1860 census of Lima in the context of changing legal codes from the late colonial period to the early decades of the republic, when laws based on corporate identities and rights were supplanted by individual rights as citizens. The emphasis on individual rights and equality paradoxically erased ethnoracial distinctions from most legal records, yet this belied census officials' concerns over racial phenotypes in mestizaje. Although liberalism theoretically promised social mobility regardless of one's race, racial categories associated with skin color were documented with greater frequency in nineteenth-century Lima through censuses.[17] As the categories for race changed in this period, they revealed elite manipulation of the city's racial demography to suit their vision of mestizaje by erasing Blackness.

The 1860 and 1866 censuses of Lima were taken within the time period Paul Gootenberg has called "a century of demographic no-man's land," when the Peruvian governments did not have the capacity to carry out accurate national surveys. As Gootenberg explains, "The best scholars can attempt at this point is to untangle the confusions of existing census documents and bring new evidence to bear on their strengths and weaknesses."[18] Keeping the limitations of these documents in mind, the local level studies of callejones offer a window into understanding the daily lives of Afro-Peruvian *Limeños* (residents of Lima) shortly after the abolition of slavery. They also offer a rare view of official perspectives on mestizaje in Lima neighborhoods as it occurred. Analyzing the process by which census officials conducted their surveys also sheds light on the inherent contradictions of the post-abolition modernizing national governments regarding race and citizenship. Both García-Bryce and Humberto Rodríguez Pastor have used the 1866 census records to provide valuable insights on Afro-Peruvian social history in terms of occupations and daily lives, but this chapter contributes further context by analyzing the general census of Lima taken just six years after Castilla's abolition decree in 1860. Despite the inherent value of such a source for historians, its rare use by historians has earned it the title "the unknown census."[19]

Castilla's Lima-centered modernization program for Peru relied on an accurate account of the city's population, showing his government's concerns regarding the nation's racial demography even as Lorente silenced Afro-Peruvians from his account of the nation's past and present. The 1860 census coincided with the promulgation of a new constitution, which went into effect on November 10 of that year. The new constitution (as analyzed in the previous chapter) set forth a classical liberal agenda for a modern republic, focusing on national and individual rights and guarantees. The same document that "guaranteed" the end of slavery and promised to revoke one's citizenship for "the traffic of slaves, wherever it is done" also included barriers to full citizenship rights that marginalized Afro-Peruvians disproportionately, in particular the requirement of literacy for voting rights.[20]

As enslaved people, Afro-Peruvians had little access to formal education. As historian Gracia Solis has noted in her doctoral work, Lima witnessed an increase in readership that corresponded with the city's demographic growth in the nineteenth century. As the capital city's population nearly doubled between 1822 and 1884, its literacy rates increased from 20 percent in 1845 to 55 percent in 1860.[21] Solis also documents elite reactions to the increase in literacy rates in this period, as some elites saw the national library as "a space for the erudition of a few men of letters and science" and saw little benefit to working classes becoming informed citizens.[22] Promoting working-class literacy, elites feared, would increase working-class participation in politics to which they now had access due to the constitution. Even as Castilla's Liberal Revolution promised legal equality between all ethnoracial groups, his government failed to implement policies aimed at promoting racial equity by refusing to address the historic exclusion of Afro-Peruvians.

The arbitrary and incomplete nature of the census records frustrates any attempt to narrate a clear social history of Afro-Peruvians, as much of the available data varies according to the census official conducting the survey. The 1860 census includes a section to indicate a citizen's race but not the type of residence. Many of these sections were left blank or are illegible. In contrast, the 1866 census records by callejón do not include a section for race, but in many cases the census officials wrote in a person's race under the "literacy" section. This crucial difference suggests that the Lima state in the 1860s increasingly associated race with literacy despite the erasure of racial categories from the census. This unique decision by census officials illustrates their tacit association of race with literacy, implying a fear of Afro-Peruvian citizenship in terms that elided race. In this instance, Afro-Peruvian erasure coincided with increased elite anxieties of a racialized working class influencing local and national governmental policies.

These inconsistencies notwithstanding, the records permit a snapshot of the perceived racial composition of specific Lima neighborhoods during the first decade after abolition. As the census form did not prompt the officials to ask a person's racial self-identification, it is safe to assume that they made the ultimate decision regarding an individual's "race." The decision to write in a person's race in the box intended to designate literacy suggests that the officials perceived race and literacy as equally relevant to an individual's social status and thus their citizenship rights. Ultimately, these records show that the state continued to associate citizenship with whiteness and masculinity.

AFRO-PERUVIAN LABOR ORGANIZING AND INVISIBILITY IN THE ARCHIVES

The census officials also recorded occupation, which related to social status and citizenship rights. The documents thus provide evidence that the "social dimensions of race" governed racial identities in post-abolition Peru, albeit in a less deterministic fashion than in eighteenth century Mexico City.[23] The Peruvian state saw racial categories, occupations, and literacy rates as important to its modernizing projects, and an incipient racial hierarchy emerges from these records. The hierarchy also hinted at regional differences and distinct social expectations in the construction of mestizo/a identities.[24]

The censuses provide insights into how notions of racial identities changed from the colonial period to the mid-nineteenth century in Peru. Hünefeldt has argued that "status, color, and occupation went together in nineteenth-century Lima,"[25] and the archival records of censuses show that this association continued after the abolition decree. Though limited numerically, the censuses permit some historical observations on the lives of working-class Afro-Peruvians in Lima shortly after abolition. The language used to categorize these callejoneros reveals power structures and exposes more continuity than change immediately following abolition. Enslaved Afro-Peruvians disintegrated the institution of slavery through rebellion, flight, and most commonly the purchase of freedom, or self-manumission. Despite the great progress in increasing the numbers living in freedom and attaining the decree of abolition, many Afro-Peruvians remained in positions of servitude that weren't that different from their labor regimes before abolition. At the same time, Afro-Peruvian Limeños had established networks of mutual support that remained vital to their survival in a racially exclusive society.

As recent scholarship on the African diaspora in Latin America has shown, Afro-Latino populations formed "Black social economies" as a necessary means of mutual support and survival under slavery. These economies were "oriented toward human sustenance as opposed to market fluctuations" and provided crucial economic support under an exploitative system.[26] Black social economies in Peru can be traced to the formation of *cofradías* (religious lay brotherhoods) in Lima, which contributed to the formation and support of collective Afro-Peruvian interests. Afro-Peruvians in Lima formed cofradías around the idea of *nación*, an identity that corresponded to the African port from which their ancestors departed.[27] The brotherhoods preserved and fomented Afro-Peruvian cultural traditions (such as the cult of El Señor de los Milagros), provided economic security to their members by helping in times of need, and assured that members received a dignified burial upon death. Such mutual support laid the foundation for Afro-Peruvian labor organization, as mutual aid societies and artisan guilds grew in importance just after abolition. These organizations became more open after abolition, thus the records ignored their racial composition in the late nineteenth century. This openness, associated with mestizaje, led both observers and participants to erase the Afro-Peruvian roots of labor activism, demonstrating how mestizaje produced a selective narrative of nineteenth-century social history that was void of Afro-Peruvian contributions.

Artisan guilds served a similar function of promoting corporate interests by regulating economic activity and limiting the practice of the trades to their members. The implicit class interests these guilds promoted in the public sphere, such as protective tariffs for handmade goods, were initially limited to each trade. Nonetheless, guild membership created a social hierarchy within the working class, as laborers could easily suffer material consequences for not joining the organizations. Guilds that were exclusively composed of Afro-Peruvians, such as that of the *aguadores* (water carriers) of Lima, furthermore, sought social mobility by acting collectively to demand higher pay. As the Afro-Peruvian intellectual Ricardo Palma documented in his *tradición* titled *Los aguadores de Lima,* this guild was formed in 1650 and made use of its bargaining power even after abolition.[28] Although such demands might have improved the living conditions of laborers, the stigmatization of such occupations associated with slavery meant that guilds could not help their members achieve honor or freedom from discrimination. As mestizos rather than negros, these actors crafted an inclusive vision of mestizaje and labor rights to benefit a broader section of Lima's working-class population. Both elites and working-class Afro-Peruvian mestizos preferred to use the rhetoric of class over race or ethnicity, allowing the hegemonic narrative to erase the unique contributions of African descendants to such labor organizing.

Afro-Peruvian artisans in post-abolition Lima expanded the scope of their organizing strategies and objectives in the 1860s. García-Bryce's analysis of the artisan press shows "a growing identification of artisans with the idea of a working class."[29] He has also found that guild members increasingly pursued their interests collectively as "artisans" rather than individually through separate trades, thereby expanding their collective class interests.[30] The political demands of Lima's artisans provide further evidence that Afro-Peruvian Limeños did not make demands based on a shared ethnoracial identity in post-abolition Lima, but these laborers demanded protectionist measures to improve their conditions associated with their respective trades through direct confrontation. As this activism relied on strategies forged by Afro-Peruvians under slavery, it demonstrates a direct challenge to the official erasure of Blackness evident in the censuses of 1860 and 1866. Afro-Peruvian artisans were not claiming whiteness, but they were maintaining, publicly, practices associated with slavery for the benefit of the working class.

CULTURAL APPROPRIATION AND DEMOGRAPHIC ERASURE

Creole elites used mestizaje to claim popular cultural forms with Afro-Peruvian origins as part of the national Creole culture, showing how cultural appropriation went together with the discourse of a raceless national identity. For example, the procession of El Señor de los Milagros (The Lord of Miracles) became popularly intertwined with a collective Peruvian identity. This ritual celebrates the miraculous survival of a painting by an anonymous enslaved African man. Called the "Lord of Miracles," the painting remained intact in the Nazarenas sanctuary in Lima after most of the city was destroyed in a seventeenth-century earthquake.[31] Afro-Peruvians have led in the creation and preservation of an annual procession in the painting's honor every October 18–20 since the earthquake. Peruvians came to embrace the celebration as an iconic national cultural manifestation, albeit with reference to abstract "Creole" origins. Between the abolition of slavery in 1854 and the early twentieth century, the historically Afro-Peruvian cofradía of Nazarenas that led the procession became more popular and more racially diverse. According to a newspaper interview with an older Afro-Peruvian member of the cofradía, as more whites joined the ranks of the lay brotherhood in the early twentieth century, they began to claim that the artist "who painted the Señor de los Milagros was white, a member of the white society."[32] This case suggests white Limeños began to see benefits to claiming such popular cultural forms as their own and denying the historic roles of Afro-Peruvians in such criollo traditions. The apparent openness of Creole culture that blended various cultures belied the elite disdain for Afro-Peruvian people, who were viewed as undeserving of basic human rights through most of the nineteenth century. Whereas previous work has shown how the popular Afro-Peruvian religious tradition "won over" whites, this chapter highlights the consequences of this process: while integrating Afro-Peruvian culture as a part of national identity, elites simultaneously denied its African roots and contributed to Afro-Peruvian invisibility. The visibility of Afro-Peruvian culture in the twentieth century, paradoxically, came at the expense of Afro-Peruvian demographic visibility.

The cofradías limited their work to social and religious affairs and mutual support, but the artisan guilds had begun to articulate a working-class political platform that included protectionist measures against foreign-made imports. These organizations laid the foundation for more politically active mutual aid societies, which began to appear in the late 1850s. In 1855, when Castilla's abolition decree was taking effect, a group of Limeño laborers formed the first mutual aid society, called the Sociedad Fraternal de San José.[33] Just a few years later, the aptly named Sociedad Democrática del Callao (Democratic Society of Callao) formed in 1858.

Sociologist Carlos A. Forment has also noted increasing numbers of Afro-Peruvians in the artisan sector after abolition, as workshop owners sometimes retained formerly enslaved people as trained laborers after they had gained freedom. Forment also points to the undemocratic structure of the cofradías (in which a king and queen made all decisions), guilds, and mutual aid societies, which established work routines and regulations, "disciplining plebian groups and protecting property rights."[34] Nonetheless, Lima's artisans voiced their collective interests in December of 1858 in Lima's port of Callao, where they protested the arrival of a shipment of finished goods (doors and windows) from the United States. After preventing the shipment from being unloaded, the carpenters' guild "presented a legal petition and a commission of artisans presented a complaint to President Castilla, demanding the protection of Peruvian artisans from competition from foreign goods."[35] President Castilla rejected their demands and allowed the shipments to enter the Peruvian market; he then ordered troops to the port to repress the ongoing protests. One protestor was killed, five were injured, and several were arrested, but the protestors continued to revolt. Contemporary reports of this collective action and violent repression elided the question of race, erasing the potential heroic portrayal of Afro-Peruvian artisans. This archival silence subsequently shaped Afro-Peruvian invisibility in what Trouillot would call "the *making of narratives*."

Following the violence, about three hundred artisans entered the congressional building to pressure its members to pass laws the guilds had requested. This peaceful protest was unsuccessful; a congressional report the following year rejected protectionist policies. Liberal politicians defended their economic policy by dispersing pamphlets attacking the guilds and by abolishing these organizations in 1862.[36] Despite such repression and exclusion from Lima politics, working-class Afro-Peruvians continued to organize for better conditions through mutual aid societies and by participating in popular political movements at the national level.

The correspondence between local civic engagement, popular politics, and the abolition of slavery is clear: "Between 1856 and 1885, Peruvians organized 403 new civic and economic groups."[37] During the first five years after abolition, Peruvians organized three times as many civic associations as had been founded in the previous twenty-five years. The rate of new civic engagement continued to increase until the War of the Pacific in 1879. The engagement in local politics benefitted Afro-Peruvians just as it benefited other ethnoracial groups, leading to the establishment of primary schools and mutual aid societies.[38] Still, the sharp increase in new civic organizations in the five years following abolition suggests that Afro-Peruvians were anxious to participate in full citizenship after decades of exclusion. As the newspaper *Zamacueca Política* shows, elites responded to Afro-Peruvian civic engagement with ridicule and scorn. The social and civic organizations they and their ancestors had established under slavery provided the local networks the experience and structure that facilitated their expansion in the first five years after abolition. As the cofradías had successfully secured money to purchase the freedom of enslaved people and thereby contribute to the destruction of slavery in nineteenth-century Lima, Afro-Peruvians expected comparable success via similar organizing strategies as citizens of a nominally inclusive democracy.[39]

Peter Blanchard has argued that the mutual aid societies that appeared in mid-nineteenth-century Peru were "heirs" of the artisan guild, both organizational structures functioning as workers' organizations that pressured the government for favorable laws. Members of Lima's artisan guilds that had been banned in 1862 joined to form the Sociedad Republicana de la "Unión Universal" de Artesanos in 1871. Manual laborers hired to tear down Lima's old city walls went on strike for higher pay in 1872, and Callao port workers went on strike for more pay in 1877 and in 1881.[40] Though absent from the historical record, the evidence from mid-century censuses suggests Afro-Peruvians were central actors in such post-abolition labor activism. As censuses condensed categories indicating African ancestry, official records rendered Afro-Peruvian agency invisible as well. Rather than contest these categories or agitate for changes exclusive to their ethnoracial identity, these actors applied their organizing strategies to improve the conditions of all working-class laborers in Lima. Paradoxically, this inclusive approach contributed to erasing Afro-Peruvians from the record of events, showing a narrative construction that denied the relevance of racial markers even as census records revealed anxieties about Lima's racial composition.

THE GENERAL CENSUS OF 1860

The most complete record of the 1860 census of Lima is that of *Calle de la Palma,* a street just south of the city center. Of the 141 people residing on this street in 1860, 110 were identified as white. Of these, the vast majority were vendors, property owners, storeowners, or students, recorded as *comerciantes, propietarios* or *estudiantes.* On this street, only twenty-eight people were categorized as African-descended. In sharp contrast with those labeled white, among those identified as African-descended (i.e., negro/a or zambo/a), nearly all were servants (*serbientes*). All of the sixteen people categorized as Black (negro/a) on this street held the occupation of "servant." One Afro-Peruvian woman on de la Palma Street, María Sentino, was recorded as a cook and servant, and she was also the only resident of African descent who could read and write. However, above her name appears the label "servant," suggesting that she served as a cook in an elite home. Children categorized as zambo/a were recorded among the servant population, including Manuela Cordera, age nine, and Bernardo Lara, age eleven. Six-year-old Margarita García was also categorized as a Black servant.[41] García was born into slavery the very year the institution was abolished, and her prospect for social mobility appears to have remained the same five years afterward.

Similarly, of the people categorized as Indian in the 1860 census of this street, all but two were recorded as servants. Five of these illiterate servants deemed *Yndio* were under thirteen years of age in 1860. The lone *Yndio* who could read and write was also the only non-servant: thirty-nine-year-old Fernando Navarrete had migrated to Lima from the northern city of Trujillo to work as a shoemaker, and being literate likely helped him maintain his occupation.[42]

The census records show slight differences in social expectations and norms among Black and Indigenous Peruvians in Lima, but they also show the proximity and integration of these groups as a racialized plebian lower class. The census officials recorded much more racial mixing between Black and Indigenous Peruvians than between other groups, as whites sought to maintain racial "purity" and the social distinction it entailed (an extension of the colonial-era notion of *limpieza de sangre*).[43] The racial category that census takers most commonly ascribed in the decade following abolition in Lima was that of zambo/a.[44]

While these records show that Afro-Peruvians held a wide variety of occupations, they also suggest social barriers based on race. Farther south of the city center, the *Calle de San Ysidro* was predominantly nonwhite. According to the census, forty-five residents of Calle de San Ysidro were white, fifty-two were Black, thirty-four were Indian, four were mestizo/a, eleven were zambo, and four were pardo (Portuguese for "brown," used in both Brazil and Peru to refer to African-descendants).[45] The most common occupations among those categorized as Black were *cargador* (carrier/porter) and *aguador* (water carrier).

Just as they had under slavery, aguadores used mules to carry barrels of water to individual homes. Although Castilla's modernizing project included building iron pipes to distribute water throughout the city, the continued existence of Afro-Peruvian aguadores in the 1860s shows that abolition did not bring immediate change to the daily working lives of such formerly enslaved people.[46] Three of those labeled Black living on San Ysidro Street were cargadores, two were aguadores, and two were *jornaleros*.[47] Before abolition, jornaleros were enslaved African descendants who worked in a separate location from their enslaver's and would pay the owner what they earned for a day's work. Following national independence and the banning of the Atlantic trade in enslaved people, coastal hacendados used this system to ease their economic troubles; however, many Afro-Peruvians took advantage of this economic crisis to earn enough money to purchase their freedom. Others simply escaped and turned to banditry, or *bandolerismo*, to survive.[48]

Combining the groups indicating African ancestry, including zambos and pardos, the African-descended population of this Calle de San Ysidro rises to sixty-seven, the number of Afro-Peruvian carriers/porters rises to five. Of the 272 people counted on Calle de la Palma and Calle de San Ysidro, all of the water carriers and porters were African-descended. Day

Figure 2.1. Pancho Fierro's *Aguador*, 1850. Wikimedia Commons/PD.

laborers or jornaleros were almost exclusively Afro-Peruvians as well: there were three *jornaleros chinos* and two *jornaleros negros*, but *chino* could signify either Chinese or the offspring of Black and Indian parentage.[49] The forced immigration of Chinese laborers began in 1849 as the abolition of slavery appeared more certain, and they were mainly utilized as laborers on northern coastal plantations to replace enslaved Black labor,[50] so a chino in a callejón of Lima at this time could indicate African ancestry.

Despite the preponderance of Black jornaleros, cargadores, and aguadores, Afro-Peruvians demonstrated adaptability and resourcefulness in gaining employment in the five years following abolition. In the predominantly white neighborhood of Calle de la Palma, most Afro-Peruvians worked as household servants. However, in the predominantly Afro-Peruvian neighborhood of Calle de San Ysidro, Afro-Peruvians worked as laundresses, carpenters, street vendors, shoemakers, basket weavers, carpenters, and small farmers (*chacareros*). Those identified as Indians residing on

Calle de San Ysidro also achieved more occupational diversity than they did in the predominantly white neighborhood of Lima. Although Fernando Navarrete was the only Indian on Calle de la Palma who was not a servant, Indians living on Calle de San Ysidro held jobs as laundresses and street vendors.[51] These census records thus suggest that post-abolition society in Lima reflected an ethnoracial hierarchy within the supposedly egalitarian ideology of mestizaje. In this hierarchy rooted in colonialism, Indigenous Peruvians could claim higher status through acculturation, but Afro-Peruvians were constrained by perceived racial (i.e., biological) difference, which elites continued to associate with slavery.

Racial and class dynamics intersected with literacy, and the ability to read and write offered a degree of social mobility for a select few Afro-Peruvians. Almost all the white adult Limeños recorded, both men and women, could read and write. Afro-Peruvians and Indians who had learned to read were more likely to attain occupations that granted them more autonomy and income than day laborers or servants. Fifty-eight-year-old Manuela Jesús, a Black woman from the bucolic town of Huaraz, could not read or write.[52] Combined with limited work experience, illiteracy likely limited her options as a wage laborer. In contrast, thirty-four-year-old Bartolomé Flores worked as a shoemaker on the same street. An Afro-Peruvian native of Lima, Flores could read but not write, and this ability likely helped him in his trade.[53] The only Black Limeño to hold a job as an "employee" (*empleado*) on this street, an occupation common among white Limeños, was also able to read.[54] Literacy offered a rare avenue to economic stability; however, the 1860 census of Lima reveals the limitations of mestizaje as a process and an ideology—the racial markers show clear barriers to Afro-Peruvian social mobility and continuities between pre- and post-abolition society in Lima.

THE GENERAL CENSUS OF 1866

The municipal government of Lima conducted another census in 1866, and in the intervening years the Calle San Ysidro was renamed *Mainas*. This more detailed census identified each callejón and in some cases the attached stores. On Mainas Street, a Señor Rivera owned the largest callejón, which held one hundred rooms. Unfortunately, the census does not include information on all of the callejón's residents, but the available data are illustrative nonetheless. The census form also changed since 1860, as race was no longer included as a column. However, the census officials frequently but not universally decided to write in the race of the residents in the literacy column. They categorized enough residents by racial category to reveal correlations among race, migration, and occupation. Mainas Street remained a predominantly Afro-Peruvian neighborhood. The limited data indicates that the callejones of Mainas Street housed thirty-six Black residents, sixty-six zambos, forty-two Indians, twelve mestizos, two chinos, and four white residents.[55] If we combine the zambo and negro categories, the number of Afro-Peruvians rises to 102, a clear majority of the 158 people recorded in this communal living space. On the same street, the Callejón del Monasterio del Prado also housed mainly Afro-Peruvians. Here just one woman was categorized as white, three residents as zambo, and eight as Black.[56] Also on Mainas Street, the Callejón del Señor Dinegro housed twelve Indians, seven zambos, and two mestizos.[57] Though incomplete, the records show continuity among the working class living in close proximity. The haphazard recordings of the census officials also reveal their continued associations of race with literacy and social status.

Because census officials used the literacy column to indicate race, or in many cases left it incomplete, it is more difficult to reach conclusions relating to occupation and literacy in the 1866 census. However, these records do reveal tendencies relating to gender, race, migration, and occupation. Black and zamba women were employed most frequently as cooks and laundresses, while men worked in a wider variety of occupations. Afro-Peruvians with common occupations and origins tend to appear together in the records, showing a relationship between racial identity, proximity, family, and job training. Five zambas under the age of eight were listed as laundresses, suggesting an assumption that daughters would pursue the same work as their mothers. Census officials recorded one zamba as able to read: twenty-seven-year-old Lima native Francisca Villegas worked as a seamstress.[58] Three young zambas under age seven were recorded as learning to read and/or in school.[59] Francisca's example again shows that literacy helped Afro-Peruvian women move beyond less skilled domestic work.

RACE AND MIGRATION IN 1860 AND 1866 CENSUS RECORDS

According to the general census of Lima for 1860, the vast majority of Afro-Peruvians residing on San Ysidro were Lima natives. These Afro-Peruvians were the beneficiaries of the efforts of generations of enslaved and freed African descendants who fought to dismantle the institution of slavery.[60] Thanks to their efforts, many Afro-Peruvians in Lima had already established themselves as free laborers in a variety of occupations. Nonetheless, even five years after abolition, many Afro-Peruvian Limeños worked in occupations and conditions similar to those under slavery.

The 1860 census suggests that Afro-Peruvian migrants in Lima were more likely to be categorized as zambo/a than Afro-Peruvian natives of Lima, who were classified as Black. Thirty-eight-year-old zamba Paula Minas, for example, was from the southern region of Ica. Although her occupation was left blank on the census, the official recorded that she was able to read and write. Similarly, forty-eight-year-old zambo José Muños migrated to Lima from Trujillo with his wife, forty-year-old Barbara Torres, also categorized as zamba. Their six children, ages twenty-five, eighteen, twenty-two, thirteen, nine, and seven, were all natives of Trujillo, meaning they had arrived to Lima no earlier than 1853. The six children carried the same racial category as both of their parents.[61] Unfortunately, census officials did not record the occupation of any members of this family, but they did note that none of them could read or write. Similarly, a thirty-year-old zambo mason (*albañil*) from Ecuador named Francisco Javier had three young children: Ana (eleven), Estevan (eight), and Faustina (four), who were also categorized as zambos. Although Francisco was literate, his children could not yet read or write and their occupations were left blank. Although Francisco was a native of Ecuador, his children were all born in Lima.[62] The Javier family presents a curious case because the children were not "learning" in school, nor were their occupations predetermined, unlike other cases examined. This family is another example of the process of mestizaje in coastal Peru, but the relationship between racial identity and occupation is less clear.

The record of the Javier family also suggests that migrants were more likely to be classified as zambo or pardo, while African-descended Lima natives were more likely seen as Black. A family categorized as pardo provides further evidence of this tendency: Ramón Cáceres was a forty-five-year-old cargador from Trujillo. His wife, twenty-year-old Andrea Ramires, a Lima native, was assigned the same racial category. Both could read but not write. Their three children, ages seven, six, and one, were not recorded as attending school or learning to read. Like the Javier family, these children were not given a predetermined occupation, but they were grouped into the same racial category as their parents.

The 1860 census reveals that the majority of Afro-Peruvian callejoneros born in Lima were identified as Black (negro/a).[63] Only four of the thirty-one residents labeled negro/a living on San Ysidro Street in 1860 had migrated from other parts of the country. Among the forty who were identified as some variant of an African-descended identity on San Ysidro (i.e., zambo/a or pardo/a), twenty-six were Lima natives.[64] But when combined with the racial identities of migrant families such as the Muños, Javier, and Cáceres, the census reveals that most Afro-Peruvians who were Lima natives were identified as Black. Moreover, the most variations of Afro-Peruvian identities were evident among those who migrated to Lima's callejones.

The snapshot view of the predominantly Afro-Peruvian neighborhood, however, does not suggest a sudden surge in Afro-Peruvian migration to the capital city following the abolition of slavery, as one might expect. Among the thirty-four people identified as Indian on the same street, twenty-three had migrated there. This suggests that Indigenous Peruvians were migrating to Lima around the time of abolition in equal or greater numbers than Afro-Peruvians. The 68 percent of the Indians residing on San Ysidro were migrants, while only 34 percent of the Afro-Peruvians on the same street had migrated there. Though incomplete statistically, the callejones of San Ysidro suggest that Afro-Peruvian migration to poor neighborhoods in Lima was meager compared with that of Indigenous migration to the capital city during the eleven years following the abolition of slavery.

The 1866 census records for the same street reveal the transient nature of its callejones and permit a better understanding of Afro-Peruvian lives during the first decade after abolition. Among the nineteen residents of Callejón de los Dolores and Callejón del Monasterio del Prado identified as Black, only two were not natives of Lima: Ysabel Lecca was a twenty-one-year-old laundress from Trujillo, and José Boza was a chacarero from Chancay, a district just north of Lima. Among the twenty-two residents identified as zambo/a in these two callejones, however, ten were migrants to Lima. The majority of these migrants came from the northern coast, from the cities of Trujillo (two), Chiclayo (one), Piura (one), Supe (one), and the department of Lambayeque (three). Thus, the 1866 census of Lima provides further suggestive evidence of perceived regional differences between racial identities of Afro-Peruvians, as census takers seemed more likely to ascribe Indigeneity to people of rural origins. While most Afro-Peruvian natives of Lima were identified simply as Black on San Ysidro street, most Afro-Peruvian migrants to this street were identified as zambo/a.[65]

Other common occupations showed clear lineages from slavery, as many negros were chacareros, cargadores, masons, aguadores, or servants. Four children labeled Black, three girls, and a boy under the age of twelve were listed as "*peones*": their father, José Boza, was a small farmer. The most common occupation among women native to Lima labeled negra was that of laundress (four). Men identified as zambo exhibited a wider variety of specialized occupations. These included carpenters (three), bakers (two), a tailor, a shoemaker, a launderer, a small farmer (*ortelano*), a cart driver (*carretero*), a shrimp vendor (*camaronero*), a *mayordomo* (which could mean either a butler/house servant or a foreman in charge of laborers), and a fireworks manufacturer (*cohetero*, a favorite subject of Pancho Fierro's *costumbrista* paintings of the cultural life of this era). However, zambos also performed lower-status occupations in common with slavery, including a cargador, a servant, a carpenter, a mason, and a *labrador* ("a farmer or low-status owner of an estate").[66] The majority of women and girls identified as zamba were documented as seamstresses (*costureras*), even twenty-one-month-old Manuela Ortiz. Again, this suggests that Afro-Peruvian women faced more challenges to social mobility following the abolition decree despite having relatively high rates of literacy in the sphere of domestic labor in eighteenth-century Lima.[67] Overall, zambos tended to have higher status and more skilled occupations in the census. This suggests that census officials were more likely to categorize African descendants with higher-status occupations as zambos rather than as negros. An eleven-year-old zambo named Adon Castellanos, for example, was a student in secondary school.[68]

Although women identified as zamba on this street also tended to follow in their mother's line of work, some also exhibited potential social mobility. Although two young zamba girls were recorded as laundresses at just five and six years of age, others were attending school. Six-and-a-half-year-old Lima native Luisa Cristin and five-year-old Lima native Juana Velarde were recorded as zambas who were "in school" and "learning" to read.[69] Although there were also five- and six year-old zamba girls who were expected to carry on their mother's work as laundresses, no schoolgirls were identified as Black. Once again, this suggests distinct social expectations associated with distinct Afro-Peruvian racial categories, demonstrating correspondence between census officials' perceptions and the ideology of mestizaje, which continued to associate Blackness with negative stereotypes and a condition that could be erased through social ascendance.

Zambos in this part of Lima exhibited more occupational variation and possible social mobility than Limeños labeled negro/a, but Indians living in the same callejones held a wider variety of occupations than most Afro-Peruvians. Similar to Black Limeñas, the most common occupations among Indian women on Mainas Street were those of cooks and laundresses. Two Indian women were recorded as "*peones*," two as fruit vendors (*fruteras*), two as market venders (*placeras*), one as a seamstress, and one as a chicha vendor (*chichera*).[70] Indian men's occupations varied more than those of their Black counterparts, but they also overlapped a great deal. Two Indian men in the Callejón de los Dolores and Callejón del Monasterio Prado worked as cigar makers (*cigarreros*), another was an ironworker, another a bread baker, another a mason, and another worked as a tailor. Only one of the Indians on this street was able to read, a forty-four-year-old *chichera* from Ayacucho.[71] Similar to the zamba girls mentioned above, just one Indian child was attending school, a five-year-old Lima native. Thus the censuses reveal slight differences between those considered zambos and those labeled negros, and more similarities between the categories Indian and zambo among the callejoneros. In1860s Lima, then, Indians enjoyed greater social mobility, a benefit that may have appealed to many Afro-Peruvian Limeños whose occupations continued to resemble the work they performed under slavery.[72] These trends in local census records correspond with the social hierarchy in the colonial *sistema de castas* and the emerging "modern" ideology of mestizaje, showing that the new ideology's claims of erasing racial differences were incomplete.

Among the thirty-one people categorized as Indian in the following *Callejón del Señor Dinegro* in 1866, seventeen were migrants, six originating from the Andean city of Ayacucho. Unlike the Afro-Peruvian migrants to Lima, almost all of the Indian migrants on Mainas Street originated in the Andean interior, from towns such as Yauyos (two), Huancayo (two), Cerro del Pasco, Jauja (five), and the nearby town of Tupicocha (three), and two from Bolivia.[73]

Among the sixty-four Afro-Peruvian residents of this callejón (including negros, zambos, and mulatos), twenty-eight were migrants. Thus, whereas 55 percent of Indian residents were migrants, only 31 percent of Afro-Peruvian residents were migrants in this shared living space. The differences in regional origins evident in the 1860 census persisted in 1866, as almost all of the Afro-Peruvian migrants to this callejón were from coastal regions, primarily from the northern region of Piura (nine). Others originated in the northern coastal regions of Trujillo (five) and Lambayeque (two) and from the southern coastal districts of Cañete (four), Chilca (one), and Pisco (four). Similar to the other callejones of this street, most of the residents identified as Black were Lima natives (ten of the seventeen). Although many of those identified as zambo/a migrated from the northern coast (sixteen), more were Lima natives by 1866 (twenty-two). As coastal Peru is the most fertile region of the country for plantation agriculture, one might assume that many of these Afro-Peruvians migrated to Lima immediately following the abolition of slavery and their freedom from forced plantation labor in sugar cane or cotton fields. Instead, however, the census shows that most of these migrants had arrived to Lima well before abolition. In fact, only a few Afro-Peruvian migrants on Mainas Street might have come directly from rural plantations: a laundress, a *cocinera* (cook), and a seamstress from Trujillo left for Lima the year of abolition. All of these women were categorized as zambas, such as Simona Reynoso, a twenty-four-year-old seamstress who migrated from Arequipa in 1855.[74]

This particular street and its callejones are unique in the census records for 1866 because officials recorded the race of at least 90 percent of the residents (seventeen of the people whose race was not recorded were not in residence at the time of the census, and nine others are simply illegible). Just as in 1860, this street housed more Afro-Peruvian and Indigenous Limeños than others that also include information about race. For example, the succeeding street recorded in 1866, *Calle Urubamba,* housed eighty-six white people and just six Afro-Peruvians, all of whom were identified as Black. Two of these women were cooks, one was a seamstress, and one man was recorded as a shoemaker.[75] Surprisingly few callejoneros remained in the same home for this six-year period. The few residents whom census officials recorded in both documents were all categorized as Black: Juan Barreto, a cargador; José Antonio Boza, a chacarero; and Maria Piamonte, a laundress who continued to live with José Antonio Boza.[76] Though limited, this correspondence suggests that Blackness limited one's social mobility, showing that census officials perceived mestizaje as a process of erasing Blackness.

CONCLUSIONS

The paucity of callejoneros who stayed in the same living space suggests these communal homes were itinerant locations, and some residents likely improved their social status and moved to locations that reflected such change. The three residents who remained in the same callejón between 1860 and 1866, however, exemplify the limited mobility of those categorized as Black. They also exhibit the continued correspondence between Blackness and enslaved labor. Literacy, occupation, and race were closely intertwined in constructions of racial identities in Lima's callejones in the first decade after the abolition of slavery. As census officials equated social status to race, they categorized most residents of lower-class callejones as negro/a, *indio/a* (Indian) or zambo/a. In contrast with the burgeoning category of zambo/a in Lima's 1866 census record, only one person was identified as mulato (a person of presumably African and Spanish descent). Considering the methodology of the census takers, which associated race with literacy and social status, this scarcity of white admixture may reflect their reluctance to admit the possibility of Spanish and African racial mixing. From another perspective, however, Afro-Peruvians may have claimed indigeneity as zambos to ascend socially, thereby denying Blackness but not necessarily denying African ancestry. In labeling people zambos, census takers and their subjects were not ascribing or claiming whiteness. As many Afro-Peruvians and zambos residing in Lima in the 1860s had migrated from the northern coast, and many Indigenous and Afro-Peruvians converged in the same neighborhoods of Lima, racial mixing likely continued in the capital city in a similar fashion. These Indigenous and Afro-Peruvians worked and lived in the same space, jointly considered "plebeian." Although people in both of these groups could be *peones* and *servientes*, these censuses suggest that Indians and zambos enjoyed slightly greater social mobility and economic autonomy, while those labeled negro and negra struggled against the legacies of slavery.

Historian José Ramón Jouve Martin's analysis of colonial court records showed that Afro-Peruvian women were more adept at using judicial language in seventeenth-century Lima than their male counterparts were; however, the 1860s censuses show that Afro-Peruvian women in Lima's callejones were no more likely to be literate than Afro-Peruvian men were.[77] Afro-Peruvian women, in particular, were more likely to work as servants or in domestic labor, and Black girls were not enumerated as school children. As the example of María Sentino on Palma Street demonstrates, Afro-Peruvian women who worked as servants in the homes of white elites may have had greater access to basic education and literacy despite their perceived Blackness.

The Lima censuses reveal clear expectations based on race, but many of these social mores had their roots in the colonial period. As historian Rachel Sarah O'Toole has argued, Indigenous laborers along Peru's northern coast "claimed a level of autonomy that slaves could not claim within a colonial legal context, but enslaved people nonetheless used extralegal spheres to gain a measure of justice." Although enslaved Afro-Peruvians also succeeded in negotiating and claiming casta categories prior to abolition, census officials reduced these categories by imposing race labels that precluded any historical claims of customary practices.[78] Indigenous Peruvians in Lima continued to hold a higher degree of autonomy than did Afro-Peruvians in the 1860s, while slavery, illegality, and immorality were continually associated with Blackness.[79]

As other scholars have noted, census and labor records additionally show the maintenance of Afro-Peruvian organizing strategies of mutual support following slavery's abolition. From cofradías to artisan guilds to mutual aid societies, such "black social economies" increased in importance as they transcended ethnoracial lines after 1855. Such networks became vital to the successes of the labor movement in the early twentieth century, yet the traditional historiography on labor has generally overlooked this connection, as the archival records on such activism ignore the question of race. In this way, the ideology of mestizaje produced sources void of ethnoracial categories, creating a narrative that perpetuated Afro-Peruvian invisibility. This contradiction is embodied in the white appropriation of the Afro-Peruvian tradition of the cult of el Señor de los Mlilagos. Because censuses did include racial categories, however, they shed some rare light on the construction of race and Blackness within the process and development of mestizaje. In this immediate post-abolition context, it made sense for Afro-Peruvians to avoid speaking of race and Blackness in favor of common mestizo interests, limiting their visibility in the historical record. Together, these sources show the challenges that Afro-Peruvians faced in 1860s Lima despite legal equality, and the spike in civic institutions in this era shows that Afro-Peruvians demanded to participate in politics despite entrenched social barriers.

Following his decree abolishing slavery in Peru, Ramón Castilla granted what should be considered an unequal universal suffrage to Peruvian citizens, excluding from the political process those who fought with Echenique's military as well as women and those without access to education.[80] The right to vote was limited to literate or moneyed men. The ability of citizens to read and write was a central concern of the "government of liberty," as the census records show. Castilla's government paradoxically granted legal equality to people they considered racially inferior while "naturalizing" racial and social hierarchies through phenotypic differences.[81] The hegemonic discourse that continued to associate Blackness with slavery incentivized claims of Indigenous ancestry, and census officials were more likely to separate higher social status from Blackness. Together, these forces contributed to shaping mestizaje by increasing zambo visibility and decreasing perceived African ancestry. Meanwhile, Afro-Peruvian mestizos challenged the dominant discourse by embracing a multiracial identity rooted in class that maintained Afro-Peruvian social organizing strategies and cultural forms. The following chapter takes a closer look at the methods, logic, and objectives of subsequent national and regional censuses centered in Lima in the late nineteenth and early twentieth centuries, which effectively rendered the Afro-Peruvian population invisible in the "official" records that compose the archives.

Chapter 3

Afro-Peruvian Invisibility in the Historical Record

Twentieth-Century Censuses, *Mestizaje*, and Demographic Decline

Following abolition, many Afro-Peruvians remained on lands on or near the lands they had worked as enslaved people along the Pacific coast. Despite the cultural vibrance of these communities, they remained marginalized by the governing elite and ignored by the wealthy families that inherited the wealth of enslaved labor. On July 15, 1878, government official Francisco Rateci reported on the challenges of endemic disease in the region of Chincha in the following terms:

> In Chincha, as in the rest of the coastal territories of Peru, bathed by rivers, wetlands and swamps are easily formed, especially in lower areas and immediacies of the sea, whose emanations or effluvia spread in the atmospheric air and brought into contact with the animal economy, cause endemic diseases, known in all parts by the name of malarial fevers. In Chincha, in addition to those common sources of infection, there are others no less unhealthy and mainly in the Chincha Alta countryside. . . . To conclude I will add something very useful for the well-being of the inhabitants of Chincha. If in Chincha drainage ditches were practiced in the vicinity of the sea, if the pools of

> compressed liquids were limited in the countryside, if the people were provided with clean water to drink, if hygienic conditions could be improved, and finally if the masses could be educated, a large number of diseases would disappear and mortality would decrease mainly among children.[1]

As an official representative of the state delegation from the Department of Medicine in the Department of Chancay, Rateci made specific recommendations for state policy and local behaviors, but he left out key information: Chincha Alta, like several other communities along the coast, included a large African-descended population. In 1868, President José Balta signed a decree elevating Chincha to the status of province (*provincia*). The decree also elevated the status of Carmen, a predominantly Afro-Peruvian community in the province, to a township.[2] The Department of Medicine thus drew attention to the challenges facing Afro-Peruvians in this coastal region without reference to race or ethnicity, demonstrating the challenges of historical research focused on the African-descendant population during a period when the state regarded ethnoracial differences as being irrelevant. Nonetheless, Afro-Peruvians had made this region profitable in the early republican period as enslaved laborers on sugar plantations and by extracting massive amounts of guano beginning in 1840. The Department of Medicine report also omitted the fact that the laboring population of Chincha Alta grew "exponentially" between 1850 and 1870 following an 1849 law that permitted local hacendados to import Chinese "coolie" laborers.[3] As the number of "raceless" laborers increased in this region following abolition, the mention of ethnoracial categories was deemed unnecessary. The history of slavery in the region was irrelevant in such government reports on conditions in Chincha Alta, rendering its legacies beyond the realm of possibility in the making of sources. Consistent with this selective recording of events in the archives, an 1899 study by state engineers reported on the main causes and consequences of flood damages in Chincha Alta, and their findings focused on how floodwaters impacted the crops on haciendas rather than their effects on the local population.[4] This "raceless" analysis paralleled a national trend in post-abolition years that erased Afro-Peruvians from the past and the present, reflected in the archives that compiled these facts, especially in Lima-centered censuses.

PERUVIAN CENSUSES IN THE CONTEXT OF SCIENTIFIC RACISM

National census records of post-abolition Peru concluded that the Afro-Peruvian population declined dramatically in the early twentieth century, constituting less than one-half of 1 percent of the national population by 1940.[5] Expanding on the approach used in the previous chapter, the following pages analyze the census survey forms, the demographic findings, and the official analyses that accompanied records of censuses in 1876, 1903, 1908, and 1940. As the reported Afro-Peruvian population declined dramatically in this period, census officials' autonomy in conducting censuses and categorizing citizens increased, showing a top-down process of erasing Blackness as the nation modernized and entered the twentieth century. Such erasure through omission was a common element that demonstrates the influence of Comtean positivism in Latin America in this period. Historian George Reid Andrews's work on the supposed disappearance of the Afro-Argentine population in the nineteenth century serves as a model by placing the Peruvian case in comparative perspective and by questioning the reliability of census data for the Afro-Peruvian population.[6] Additionally, historian Theodor Cohen's recent research on the Afro-Mexican population has provided insights on the limitations of censuses to represent and recuperate Blackness in modern Latin America. As Cohen suggests, contemporary demographic studies can provide insights into the modernizing nation state's top-down processes of state formation projects that render African-descendants "insignificant."[7] As the previous chapter suggests, census officials' decisions regarding how to categorize race were subjective. The twentieth-century census records provide a broad overview of demographic trends but do not include data recorded at the level of neighborhoods or homes. Nevertheless, the censuses and their accompanying analyses utilized in this chapter suggest how national modernizing projects influenced census officials' decisions regarding how to categorize a person's race.

As historian Eduardo Zimmermann has argued, "the idea of race provided a common language and a 'scientific' foundation" for social reformers of this period throughout Latin America.[8] Political scientist Juliet Hooker has brought to light crucial transnational insights on discourses of Blackness, mestizaje, and national identities in this period as well, emphasizing that Frederick Douglass, W. E. B. Du Bois, Domingo F. Sarmiento, and José

Vasconcelos "were all operating within a common discursive field, which was the scientific racism that dominated US and European intellectual circles from the second half of the nineteenth century through the first half of the twentieth century."[9] These factors influenced the census-taking methods and their intended outcomes, and they contributed to an official narrative asserting the assimilation and disappearance of the Afro-Peruvian population. Legal resolutions and explanations of census procedures provide further clues to understand the diminishing numbers of Afro-Peruvians in national censuses. The surveys of Lima in 1903 and 1908, carried out under José Pardo's presidency, identified the officials and their roles in the national project. The state-appointed officials supplemented the colonial-era provincial local strongmen and priests but did not replace them, and they worked as a council to render a more accurate and inexpensive census. Like the censuses of 1860s Lima, the early twentieth-century national surveys were a crucial first step in modernization projects by quantifying Peru's inhabitants and identifying the public services they required.

Historians of racial classification in US censuses have argued that these surveys help "to construct [a nation's] social and political order. Censuses provide the concepts, taxonomy, and substantive information by which a nation understands its component parts as well as the contours of the whole. A census both creates the image *and* provides the mirror of that image for a nation's self-reflection." Censuses do not single-handedly create racial hierarchies of a nation; however, they provide "the taxonomy and language of race; generating the informational content for that taxonomy: facilitating the development of public policies; and generating numbers upon which claims to political representation are made."[10] In Peru, the declining categories indicating African ancestry in the twentieth-century censuses contributed to their perceived disappearance, precluding Afro-Peruvian claims of racism and exclusion from discourses of national identity. Failing to recruit European immigrants to "whiten" the population through mestizaje, these social engineers erased Blackness in the making of archives by manipulating the censuses to erase the existence of African ancestry. The silences in these records shaped the post-abolition discourse on Peruvian national identity and the nation's unique ideology of mestizaje, which relegated African descendants to the colonial era and denied their existence in the twentieth century. Failing to recruit significant numbers of European immigrants to "whiten" the population, in contrast with Brazil and Argentina, these social engineers erased Blackness in the archives through the ideology of mestizaje, which implicitly maintained blackness as "inferior." This presumed inferiority led governing elites to assume that Blackness would be erased through mestizaje, in a form of circular logic that bent the "scientific" findings to suit a narrative of white supremacy, a malleability inherent to the pseudoscience of race.

Furthermore, the process of racial reorganizing in early twentieth-century Peruvian censuses bears similarities to the concurrent process in the United States between 1850 and 1940. Peruvian census officials, like those of the US Census Office, applied European-derived discourses of race and nationality to categorize the citizens they surveyed. Similar Eurocentric assumptions about race led Peruvian census officials to be influenced by a mixture of "political, scientific, and ideological" motivations when constructing ethnoracial taxonomies in early twentieth-century censuses. Such factors led the US Census Office to identify, elaborate on, and eventually drop mixtures between Black people and others. Just as in the United States, categories indicating African ancestry aside from "Black/negro/a" disappeared completely from Peruvian censuses in 1940.[11]

Documentation of national census of 1876 included specific instructions for *empadronadores* (enumerators) to collect racial data with limited input from the citizens they surveyed. Instructing these census officials to categorize subjects into one of five racial "subdivisions: *blanca, india, negra, mestiza, asiática*," the authorities urged "great caution not to injure peoples' vulnerability, especially those of the fourth subdivision, which understood all mixtures without distinction."[12] The specific instruction to disregard the ancestry of those labeled mestizo/a flattened the diversity of this population, which posited a facile resolution to potential racial animosities through mestizaje. As an ideology, then, mestizaje rendered the history of race-based slavery and contemporary racial differences irrelevant. The census of 1876 thereby reduced a significant population of mestizos with African ancestry (e.g., zambo/a and pardo/a) to the category mestizo/a, erasing their African ancestry in the official records.

The 1903 and 1908 censuses of Lima sought to project an image of the city as modern and civilized. A 1903 law explained that local industry, public services, and visiting tourists would all benefit from "a guide of Lima similar to those that with so much variety and great usefulness are published in the great cities of the world."[13] Although this document rationalized the census process for the entirety of Peru, it demonstrates that Lima was the focal point of modernization programs that sought to project an image of a nation that Europeans would respect. The outward-looking nature and transnational connections of the censuses resulted from the broader scope of these surveys, in contrast with the municipal-level censuses of Lima callejones. The officials used the same census survey forms used in Argentina, and their analyses of their findings demonstrate concern for how "modern" nations would view Peru.

The census resolutions of 1908 divided Peru's departments into zones based on prior numbers and enlisted a *jefe* (boss), a *receptor* or *inspector*, and several empadronadores to count and categorize the population of each zone. After census officials completed a provisional census and collected local registries of homes and their inhabitants, the enumerators went door-to-door to categorize and record the residents. They reported their findings at the end of each day to the receptor or inspector, who then checked the new data against the provisional findings and made the necessary adjustments.[14]

The *cédulas* (forms) that the enumerators completed for each household required them to ask each inhabitant his or her religion, age, place of birth, level of education, and race. This appears to be an important difference from the nineteenth-century censuses, in which the enumerators had greater autonomy in racial categorizing.[15] However, the official questionnaire limited the categories connoting African ancestry to one among five classifications, thereby contributing to the process of erasing the existence of African-descended people in Peru. The official analysis that accompanied the 1908 census first points out that Lima's history produced a *mestizaje especial* (special racial mixing) that created the *criollo blanco* (white Creole). Although this language supports the conclusion that elites (such as Clemente Palma) denied the existence of Afro-Peruvians as part of the Creole identity and culture, the census official also summarized the history of "black slavery" along the Pacific coast, stating that the census of 1614 counted "10,386 blacks out of a total of 26,441 souls." The number of Africans and African descendants along the coast continued to grow until the colony stopped importing enslaved Africans in 1793.[16] The analysis also asserted that the number of Black people continued to diminish over the national period due to racial mixing, citing colonial descriptions of their "inferior" cultural practices as the only explanation for their erasure through mestizaje. Thus the census analysts equated Blackness with cultural inferiority and assumed that Afro-Peruvians accepted and internalized this ethnoracial hierarchy to suggest they took part in their own disappearance. At the same time that census officials acknowledged that African-descended people had mixed with and become a part of the criollo identity, they disregarded Afro-Peruvian contributions to this racial and cultural construct.

In contrast, the 1908 census's analysis admitted that it could not prevent Limeños of the "Indian race" from claiming to be white in the census. The officials noted that "many *indios,* above all, those who enjoy certain economic advantage and some social elevation, have written themselves, in fact, as whites. . . ."[17] The census officials saw this as a problem due to the perceived inferiority of the "indigenous race," which they understood as a stable, inherited condition that could not be jettisoned through economic ascendance. However, such "passing" was more difficult for Afro-Peruvians, as skin color inhibited their perceived ability to claim whiteness.[18] These census records lend further support to this claim, as officials used culture as a euphemism for race as phenotype, displaying the influence of racial pseudoscience on their recordkeeping.

The author of a study of 1903 census data of Lima, whose work is cited in the official analysis, provides evidence to support this claim. León García asserted that Afro-Peruvians had more difficulty if they tried to "pass" as white, stating that unlike Indigenous Peruvians, "Blacks and yellows do not present any confusion; but one should not consider the possibility that a certain number of Chinese have escaped the census inscriptions by their resistance to enumeration."[19] Whereas Asian and Indigenous Peruvians could claim and perform whiteness, Afro-Peruvians had more difficulty due to the rise of racial pseudoscience, which presented "race" as an inherited set of biological characteristics. The official analysis thus contradicted the dominant narrative that Afro-Peruvians claimed whiteness and were the agents of their own disappearance.

Taking cues from nations they considered models of civility and progress, officials placed special emphasis on women's fertility, which they saw as essential to population growth and national sustainability. Such demographic research had first developed in Europe, the officials pointed out, to understand the "vital political and economic nature" of the nation, which was "intimately connected to the future of a people." This knowledge, they continued, had been useful in the cities of Berlin, Oldenburg, Copenhagen, Budapest, and other European centers during the second half of the nineteenth century, legitimizing its study in Peru.[20] The authors prejudicially asserted that "black women—those who reproduce the most outside of marriage—are the most fertile, followed by white and *mestiza* women."[21] The organizer of the 1904 census of Buenos Aires wrote the preface to this section of the census, subtitled "Fertility of the Woman in Lima," suggesting that Limeño elites might have viewed their southern neighbor as a model for such a modernizing survey. The Argentine census prompted women to answer how many of their children had died, and the Peruvian census followed suit with the same question to document child mortality rates in Lima. In fact, Peruvian census officials used the same questionnaire published from the 1904 census of Buenos Aires to assess the fertility rates of Lima women, as well as child mortality rates.[22] As Erika Denise Edwards has shown, these Argentine censuses contributed to the erasure of Afro-Latinas from the nation's identity and history,[23] and the same survey forms carried out a similar process in Peru.

The analysis that accompanied the 1908 census took cues from model nations, but the author did not see the high fertility rate of unmarried Afro-Peruvian women as a problem. Rather, Afro-Peruvian women in Lima were contributing a national average of five children each, a "strong performance that allows us to maintain our population and still grow productively despite our intense depopulation due to death, principally the deaths of children."[24] Much like Andrews's findings on fertility rates of Afro-Argentine women in nineteenth-century Buenos Aires, such high rates of fertility contradict the final numbers asserting a diminishing African-descended population.[25]

In contrast, the low fertility rates among Indigenous women in Lima and along the coast perplexed the census official, who noted that the "reproductive aptitude" of Indigenous women in the Peruvian interior "could not be missed."[26] Typical of the elite intellectual emphasis on "social *mestizaje*," this concern may have reinforced the "progressive" position of *indigenistas* that "the regeneration of the 'Indian race' should take place in its 'natural habitat.'"[27] When the census findings did not match the official expectations, elite intellectuals provided a remedy that fit their vision of Peru's racial geography. Similarly, they interpreted Afro-Peruvian women's fertility in ways that suited this vision, erasing the African ancestry from their mestizo/a children.

The reportedly high fertility rate of Afro-Peruvian women contradicts the findings of the census itself with regard to race, as the 1903 and 1908 censuses display a sudden decrease in the number of Afro-Peruvians in Lima: whereas Black people constituted 9.4 percent of the city's population in the 1876 census, officials recorded only 5.6 percent of the Lima's population as Black in 1903, marking the most significant decline during the national period.[28] As long as Afro-Peruvian women were bearing mestizo children, elites seemed to perceive their high fertility rates as a virtue, interpreting their findings to fit the narrative of mestizaje. Furthermore, government officials interpreted this data to assert that Afro-Peruvian women were contributing to the disappearance of the Afro-Peruvian population, a top-down analysis that disregarded the perspectives of the subjects under scrutiny.

In some ways, the census's accompanying analysis reified earlier notions of race as related to socioeconomic class, rendering little difference between Indigenous and African-descended populations whom census officials viewed as common plebeians oppressed by a white aristocracy. Reflecting on findings of the 1903 census of Lima neighborhoods, the officials noted that in this study "the race of the inhabitants ostensibly influences the conditions of their dwelling; the daily observations and proximity of rooms and inhabitants, shows us that the worse the race, the worse the room: the Chinese stay in worse conditions than Indians and blacks; and these, worse than the *mestizos*, the whites enjoy the most *comfort* and living space. In view of this observation, which is only contradicted in few exceptions, we have compared the distribution of homes by district according to the good or bad quality and the population divided by race in two groups with the categories *blancos* and *castas,* the latter group assigned to all subjects who do not pertain to the first race."[29]

The language of the analysis reinforced racial determinism. While the analysis lumps all nonwhites together as a racialized underclass, it also reveals the lived reality of the dominant discourse of mestizaje: those perceived as mestizos enjoyed better living spaces than did those labeled Indigenous, Chinese, and Black. Thus African-descended Limeños may have seen material benefits in publicly identifying as mestizo/a rather than as negro/a, and the elimination of intermediate categories connoting African ancestry (i.e., zambo and pardo) facilitated the erasure of African ancestry among such ethnoracial mixtures. Alternatively, census officials may have been more likely to categorize a subject as mestizo/a if that person had risen in socioeconomic standing despite their insistence on race as biological difference. Lima censuses of the 1860s suggested a diminishing number of whites in Peru after abolition, showing that Afro-Peruvians were not simply "whitening." Instead of denying any association with African ancestry in order to "approximate white norms," many African-descended Peruvians simply reported mixed ancestry among a series of labels that wrote out African ancestry. Rather than whitening, African-descended Peruvians increasingly identified as mestizos in a process facilitated by elites. Despite elite interests, however, many Afro-Peruvian mestizos maintained cultural practices and identities rooted in African ancestry while officials erased African ancestry in the censuses.

Educated elites seemed aware that the broad category of mestizo enveloped those of African descent who had mixed with Indigenous and white Peruvians. In his official analysis of the 1908 census, León García wrote that the majority of those classified as mestizos were known, "among us, as '*zambos*' and '*mulatos*.'" He explains that he reduced these categories under the blanket of "mestizo" so as to "not increase divisions," but does not elaborate on his reasoning.[30] León García and his contemporaries may have seen it as more practical to condense such categories connoting African ancestry in order to mitigate social tensions, which was in keeping with the ideology of mestizaje producing a raceless, mestizo national identity. Regardless of intent, the decision to stretch the boundaries of the mestizo label shows the early emergence of "the cult of the mestizo" in Peru, which exalted racial mixing to uplift Indigenous populations and erase ethnoracial distinctions.[31] León García also pointed out a continuity regarding migration patterns and racial categorizing in line with censuses of the 1860s. More Indigenous Peruvians continued to migrate to Lima from rural areas, while those categorized as Black were more likely to be Lima natives.[32] This analysis demonstrates continuities with the perspectives of census officials of the 1860s and a continued association of Blackness with slavery in the early twentieth century.

CENSUS PROCEDURES IN THE RURAL NORTH: ERASING BLACKNESS THROUGH *MESTIZAJE* IN ECCLESIASTICAL RECORDS OF CHULUCANAS, PIURA

A similar process of racial categorizing appears in the baptismal records in the district of Chulucanas, in the northern department of Piura. This region has a historic concentration of African-descended people, many of whom were enslaved on plantations, such as Yapatera. Baptismal records from the late nineteenth century show a growing mestizo population, while the number of children categorized as white declined. Between 1854 and 1900, priests recorded the "*condición social*" ("social condition," a euphemism for race) of hundreds of children. Although the records are incomplete and inconsistent regarding children's "social condition," they reveal a trend similar to that of the national censuses in Lima over the same period: categories indicating African ancestry declined, minimizing the perceived presence of Afro-Peruvians there. In 1854, the first 150 children recorded were all categorized as casta, indicating African ancestry with use of a term dominant in the colonial period. In contrast, priests recorded only five children as blanco/a (white), and thirty-seven were categorized as indio/a (Indigenous).[33] The generalized category of casta appears to have absorbed more specific categories indicating African ancestry, however, such as negro/a and zambo/a. These records show that parish registers mirrored those of the state in diminishing categories indicating African ancestry, contributing to Afro-Peruvian invisibility through the hegemony of mestizaje.

Despite the distant contexts, the records in Piura and Lima demonstrate a similar method of erasing Blackness, suggesting a systematic process at the national level. Between 1885 and 1889, priests categorized just six children as casta, fifty as white, seventy-five as mestizo/a, and seventy-nine as indio/a.[34] The decline in castas and increase in whites, mestizos, and Indians suggest that Afro-Peruvians were mixing with other groups and that more white Peruvians had settled in the region in the decades following the abolition of slavery. Considering this was not a period of heightened migration to Piura, however, the records indicate an increasing reluctance among church officials to note the African ancestry of the children they baptized. In contrast with Lima, the isolation of this region may have facilitated Afro-Peruvian claims of mestizo or white identities for their children.

Nonetheless, in 1889 priests recorded fewer white baptisms as the category of mestizo waxed. These registers show 49 children categorized as white, 154 as mestizo/a, and 109 as indio/a.[35] In this case, priests perceived a surge in the white population, followed by increased mixing between Afro-Peruvian, Indigenous, and white residents of the parish.[36] The demographic changes over this four-year period suggest that fewer people were perceived as white, providing further evidence that Afro-Peruvians were not claiming whiteness, but many were identified as mestizos, which effectively distanced them from African ancestry. The lack of categories indicating mixed African ancestry, much like the Lima-centered censuses of the early twentieth century, appears to have minimized the perception of African-descended people in Chulucanas. Furthermore, by 1897 priests abruptly stopped recording the "social condition" of the children they baptized, apparently believing that race labels did not matter, as all are equal in God's eyes. The decision carried unforeseen consequences, especially that of contributing to the perceived disappearance of the Afro-Peruvian population.[37]

A contemporary analysis of the early twentieth-century censuses of Lima also lamented the common usage of the singular category of casta by parish priests in the capital, arguing that their meaning was unclear: "It is not possible to know the distribution of races understood by the generic term 'castas' employed in this statistic because the data comes from parish registers, whose priests, devotees of the aristocratic spirit of the era, always confused all people of color, as equally inferior, under the vague rubric of castas."[38] León García's perspective on race influenced the official analyses of early twentieth-century Lima, and his analysis of nineteenth-century parish registers suggests that such Lima elites saw racism as an element of Peru's colonial past that was eliminated through independence and abolition. He distanced himself and his early twentieth-century contemporaries from overt racism while simultaneously accusing priests of racist, traditional, "aristocratic" attitudes associated with the past. Between 1876 and 1940 such distancing from overt racism contributed to the diminution of discourses of racial difference and the invisibility of Afro-Peruvians.

Historian Steve Stein provides context for the logic behind censuses in this period, marking the period between 1900 and 1930 as one of "dramatic transformation," as public services continually expanded and the "popular masses" doubled in size. Whereas the census data is vague in terms of socioeconomic indicators and neighborhoods, Stein finds that residents of callejones increased over this period, a detail beyond the scope of the city's published censuses.[39] Instead, Stein analyzes newspapers, records from labor unions, and sports and social clubs to reconstruct the existence of a collective Afro-Peruvian identity during the first three decades of the twentieth century. Such sources provide crucial insights on Afro-Peruvian contributions to national culture and daily life beyond the purview of census records.

Afro-Peruvians found camaraderie in sports and cultural performances that connected them to a sense of national pride and peruanidad. In contrast with elite attempts to appropriate the popular religious cult of El Señor de los Milagros (discussed in the previous chapter), *fútbol* (soccer) became an outlet for Afro-Peruvian collective identity, in particular through the club Alianza de Lima. Established in 1900 as "Sport Alianza," the club played against other working-class teams, which differed greatly from the elite, formal, and "exclusive" fútbol clubs that practiced and competed in cricket clubs only accessible to members of the city's oligarchy. Historian José Antonio del Busto Duthurburu has pointed out that contemporaries referred to Club Alianza as the "team of blacks," with strong support in the "black neighborhood of Lima," la Victoria.[40] Unlike other "popular" fútbol clubs of Lima at the time, Stein argues, Alianza de Lima fomented a strong racial connection between its members and its supporters by the 1920s. The majority of the players identified as Black and held "traditionally Afro-Peruvian occupations," which their meager club earnings supplemented.[41]

Unlike the popularity of El Señor de los Milagros, Alianza Lima elicited racist anxieties among the city's white population by the late 1920s due to its unapologetic public image as a Black team. When the club sought entry to the South American fútbol championship in 1929, a Peruvian commentator lamented, "How can we send a team of blacks to a championship!—they exclaim. They'll say we are a country of that race!"[42] Although Afro-Peruvians were creating and maintaining avenues for collective identity, white elites continually distanced the nation's public image from any associations with Blackness.

In a 2015 study published by Peru's Ministry of Culture, historians Maribel Arrelucea Barrantes and Jesús Cosamalón Aguilar bring together demographic data from a variety of sources to reach a similar conclusion regarding Lima's Afro-Peruvian population during this period. Their use of demographic records from the national treasury (*Ministerio de Hacienda*) and the municipal government of Lima corroborates the national census account to show that "the most pronounced [demographic] decline occurred in the case of blacks . . . between 1876 and 1931." The records show an annual increase of 1.5 percent in the white category, while those labeled as mestizos and castas increased at an annual rate of 3.4 percent in this period. Those categorized as Indian declined at a rate of 0.4 percent per year, and those categorized as Black declined at a yearly rate of 0.18 percent. In 1931, 152,771 people were identified as Black, mestizo, and casta in Lima out of a total population of 275,905. Although those categorized as Black (8,244) composed only 0.03 percent of the city's total population that year, the combined categories indicating mixed and African ancestry were over 55 percent of the city's inhabitants. As the population categorized as white remained a minority, comprising 34 percent of the city in 1931, the categories indicating possible African ancestry grew to a majority. Taken together, these records challenge the official narrative of Afro-Peruvian disappearance through "whitening." While many Afro-Peruvians may have "avoided the dishonor of being labeled 'Black,'" these alternative statistics suggest that Limeños perceived as Indigenous were declining at a faster rate between 1876 and 1931.[43] While mestizaje increased cultural and racial mixing between Indigenous and Afro-Peruvians in this period, the process fomented collective interests based in class rather than race. As Limeños distanced themselves from Blackness and indigeneity, moreover, they did not necessarily claim whiteness or shed cultural traditions. Institutional whitening, as a top-down process, could not erase the cultural traditions that maintained a unique Afro-Peruvian collective identity.

Marisol de la Cadena's analysis of the changing vocabulary of race and class in early twentieth-century Peru provides evidence that indigenista intellectuals of the 1930s contributed to Afro-Peruvian invisibility, a dominant discourse and interpretation of Peruvian history that I analyze in more detail in chapter 5. As this literary movement coincided with the "international discredit of racial thought, 'class' gradually absorbed everybody's race, and became the sole element in leftist rhetoric. . . . Workers of coastal haciendas were identified as '*asalariados rurales*,' while 'proletarian' referred to urban factory workers. These two categories were used instead of the labels *mestizos, cholos* or *zambos*, to name the *gente del pueblo*—those excluded from the *gente decente*. . . . Replacing race labels with class rhetoric, leftist parties assumed the leadership of a nationwide social movement to organize rural unions."[44] Like the official narrative provided by census officials, this class rhetoric rendered Afro-Peruvian participation in such movements invisible. While elites erased Afro-Peruvians from the historical record from above, sociopolitical movements from below elided race in favor of class and erased Afro-Peruvian roles from within these movements.

ERASING BLACKNESS IN THE 1940 NATIONAL CENSUS

In the modernizing era, political elites promoted an image of the nation as civilized, white, and sanitized of its African ancestry. This is evinced in the mechanics of the 1940 census, when officials completed the "whitening" of their population. The officials combined the race labels of mestizo and blanco ("mixed" and "white"), resulting in the lowest-ever recorded number of Afro-Peruvians in the nation's history. Whereas Lima records from 1931 included mestizos and castas as a single category that could indicate African ancestry, the national census of 1940 eliminated the term "casta" and replaced it with "white," thereby erasing the potential for African ancestry to be read in the census. The singular category of mestiza/blanca became the default race label in the 1940 census, as officials were instructed that "people who do not have a definitive race . . . will be recorded as mestizos."[45] Officials thus celebrated Afro-Peruvian women's fertility inasmuch as they could manipulate it to report increasing numbers of mestizos and a decreasing Afro-Peruvian population.

The decision to combine the categories of mestiza and blanca may suggest a growing openness to mestizos as a socially mobile group, but it also reflects a common desire among Latin American elites to draw the boundary between mestizo and Indigenous more clearly—in Central America, for example, the Guatemalan officials began labeling all non-Indigenous citizens as "Ladinos" to provide legal benefits to the emerging coffee elite in the 1870s.[46] As historian Jeffrey Gould has concluded in the case of Nicaragua, the "myth of mestizaje" rendered the Indigenous population invisible between 1880 and 1965.[47] Similar to Gould's emphasis on the economic and political contributions of Indigenous Nicaraguans to counter this invisibility, the Peruvian censuses presented a "seriously distorted image" of Peruvian history.[48] The legal intentions of racial categories in the Peruvian censuses are obscure, but the process contributed to an emerging elite racial ideology that de la Cadena calls "silent racism": absorbing African-descended Peruvians into a broader category of whiteness and defining race in terms of culture, as de la Cadena explains, "provided academics with a comfortable self-acquittal of racist guilt, without eradicating racism."[49]

An official recognition of mestizos as whites thus served to support an ideology of a "raceless" nation while erasing Peru's African ancestry. This is evident in the census records for the Pacific coastal regions with well-documented histories of Afro-Peruvian presence, such as Zaña, Piura, Trujillo, Chiclayo, and Lima, where officials recorded 0.02 percent of the local populations as "Black" in 1940. However, the officials documented at least 77 percent of the citizens as "blanca y mestiza."[50] This manipulation of the census records created a distorted view of the Peruvian population with significant repercussions for Afro-Peruvians. As Andrews has argued regarding the Argentine case, "demographic distortions in turn form part of a larger phenomenon, that being the obscuring, be it intentional or unintentional, of the role of the Afro-Argentines in their nation's history." In broader terms, such a manipulation of the historical record "has formed an enormous obstacle to our efforts to understand present-day patterns of race relations in Latin America, how they vary within the region, and how they compare with those found in other multiracial societies."[51] The manipulation of racial categories of Peru's national census of 1940 underscores this point.

The analyses that accompany the census data offered an "official" (that is, state-sanctioned) explanation of the history of Afro-Peruvians, which completely denied their historical agency. The official analysis of 1940 surmised that "the political hatred between two military *caudillos* [Echenique and Castilla] was the authentic liberator of the blacks. The unconscious, as such, was the protagonist of this memorable episode in the history of our *patria*."[52] This narrative denied the efforts of generations of Afro-Peruvians to dismantle slavery before the revolution of 1854, which combines with demographic distortions to create persistent obstacles for historians interested in documenting Afro-Peruvian history before and after the abolition of slavery.

The census officials of early twentieth-century Lima modeled their survey on that of Buenos Aires with the hopes of engineering a comparable modern city as a public image of Peruvian national identity. They went so far as to use the same questionnaires as their Argentine counterparts and frequently cited censuses of major cities throughout Europe and as far north as Norway. Their desire to create an image of a modern nation led to contradictory findings: Afro-Peruvian women were birthing healthy children at a sustainable rate, yet the early twentieth-century censuses reported the smallest-ever Afro-Peruvian percentage of the national population. The final lines of analysis of the 1940 census attempted to explain this sudden decline despite their insistence on Afro-Peruvian women's fecundity:

Table 3.1. Peru's national census report of 1940 (Departamento de Lima, Cuadro No 16.—Poblacion censada, segun religión, por raza y sexo)

Religión	Poblacion			Blanca y Mestiza		India		Negra		Amarilla		Raza no declarada	
	Total	Hombres	Mujeres	Hombres	Mujeres	Hombres	Mujeres	Hombres	Mujeres	Hombres	Mujeres	Hombres	Mujeres
TOTAL	828,298	424,656	403,642	331,042	327,375	67,074	59,631	6,800	6,932	19,372	9,298	368	406
Católica	799,673	405,022	394,651	324,028	322,643	66,797	59,417	6,771	6,915	7,066	5,279	360	397
Budísta	9,832	6,251	3,581	31	23	5	—	—	8	6,214	3,549	1	1
Protestante	7,241	4,184	3,057	3,988	2,902	170	141	—	—	26	14	—	—
Confucista	5,724	5,511	213	19	26	2	—	10	—	5,479	187	1	—
Judía	1,812	974	838	945	828	—	—	1	—	28	10	—	—
Mahometana	49	34	15	25	13	4	1	—	—	5	1	—	—
Otras religiones	1,208	755	453	579	357	17	6	2	1	157	89	—	—
Sin religión	1,652	1,291	361	962	229	41	22	7	4	281	106	—	—
Religión no declarada	1,107	634	473	465	354	38	44	9	4	116	63	6	8

Source: Collection of Archivo Histórico Municipal de Lima.

> The demographic and census data *affirm* a decline in the black race. A race is maintained through genetic aggregation or through immigration. Legions of blacks no longer come to Peru, as in the era of slavery. Free immigration also fails to add [to the black population] because our country does not offer any special perspective for men of color that might explain such migratory movements. *The productive growth of blacks in Peru is null.* Statistical studies by Dr. Leon Garcia, in Lima, proved that over a six-year period only 249 blacks were born, despite the census findings that demonstrate that black women were the most [reproductively] prolific in our capital. The convergence of two negative factors—lack of genetic aggregation and the absence of immigration—explain why the demographic volume of the black race is diminishing from one century to the next.[53]

The analysts grounded their explanation of the declining Black population in Eurocentric environmental and racially deterministic language. This official narrative contradicts the popular understanding of race as culture, offering a uniquely transparent view of elite anxieties and persistent understandings of race as biological and social. Afro-Peruvians did not inhabit the Andean interior, according to this analysis, because the climate did not suit their race. The hot sun of the Peruvian coast that "burns the skin," however, was similar to the environment of the "black continent." The 1940 census offered the forgone conclusion that Afro-Peruvians would be absorbed into the broader national identity by conflating mestizos with blancos and erasing categories that indicated African ancestry, such as zambo/a. The official analysis and explanation of the disappearance of "blacks" in the census did not consider the children of Afro-Peruvian women as African-descended, effectively denying the existence of African ancestry as part of the Peruvian nation.

León García's study of the early twentieth-century censuses of Lima concludes that racial mixing in the capital city was producing a "progressive amalgamation of all of the bloods." This was a "simply natural process," he argued, "concordant with what has occurred" in other parts of Latin America, such as the Antilles, Brazil, and Mexico. In all of these cases, the "force of the victors over the vanquished" influenced the majority of the new nation's citizens to identify as "white in origin" despite their "mixed blood."

The mixing of new racial elements, he suggests, comes together in "sensible ways" under the "strong bond of nationality."[54] Despite the aforementioned obstacles to Afro-Peruvians who may have desired to claim whiteness, the census itself changed to accommodate this concern: by including Afro-Peruvians of mixed racial ancestry in the same category as whites, these Lima elites rendered such ethnoracial differences as irrelevant to a common national identity. As Peruvian officials worked to modernize the nation, their censuses did the work of relegating the history of slavery and Blackness to the colonial past, denying the relevance of African ancestry in the "modern" twentieth-century nation.

CONCLUSIONS

The racial reorganization of Peruvian censuses in the twentieth century reveals some similarities to the reduction in racial categories in contemporaneous US censuses, as well as to the flawed processes of census taking in other parts of Latin America. The Peruvian censuses eliminated categories indicating African ancestry between 1876 and 1940, just as the US Census Office (which became the US Bureau of the Census in 1903) did. The same questions that George Reid Andrews has raised regarding the underestimation of Afro-Argentines in Buenos Aires can be applied to Lima, where census officials categorized children of Afro-Peruvian women as mestizos to offer positive evidence of population growth but also to deny Blackness.

The politics of censuses are historically contingent, and Peruvian census officials expressed and reflected elite concerns that disparaged Blackness and constructed an image of Lima as modern and white. This case presents a process similar to the construction of racial identities in censuses of São Paolo, Brazil. Through her analysis of the myth of the "vanishing Indian" in Sao Paolo, Muriel Nazzari has argued that "censuses are not neutral documents that report only 'facts' but are themselves instruments of state and elite control that reflect the social construction of race."[55]

The reorganization of racial taxonomy in twentieth-century Peruvian censuses presents the inverse process to that of Brazil in the eighteenth century, however. Where Nazzari documents declining categories indicating Indigenous identities and ancestry, this chapter finds similar reasons for declining categories indicating African ancestry in Peru. In early eighteenth-century São Paulo, historians estimate that Indians were 80 percent of the population. By the early nineteenth century, however, the censuses of São Paulo used only the categories "white, black, and *pardo*, a synonym of mulatto," which denied the existence of an Indigenous population (or even Indigenous ancestry) in the city. The racial reorganization of São Paulo censuses was opposite to that of Peru and Mexico. As Nazzari points out, "In Sao Paulo by 1800 the Portuguese-Indian-African triangle had collapsed into a Portuguese-African continuum."[56] Nazzari cites R. Douglas Cope's related work on colonial Mexico City, where the Spanish-African-Indian triangle collapsed into a Spanish-Indian continuum by 1800. Between 1866 and 1940, records of the Afro-Peruvian population thus underwent categorical changes in censuses similar to those of Mexico City's African-descended population and similar to São Paulo's Indigenous population in the eighteenth century.

George Reid Andrews's analysis of census records of Buenos Aires demonstrates that 30 percent of the city's population was identified as Black in 1778, yet the census of 1887 enumerated less than 2 percent of the city's population as Afro-Argentine.[57] In contrast with Peru, however, Argentina welcomed nearly one million European immigrants over the nineteenth century. The application of positivist policies to "whiten" the Argentine population increased European immigration after 1895, contributing to the doubling of the nation's population between 1890 and 1914.[58] In contrast, Peru received fewer European immigrants than Brazil and Argentina, even as Europeans immigrated to the Americas by the millions between 1870 and 1900. Despite Civilista efforts to recruit European immigrants due to their associations with development and modernization, the labor demands on Peruvian coastal haciendas did not match the interests of such immigrants. Peru's large peasantry and its peripheral location in relation to the Atlantic world made it a less desirable destination to Europeans seeking economic opportunities and social advantages.[59] Thus, whereas European immigration contributed to the invisibility of Afro-Latino populations in other countries during this period, the Peruvian narrative of mestizaje is unique in rendering its African-descended population invisible in the absence of such immigration and racial "whitening."

The demographic distortions of Lima's censuses regarding the Afro-Peruvian population between the late colonial period and the early twentieth century are even more dramatic, as Afro-Peruvians declined from over half of the city's population to below one percent by 1940. Andrews cites "the frequency with which Afro-Argentines appear in random newspaper and magazine photographs" as alternative evidence to counter the official narrative of disappearance offered by the census data.[60] Steve Stein's use of photographs, print, and popular culture offers similar "alternative evidence" to the official narrative offered in the analyses that accompanied the censuses of 1903, 1908, and 1940. The Lima records analyzed by local historians Cosamalón Aguilar and Arrelucea Barrantes provide further evidence of the underrepresentation of Afro-Peruvians in the national surveys. But as Afro-Peruvians created and maintained associations based on a collective ethnoracial identity, Lima elites resisted Afro-Peruvian visibility in the public image of the city they sought to project internationally. This carried significant consequences for Afro-Peruvian subsequent demands for social equality and their place in the nation's identity.

The declining use of racial markers among intellectuals, state officials, and clerics in the early twentieth century contributed to the historic invisibility and even the erasure of Afro-Peruvians in the nation, a product of the selective recording of events in the "moment of fact creation (the making of sources)" and "the moment of fact assembly (the making of *archives*)."[61] If census officials in Lima understood censuses as tools to push progressive agendas and create the appearance of a modern nation, the denial of African ancestry also meant the denial of social services for, and discrimination particular to, Afro-Peruvians. Just as importantly, this erasure and invisibility denied Afro-Peruvians their rightful place in the official narrative of the nation's history and identity. The following chapter examines the ongoing construction of peruanidad in the late nineteenth and early twentieth centuries, which corresponded with the census records' erasure of Afro-Peruvians as a category of contemporary analysis. The following two chapters show how the making of sources and the making of archives produced silences in the subsequent making of narratives, which rendered Afro-Peruvians invisible in discourses of mestizaje as national identity.

PART II

"The Making of Narratives"

Chapter 4

Peruanidad and Blackness in National and Local Perspectives

Popular Literature and Racial Science

A wide array of discourses on race and nation contributed to the construction of Peruvian national identity in the late nineteenth and early twentieth centuries. Elite and popular literature constructed peruanidad in influential ways during this period. I define peruanidad in this context as a narrative of national identity based on the idea that mestizaje erased racial differences and strengthened the democracy. However, this narrative process cast Afro-Peruvians in the past and envisioned a future void of African ancestry. Paradoxically, this shaping of peruanidad entailed the celebration of Afro-Peruvian cultural forms while denying their existence in the present. Many studies have examined the emerging notion of peruanidad in this period, but fewer have questioned the roles assigned to Afro-Peruvians in this process.[1] Indigenous populations of Peru have dominated elite and popular narratives constructing the nation's identity, with Afro-Peruvian history and culture positioned in a more ambiguous place in the construction of peruanidad.[2] This chapter builds on sociologist Edward Telles's assertion that "the 'imagined construction' of ethnic and racial differences in Peru has its roots in the different debates and projects of nation building during the nineteenth and the twentieth centuries. These discourses produced a social structure of ethnic and racial boundaries and an 'ethnoracial grammar' used by social actors to describe and interpret their differences and inequalities."[3] This chapter also builds on Marisol de la Cadena's work on the fluidity of the mestizo identity in twentieth-century Peru, as well as anthropological work on racism and Blackness in northern Peru, by examining the intellectual connections between regional literature and various strains of nationalist writing in Lima.[4]

The 1870s through the 1920s witnessed the rise of positivist philosophy among Latin American elites, and this chapter traces a shift from classical liberalism to positivism in terms of race, mestizaje, and national identity. I contrast pseudohistorical and pseudoscientific writings of Lima elites with literature from the northern region of Piura to expose differing regional and local conceptions of peruanidad as well as distinct interpretations of colonial history in shaping the nation. Limeño Ricardo Palma and Piuran Enrique López Albújar made visible the Afro-Peruvian presence in their "foundational fictions" in disparate ways, yet these interventions in the national imaginary have largely been overlooked due to the dominance of indigenismo (the 1920s elite-driven intellectual, social, and political movement that identified the Indigenous population as the basis of Peruvian national identity, analyzed in the following chapter).[5] The literary and discourse analysis thus suggests the need to consider how distinct local political concerns shaped a variety of perspectives on peruanidad, with a particular focus on the role of Afro-Peruvians in national literature. Popular understandings of Afro-Peruvian culture and history influenced elite perceptions of race between the 1860s and the 1930s, revealing the discursive parallels between popular literature and elite constructions of ethnoracial boundaries. Following abolition in Peru, this period also coincides with the perceived disappearance of the Afro-Peruvian population in the official record. This chapter provides a rare glimpse of an Afro-Peruvian mestizo intellectual whose family ascended socially and were compelled to grapple with their African ancestry in ways that limited the visibility of Blackness. The range of literature analyzed in this chapter—pseudoscientific writings on race and mestizaje, popular literature on history and culture, romantic novels, and, finally, an antiracist and anti-imperialist essay—displays the complex shaping of peruanidad.

The writings of Lima intellectual Ricardo Palma (1833–1919) are a well-known source of national identity for Peruvians. Today, Palma is remembered officially as "the most important Afro-Peruvian writer in history who made visible the black presence in Peruvian society."[6] His celebrated *tradiciones* (traditions) were short stories blending fictional satire with history, celebrating the mixed heritage that came to compose Peruvian culture. He is remembered as an "integrationist" for his criticisms of institutional mistreatment of lower classes and his celebration of Afro-Peruvian and Indigenous cultural contributions. The morals or lessons of his tradiciones often criticized the colonial legacy of white superiority, suggesting Palma's inner conflict as a Lima elite with African ancestry. This internal tension, I argue, influenced his foundational fictions in contradictory ways: both his political career as a social elite and his writing reflected a simultaneous recognition of and distancing from an Afro-Peruvian identity. His son, Clemente, went one step further by spurning any association with Blackness, using his elite education to apply nineteenth-century pseudoscientific theories of race to explain Peruvian backwardness when compared with Europe. This perspective stood in contrast with Piuran author and sociologist Enrique López Albújar, whose literature and poetry celebrated Afro-Peruvian culture while identifying ethnoracial inequality as a legacy of slavery. Despite Clemente's Eurocentric and pessimistic vision of Peru's destiny while he was a student, his later writings show a closer association with both his father's and Albújar's integrationist perspectives. Whereas integrationists included African descendants and Indigenous populations in their visions of mestizaje as national identity, most eugenicists believed in applying the European pseudoscience of race to "uplift" and "whiten" racialized populations they deemed inferior. However, ideas of race and nation changed and varied in Latin America and in Peru between the 1860s and 1930s, showing how an emerging science and popular understandings of race and mestizaje informed each other in historically contingent ways. The discursive shifts evident in Clemente Palma's writings also bear similarities to Peru's leading eugenicist of the 1930s, Roberto MacLean Estenós, demonstrating the interplay between popular culture and the pseudoscience of race.

Whereas a great deal of excellent scholarship on social engineering in early twentieth-century Latin America focuses on government policies taking cues from imperial powers, this chapter emphasizes the importance of cultural work in contextualizing such flexible yet powerful pseudoscience.[7] By examining the construction of peruanidad and Blackness in a transnational perspective, the chapter exposes similarities in discourses of race and nation across the Americas while highlighting diverse perspectives that were ultimately constrained by a dominant discourse of mestizaje.

Furthermore, the contrasting views of Afro-Peruvians belonging to Ricardo and Clemente Palma illuminate the complex process by which elites conveyed Afro-Peruvians in the construction of a national identity. While divergent, the hegemonic narrative placed Afro-Peruvians in a romanticized, sensual environment of the past while suggesting that they existed only as mestizos in contemporary Peru.

RICARDO AND CLEMENTE PALMA: INTERNALIZING BLACKNESS

Ricardo Palma's early career demonstrates his contempt for the "Great Liberator" Ramón Castilla despite his abolition of slavery. Palma's perspective on Castilla heavily influenced his literary and political career. Born in the young Peruvian republic in 1833, Palma witnessed the rise of Castilla to the presidency in 1845 and his authoritarian hold over the office until 1863. Although the "Government of Liberty" abolished slavery and brought needed stability to the country after years of upheaval and caudillo rivalries, Palma saw Castilla as a dictator. This is evident in Palma's early political activism as well as his initial support for a more inclusive political left in the 1870s.[8] While his writing was groundbreaking in its representation and inclusion of the Afro-Peruvian population and history, his representations were not always celebratory or even sympathetic. Thus, his legacy as a representative of Afro-Peruvian culture and identity is mixed, and his contradictions are emblematic of the paradox of mestizaje.

Ricardo Palma's political activism began with his involvement in the failed storming of Castilla's home in 1860, for which he was exiled to Chile. When Palma returned to Peru in 1863, Castilla's democratically elected successor (of the opposition party), President José Gálvez, named Palma consul to Pará, Brazil. After traveling in Brazil, Europe, and the United States, Palma returned to Peru and supported José Balta's successful revolution against President Mariano Prado in 1867. This earned him the position of Balta's private secretary, and shortly thereafter he was appointed senator of the district of Loreto (the largest Peruvian department, located in the far northern region). His position as senator of such a remote yet large district exemplifies the Lima-centered politics of this era, as Palma was not from Loreto nor did the district's constituents elect him.

Ricardo Palma wrote a popular tradición about Balta's 1868 revolution that provides a cultural perspective not visible in the institutional accounts of this period of tumultuous politics. Ricardo Palma's tradición titled "La Conga" celebrated the Afro-Peruvian contributions to this revolution. Palma's account repeats a song and dance by the same name that the people of Chiclayo sang while defeating the government forces. "La Conga" falls under the genre of a *zamacueca*, and Palma's account of this "dance of the land, creole dance, purely national" places Afro-Peruvian culture at the center this northern political movement. The title suggests the African roots of the politically expressive song, with a refrain praising José Balta as "the best" among the colonels.[9] By highlighting such cultural expressions in sociopolitical movements along the coast, Palma located the Afro-Peruvian presence in support of Balta's revolution. However, even this account did not explicitly state that Afro-Peruvians (negros/as) played key roles in the revolution even though its success directly benefited them.[10] Instead, Palma occludes and appropriates the expression of Blackness in this movement as "creole" and "purely national," showing how his "integrationist" approach also entailed the erasure of Blackness in favor of a celebratory raceless discourse of peruanidad.

Palma published his first collection of tradiciones in 1872, the same year that he would retire from politics. This year saw the election of Manuel Pardo, which was contested by four colonels (the Gutiérrez brothers) who supported Balta. However, Balta refused to bar Pardo from the presidency, so the brothers imprisoned the former president on July 22. News of the coup reached the Lima public through other military officials who had opposed the instigators. The Gutiérrez brothers quickly found themselves besieged in the government palace, as Lima "masses" took to the streets and revolted against the military intervention in the city center. To intimidate the masses and quell the uprising, one of the colonels executed Balta in his cell, and General Tomás Gutiérrez declared himself "supreme chief," president of the republic. The assassination only fanned the flames of revolt, as mobs pursued three of the brothers to their deaths by burning just four days later (one brother, Marcelino, fled and found shelter at a friend's house nearby).[11]

Until the 1970s, the historiographical treatment of the popular uprising that ended the lives of the Gutiérrez brothers either exalted the righteous political retribution of the urban masses, lamented the brutality of the violence, or attempted to explain the uprising as the manifestation of a psychosis of mass hysteria. Historian Margarita Giesecke revised these one-dimensional analyses in her close study of the event in her 1978 book, *Masas Urbanas y Rebelión en la Historia. Lima: Golpe de Estado, 1872.* Giesecke's important intervention restored the political and social dimensions necessary to understand the rational interests of the Lima "masses" who decided to retaliate against the military coup. Rather than examining an outbreak of violence between the power-hungry military and a raucous mob, Giesecke examines a variety of local documents to understand the occupations and income levels of the Limeños who decided to storm the national palace and execute the Gutiérrez brothers, showing how class interests shaped a popular response to the attempted coup. Working-class Afro-Peruvians had similar motivations to demand the integrity of the electoral process to which they had recently gained access.

The mob's outrage and extreme violence shocked many onlookers, especially the Lima elite. Newspaper accounts provided gruesome details of how the brothers' bodies were mutilated (including the removal of one brother's heart). The angry mob later captured and killed Marcelino Gutiérrez as well, and in the process they demolished the homes of the colonels. The horrific scenes of mutilated corpses in the Plaza de Armas, according to Giesecke, caused the historical narrative to focus on the mob mentality of these actors rather than consider the socioeconomic motivations underlying their public display of contempt for a conservative military coup. The Gutiérrez brothers had executed José Balta to prevent the rise of Manuel Pardo to the presidency, both of whom can be considered part of Peru's "new liberal" movement. These politicians were the first to break from elite-centered politics by rejecting the close relationship between the military and government and praising the daily efforts of the working classes of Lima. Pardo embodied the progressive politics of the "new liberals" who reinterpreted literature from the French Enlightenment to draw the support of working-class Limeños: these laborers could use their material skills to break from the chains of slavery, and the labor "union was [now] to the artisan what the club had been to the intellectual."[12] Rather than having to pursue honor through military service, the new liberals supported the efforts of Afro-Peruvian Limeños tacitly by echoing their demands for better working and living conditions.

Giesecke identifies several intellectuals who exalted the virtuous labor of the working classes and even cited Rousseau in support of their demands for equal civil rights and political representation. Thus, her work provides further context for understanding why the negation of voting rights (by means of a coup) would elicit such a violent response. Her analysis of the coup also addresses the understudied political interests of working-class Lima residents, many of whom held occupations common among Afro-Peruvians, such as aguadores (water carriers) and *artesanos* (artisans).[13] Despite the book's analysis of social divisions that resemble discourses of racial difference, Giesecke does not address the question of ethnoracial identities in her analysis.

Even more poignantly, this context further elucidates Ricardo Palma's own political perspective and decision to separate himself from the new liberal movement. Palma's distancing from the popular politics of Lima may reflect his personal anxieties regarding African ancestry, as his partial African ancestry could have barred him from academic circles. However, his writings tended to include the influence of Afro-Peruvians on national and local politics. Palma's tradiciones integrated Afro-Peruvian culture as a major part of national identity. Even though "blackness was a synonym of plebian, uncultured, barbarism, degradation, etc.," Palma's tradiciones frequently included African-descended people set in the colonial era, and not always simply as enslaved people.[14]

A recurring historical figure in the tradiciones is a mulato Dominican friar born in sixteenth-century Lima, Fray Martin de Porres, who was beatified in 1837. A tradición titled "Los Ratones de Fray Martín" ("Brother Martin's Mice") was included in Palma's first collection published in 1872. Here Palma factually presents the friar as the son of the Spaniard Juan de Porres and an unnamed Afro-Panamanian enslaved woman. Palma blends comedy smoothly with the historical narrative, explaining "and, opting for the career of a saint, which in those times was a career like any other, he visited the Convent of Santo Domingo, where he died on November 3, 1639, in an odor of saintliness." Identifying the saint as an emblem of peruanidad, Palma praises "our countryman Martin de Porres, [who] in life and after death, performed miracles above all. He made miracles with such facility as others made verses."[15] Read as an allegory for the construction of the nation, the Afro-Peruvian saint brought harmony to early republican Peru by means of the Catholic Church. This foundational fiction depicts the church as integrating three distinct ethnoracial identities in Peru: the Spaniard, the Indigenous, and the African.

As literary scholar Larissa Brewer-García has pointed out, white Creole elites have used the image of the seventeenth-century Afro-Peruvian saint to their own ends. Brewer-Garcia argues that his "visual and textual composite . . . could simultaneously embody black and white characteristics," ultimately arguing that this strategy "represents an effort made by white Creole elites in Lima in the mid-to-late seventeenth century to fashion themselves before the larger Catholic world as inheritors of classical forms and successful evangelizers of the region's dark-skinned populations."[16] Similarly, historian Rafael Castañeda García has argued that such manipulation occurred throughout the Atlantic world: "On both sides of the Atlantic the presence of black saints formed part of the constructed imaginary of the Church to foster cohesion and establish ties of identification between the African population and their descendants, enslaved and free. In Ibero-America there was devotion to San Antonio de Noto, San Benito de Palermo, San Elesbán, Santa Ifigenia, San Baltasar (the black 'wise king'), and later San Martín de Porres."[17] The church and white Creoles certainly used the imagery of Porres for their own ends, but Palma used this historical figure to critique the contradictions and power of the church in his own era.

In contrast with this harmonious depiction of the Afro-Peruvian saint and the church, other tradiciones criticize the church's authority while praising the Afro-Peruvian San Martin de Porres. Palma asserted that the saint's ability to perform miracles in "El Virrey de los Milagros" ("The Viceroy of Miracles") would compare favorably to any European saint. Yet Palma notes that the Dominican order at one point forbade the lay brother from performing the acts, a reference to the historic policy barring people of African ancestry from full membership in such religious orders. In another tradición narrating his life, Martin de Porres was passing a scaffolding when a worker fell from it. As the worker fell to the ground and his sure death, Porres miraculously stopped the man midfall. While the man awaited his fate, Porres ran to the prior of the Dominican order to ask permission to complete the miracle and save the man's life. The prior begrudgingly allowed Porres to complete the miracle. The tradición thus comments on the church's racist past while reinforcing the Afro-Peruvian saint's hallowed place in the Peruvian imaginary.[18] Considered in the context of debates surrounding Catholicism in the 1860 constitution, the tradición was likely read as a criticism of the church's authority.

As a young professional, Ricardo Palma had weathered several public criticisms of his Blackness intended to deprecate him among his high-society peers. Yet he did not completely deny his ancestry and later responded, famously, that in Peru "*el que no tiene de inga tiene de mendinga*" ("he who does not have some Inka has some African").[19]

Ricardo Palma's assertion that all Peruvians share mixed ethnoracial heritage reflected his writings to such an extent that many have mistakenly assumed that he coined the phrase. However, linguist Augusto Alcocer Martinez has shown that the "popular saying" predates Palma's inclusion of the phrase in his 1899 publication *Neologismos y Americanismos* (*Neologisms and Americanisms*). Furthermore, Alcocer argues that the saying has its roots in the colonial era, when mixed-race plebians uttered the words "to insult and make fun of the aristocracy," who clung to the idea of *limpieza de sangre* (purity of blood) and "rejected the mixture of races and any type of *mestizaje*."[20]

Thus Ricardo Palma's association with the phrase at the turn of the century, as an educated member of elite society, was remarkable because it challenged the aristocracy's carefully manicured self-image and the idea of the purely white Creole. Palma's openness, however, elicited several attacks on his public image, and his vision of Peruvian mestizaje did not hold African descendants as equals.

Venezuelan author Rufino Blanco Fombona's attack of Ricardo Palma's character was the most infamous. Palma served as the director of the national library from 1881 to 1912 and helped rebuild the building and its collection following its destruction during the War of the Pacific. Another "man of letters," Manuel González Prada, who had been critical of Palma's tenure, took over the role as the library's director and discovered some of his predecessor's notes written in the margins of a book by Blanco Fombona. The notes allegedly criticized the Venezuelan author's libelous writings published against another Venezuelan poet named Andrés Mata. Blanco Fombona learned of the critique and subsequently disparaged Palma's race and parentage in the prologue of González Prada's *Páginas Libres* (*Free Pages*) in 1894. Specifically, the Venezuelan author declared that Palma's father was a "lascivious Negro soldier who had accompanied Bolívar to Peru and raped a poor, humble woman from Lima. From that crime of passion was born Ricardo Palma."[21] By 1912, however, Palma had achieved such esteem in Peruvian elite society that Lima newspapers printed opinions in defense of the writer, and people gathered en masse to publicly defend and praise him.[22] This moment in Palma's life is emphasized in the memory represented at the Casa Museo Ricardo Palma today.

Whereas Ricardo Palma navigated the sensitive terrain of racial identity without completely denying his own Blackness or disparaging Peru's African ancestry, his son, Clemente, responded differently to the attacks against the family's lineage. Clemente Palma was born on December 3, 1872, the year of the coup. Scholars have noted that Clemente was of a lighter complexion than his father, and he witnessed numerous incidents of prejudice against his father for his African ancestry, which likely contributed to his developing philosophy of race. Clemente Palma was raised in Miraflores, an upper-class neighborhood in the outskirts of Lima. Like his father, he attended the prestigious Universidad Nacional Mayor de San Marcos (UNMSM), where he earned his bachelor's and doctoral degrees in literature. There Clemente read European pseudoscientific racial theories and integrated those ideologies into his theses, demonstrating a shift to positivism, which suggested that authoritarian social control and "whitening" were the keys to social improvement and modernization. Positivism provided presumed "scientific" backing to theories of racial degeneration, but a nation's racial and social composition could be improved by a process of mestizaje, which was controlled by elites. Evidence of Clemente's disdain for the Afro-Peruvian population is hidden in plain sight in the Casa Museo Ricardo Palma on General Suárez Street on a small bookshelf behind Ricardo Palma's desk. Adjacent to the father's famous spectacles, private letters, and famous works that remain on public display at the home are Clemente's bachelor's and doctoral theses, which reveal his ambivalence regarding Peru's history of mestizaje.

Clemente Palma's theses reveal a more sinister perspective on the racial composition of Peru, in contrast with his father's "foundational fictions." They demonstrate the influence of European pseudoscientific racial theories on elite concepts of national identity in the late nineteenth and early twentieth centuries. In particular, Clemente Palma's first thesis constructed the common characteristics of the "*raza criolla*" (Creole race), which celebrated certain outcomes of racial mixing and lamented others. His ambivalence toward a racialized national identity, while disputed by some elite contemporaries, exemplified the contradictory process of nation-making in Peru. Regardless of its limited reception and popularity among Clemente

Palma's contemporaries, his 1897 thesis coincides with the dramatic decline in Afro-Peruvian demography in the censuses and reveals the anti-Black racism inherent to the ideology of mestizaje.

The bachelor's thesis, "El Porvenir de las razas en el Perú" ("The Future of the Races in Peru"), synthesized the discordant intellectual currents regarding race and nation in late nineteenth-century Peru. As his father's troubled career demonstrated, as well as González Prada's 1904 essay "Our Indians" (examined in the following chapter), the integrationist perspective was not the dominant discourse among Lima elites during this era. Indeed, Clemente Palma's professors Javier Prado y Ugarteche and Pablo Patrón approved his adoption of European civilizations as a model.[23] His 1897 thesis includes a section about theories of racial mixing among the principal races that have constituted the Peruvian population: specifically, the Indian, the Spanish, the Black, the Chinese, and the mixed (mestizo) races. Another section focuses on the "Indian race," which "forms the ethnic base of the Peruvian ethnicity," consistent with Sebastián Lorente's and González Prada's racial constructions prior to indigenismo. For Clemente Palma, race explained society's successes and failures. Racial difference was the basis of all social distinctions, and distinct processes of "degeneration" could be traced through the historical experiences of separate "races." However, he assumed the process of Spanish degeneration deserves more historical analysis than the innately negative characteristics of the Black, Chinese, and Indian races did. Perhaps most interesting is Clemente Palma's analysis of the national history of "mixed races" (*razas mestizas*). Palma initially classifies mestizos as the offspring of Indian and Spanish parents, which he attributes to the scarcity of Spanish women in colonial Peru. Later, however, he analyzes the addition of Black people to racial mixing in Peru, whose mixture with Spanish created a subcategory of mulato, and he further divides mulatos into various subfields, or "classes."

Following these quasi-historical analyses, Palma arrives at his pseudoscientific construction of the "Creole race," defined as the mixture of all the aforementioned ethnicities. The raza criolla, for Palma, is the "psychic tonality" of the subsequent mixture of all ethnicities in Peru that form its national identity, explaining its positive and negative characteristics. "The march of civilization," Palma asserted, "will exterminate the Indian race," and "the black race will disappear, as a pure entity, by absorption." After asserting that the "Chinese race" would meet a similar fate, Palma concludes that "the only race with a future is the Creole, which is the mixed races unified by common interaction."[24] Although Clemente Palma's notion of the Creole race bore some similarities to Mexican intellectual José Vasconcelos's theory of the "cosmic race," such connections would not be developed in a clear sense until Peruvian intellectual and politician Victor Raúl Haya de la Torre discussed his idea of *Indoamericanismo* in Mexico City with Vasconcelos in the 1920s. Vasconcelos's ideas on race were still evolving at the turn of the century, but his influential book *The Cosmic Race*, published in 1925, expressed a positive outlook on mestizaje in Mexico in opposition to a lack of racial mixing in Anglo-America.[25]

Throughout the thesis, Palma uses the terms "ethnicity" and "race" interchangeably, but his definition of race is a departure from previous nineteenth-century understandings that allowed for some fluidity based on socioeconomic status. For Clemente Palma, race was determined by ancestry, and thus one's ethnoracial identity was fixed. Citing the French racial theorist Gustave Le Bon's (1841–1931) theories that "man is always the representative of his race" and that race forms the "soul" of a nation's identity, Palma concludes, "Race should be considered a permanent being. This being is comprised not only of the living individuals that form it in a given moment, but also of the long series of dead who were their ancestors. Thus it is necessary to understand the prolonged past and future of a race to understand its "true significance."[26] For Clemente Palma, race was not just an indicator of social status but the core of any nation's identity, predetermined by ancestry and the single factor that would shape the nation's fate.

Clemente Palma's observations combined discourses on the "glorious indigenous past" with theories of racial degeneration espoused by Peruvians and Europeans, like Gustave Le Bon and Javier Prado.[27] He argued that "physically, the Indian is weak: he appears to carry on his shoulders the weight of a past ill-fated ideal and that the memory of a glorious past has paralyzed his physical development."[28] In addition, the history of the "black race" made it "inferior" and "incapable of assimilating to the civilized life." Palma feared the "atavisms of the savage life" that African slavery had introduced to the Peruvian race.[29] Tracing African genetic inferiority to the "ferocious jungle" climate of the continent, Palma concludes, "the black race is inferior because it does not meet the intellectual and character conditions that sociology assigns to perfectible races predisposed to a prosperous nation."[30] Whereas Ricardo Palma situated Afro-Peruvians in the colonial past and celebrated Afro-Peruvian contributions to mestizaje, his son employed Eurocentric biological understandings of race to erase such contributions completely. However, their writings correspond in assuming that mestizaje would erase Blackness in Peru.

Clemente Palma's negative assessment of the races of Peru meant that the nation (as a collective race-based identity) was destined to fail. The mixture of African blood in the making of Peru's raza criolla was thus prone to degeneration, but Clemente Palma also offered a solution. Asserting that Argentina was composed of "superior bloods," due to the "beneficent waves" of Italians to their country, and that Chilean racial superiority was due to English immigration and lack of African admixture, Palma offered his "humble concept." His proposed solution was to mix the raza criolla of Peru with "another race that will give it what it lacks: character." Reflecting the ideas of other Peruvian social Darwinists, Palma asserted that the positive characteristics that the raza criolla lacked could be improved by introducing "the German race." Palma assumed that German immigration would bring "solidity to the mental life of our race" and "more respect for the law and duty."[31] Clemente Palma thus interpreted mestizaje in Peru through the lens of leading European eugenicists, and he believed racial "degeneration" could be mitigated through the introduction of European genes.

Clemente Palma's racially deterministic interpretation of Peruvian national identity ran counter to his father's inclusive vision of the nation's ethnoracial and cultural heritage. Furthermore, Clemente's elite discourse on Peruvian inferiority placed Peru below Chile to help explain why the neighboring nation had humiliated Peru in the War of the Pacific eighteen years earlier. As his father had gained popular recognition for his valor in defending Lima during the Chilean invasion and for helping rebuild the capital city afterward, Clemente Palma's analysis could in no way be considered "popular." Rather, his bachelor's thesis reflected the concerns of white elites seeking to distance themselves from the "atavisms" that explained their failures as a nation. When analyzed alongside the writings of his father, Clemente Palma's writings underscore the discordant perspectives on race, nation, and mestizaje even within the same family. The differences also highlight a transition from the contradictions of liberalism to those of positivism, when elites understood race as phenotype and biological difference. In this context throughout much of Latin America, social engineers sought to "improve" a nation's race through an elite-controlled process of mestizaje that usually entailed "whitening."[32]

ENRIQUE LÓPEZ ALBÚJAR: ROMANTICISM AND REALISM IN NORTHERN PERU

In contrast with Clemente Palma's elitist and racially deterministic narrative of Peru's past, present, and future, his contemporary in northern Peru constructed a divergent vision of the nation's identity. Writer Enrique López Albújar was born in the northern region of Piura just two weeks before Clemente Palma was born in Lima. Although Albújar did not study literature, he earned his law degree from UNMSM before serving as a judge in various parts of the country. He is mainly remembered as one of the founders of indigenismo, as he first gained fame for publishing *Cuentos Andinos* (*Andean Stories*) while working in the highland city of Huánuco in 1920.[33] This collection of stories is based on his observations of the Indigenous population as an arbiter of justice in this interior department. Given the nature of his profession, it is not surprising that many of his stories examined conflict, criminality, and violence as cultural phenomena.

Violence is a central theme of his later and perhaps best-known work, for which the setting was his home region of Piura. Albújar published the novel *Matalaché* in 1928, which tells the tragic story of a love affair between an enslaved Afro-Peruvian man and the daughter of a soap factory/hacienda owner north of the city in early nineteenth-century Piura. When the hacendado learns that his daughter is pregnant with the enslaved man's baby, he orders two other enslaved men to throw the transgressor, José Manuel "Matalaché," to his death into a vat of boiling soap.

The love story between María Luz and José Manuel is written in melodramatic style, as María Luz develops "a horrible obsession that devours her soul."[34] After falling in love during their first encounter, they meet again in a romantic scene in which they confess their love for each other in the anonymity of darkness. The novel's romanticism resembles the plots of several Latin American abolitionist novels written a century earlier, but the differences outweigh the superficial resemblances, as Albújar's novel was intended for contemporary audiences concerned with race, mestizaje, and Afro-Peruvians in the twentieth century. It is worth underscoring the fact that their "true love" could be expressed only when both characters were invisible to each other, a unique circumstance that temporarily erased their perceived racial and social differences.

The novel's setting in 1816 predates the first abolitionist novel of the Americas, Cuban author Anselmo Suárez Romero's *Francisco, el Ingenio o las Delicias del Campo (Francisco, the Mill or the Delights of the Countryside)*, first published in 1838. The Cuban abolitionist novel tells the story of Francisco, an enslaved coachman (*calesero*), who falls in love with a mulata Dorotea, enslaved as a domestic laborer. The son of the hacendado, Ricardo, also falls in love with Dorotea and forces her to sleep with him in order to save Francisco from a prolonged death by torture. At the novel's end, Dorotea tells Francisco she is pregnant with Ricardo's child and that she must leave in order to save Francisco. Overcome with grief, Francisco then commits suicide by hanging. The novel has been criticized for its unrealistically romantic depiction of slavery in the Caribbean, in a manner intended merely to humanize Afro-Cubans for an audience of slaveholding elite Spanish Creoles.[35] The positioning of the protagonist who is enslaved was atypical of Cuban slavery, implicitly relegating enslaved fieldhands to a position less deserving of abolition and citizenship. Nonetheless, the tropes of the "dandified *calesero* (coachman), and the tragic/erotic *mulata*" are persistent in the Cuban national imaginary, which film scholar Alison Fraunhar argues "have tremendous power in articulating and maintaining the colonial order through an intricate system of social and economic valuation."[36] The characters of *Matalaché* resemble such tropes from Cuban abolitionist novels, revealing a similar construction of Afro-Peruvian belonging in the twentieth century. The transnational comparison reveals a trend in narratives on slavery and mestizaje from the early nineteenth through the early twentieth centuries: even when testifying to the violence of race-based slavery, these writers implied that whitening through mestizaje was the source of moral virtue, revealing the maintenance of colorism within an ideology that claimed to erase the relevance of color.

The first Latin American woman to publish an abolitionist novel also maintained these tropes, although with reversed roles to emphasize the point of her criticism. Cuban author Gertrudis Gómez de Avellaneda published the novel *Sab* in Spain in 1841, which tells the story of an enslaved mulato named Sab who falls in love with Carlota, the white daughter of his master. Perhaps to emphasize the parallels between the condition of white women and enslaved men, Avellaneda's plot tells the story of Carlota's marriage to a man from another white elite family. Enrique Otway's love for Carlota is similar to Ricardo's lust for Dorotea in *Francisco*, portrayed as profane and bleak in contrast with the perfect and "virtuous" love Sab develops for Carlota. At the very hour that Carlota and Enrique marry, Sab dies of heartbreak. Sab does not represent the typical Cuban enslaved man, as he is both mulato and an enslaved overseer who eventually wins his freedom through a lottery but remains enslaved to be close to Carlota. The plight of enslaved people on a plantation is hardly discussed in the novel, yet "his face presented a singular composite in which the crossing of two distinct races converged, and in which amalgamated, to put it as such, the features of the African caste with those of the European, without being a perfect *mulato*."[37] Avellaneda thus implies that his whiteness is his virtue. When Carlota reads Sab's letter to Teresa, another enslaved person and Carlota's closest companion, at the end of the novel, she learns of Sab's heartbreaking love for her. Although Carlota is disappointed by her loveless marriage with Enrique, she does not completely regret her neglect of Sab. Instead, she simply seems to recognize his humanity for the first time, and the narrator wonders whether she will ever forget him.

Both of these Cuban abolitionist novels evade the daily brutalities of plantation slavery, instead conveying romantic plots with the limited objective of humanizing enslaved Afro-Cubans whose enslavers considered them subhuman. The tropes of the tragic/erotic mulata/o and the "dandified" enslaved man served to promote a problematic discourse of Cuban national identity while favoring abolition, so the similarities of these plots and the narrative of *Matalaché* suggest a similarly problematic vision of Blackness in the construction of a Peruvian national identity. Including Afro-Peruvians in the sensual environment of national discourse stipulated the parameters of their belonging in peruanidad: their reproductive roles in mestizaje were undeniable, but this same process meant that Afro-Peruvians existed only in the past. Furthermore, this limited inclusion played on historic tropes of African sexual immorality dating to the late colonial period. In contrast with the romantic depictions of slavery and the supposed moral superiority of mulatos as opposed to Blacks, however, Albújar's 1928 novel lays bare the violence of race-based slavery.

Matalaché is set in late colonial Peru, during the same era of the Cuban abolitionist novels. Unlike *Sab*, Albújar's novel tells the story of forbidden love between an enslaved man and the daughter of his enslaver. The virtue of Avellaneda's Sab lies in his persistent yet unrequited love for Carlota. And whereas Suárez Romero's Francisco suffers from the erotic desire of an hacendado's son for a mulata, José Manuel Matalaché as an enslaved man faces the more realistic punishment for damaging an elite family's honor. María Luz, the hacendado's daughter and Matalaché's secret lover, attempts an abortion upon learning that she is pregnant with the enslaved man's child, in hopes that her family will not find out. When this fails, she drinks poisonous herbs to commit suicide before the novel ends with the brutal murder of Matalaché. Even though the male protagonist is also a "black mulato" overseer who is enslaved, like Sab and similar to Francisco's privileged position as a *calesero,* Matalaché's death is not caused by heartbreak but by being thrown into a vat of boiling soap by the enslaved people whose labor he had enforced throughout the novel. The novel thus implicitly criticizes the relationships of power that enslavers enforced through slavery, which diminished Afro-Peruvian solidarity. It also represents the conflicted position of women like María Luz, whose love for an Afro-Peruvian man clashed with her desire to maintain her family's honor. *Matalaché*'s more realistic depiction of slavery notwithstanding, the love between the enslaved Afro-Peruvian man and his owner's daughter can be read as symbolic of the future of Peru—an ethnoracial mixing that white elites aimed to prevent through violence. Just as poignantly, ethnoracial hierarchies remained even when such mestizaje did occur.

The Piuran novel clearly presented a more "realist" account of race relations under slavery and after abolition, which avoids more problematic representations that romanticize and soften the historical reality. The plot also resembles abolitionist narratives in the United States, similar to Frederick Douglass's autobiography, which opens with an account of terror that "establishes the centrality of violence in the making of the slave." Similar to the implicit "reader contract" in recent *testimonio* accounts and as Sadiya Hartman suggests, reading such narratives of violence requires special consideration: "Are we witnesses who confirm the truth of what happened in the face of the world-destroying capacities of pain, the distortions of torture, the sheer unrepresentability of terror, and the repression of the dominant accounts? Or are we voyeurs fascinated with and repelled by exhibitions of terror and sufferance . . . ? At issue here is the precariousness of empathy and the uncertain line between witness and spectator."[38] As *Matalaché* was written nearly eighty years after slavery was abolished, these questions seem pertinent. The novel's setting in late colonial Peru relegates such violence and slavery itself to colonial rule, dissociating the republic from the reality of Afro-Peruvian suffering after independence. The setting helped separate the reader from the suffering, and the novel's narrative of mestizaje suggests a facile resolution to the troubled history of abuse even while holding up whiteness as aspiration in the process of mestizaje. The account of the brutal murder provided a voyeuristic window into the nation's past for twentieth-century readers who could congratulate themselves on the nation's progress toward racial equality since independence and abolition.

Albújar's decision to represent his protagonist as a "mulato" overseer rather than an enslaved fieldhand, as well as the romanticism of the novel, resembles the problematic decisions of nineteenth-century Cuban abolitionists to convey the "delights" of slavery rather than emphasize the harsh conditions to which enslaved people were subjected. Even with its violent final scene, the reader may wonder why the author saw the need to write about Peruvian slavery so long after abolition. The Piuran author's other works on the cultures of northern Peru provide further perspective on his vision of peruanidad and the challenge of overcoming ethnoracial differences.

Although he is remembered as an influential *indigenista* (a founder and proponent of the *indigenismo* movement), Albújar's many publications set in his home region of Piura romanticize the history and cultural contributions of Afro-Peruvians. Eight years after publishing *Matalaché,* Albújar published a novel on Afro-Peruvian outlaws who gained notoriety for their extralegal exploits in the lawless regions of the north. His 1936 book, *Los Caballeros del Delito* (*The Gentlemen of Crime*), combines sociological analysis with criminology in its study of bandolerismo in Piura and Tumbes (the two northernmost coastal regions of Peru formerly unified as Piura). The collection of semimythical stories of famous *bandoleros* (bandits) combines racially and environmentally deterministic analyses with "criminal sociology," and was written in direct response to a criminal sociological study conducted by. José Varallanos shortly before Albújar began writing the four-hundred-page work in 1932. In response to the negative interpretations of Varallanos, Albújar began writing the many "impassioned stories" of bandoleros he had learned from his family as a young child, specifically the stories his father shared with him of the "intelligent and gentlemanly bandolero called Sambambé." This famous bandolero also shared oral histories of "the fearsome Carmen Domador" and the "celebrity bandolero" Rosa Palma.[39] Despite the positivism and determinism of Albújar's analysis of his region, this tome helps clarify the author's vision of race, regional, and national identity, with particular emphasis on the influence of African ancestry on the region's culture and identity.

Being that he was a lawyer and judge, the Piuran author's focus on the topic of banditry and crime seems natural. His passion for local cultural iconography and desire to understand the social phenomenon of banditry pushed him to seek a sociological explanation, but he did not apply the negative interpretations of racial determinism that one might expect from the dominant pseudoscientific theories of his era. Such theories influenced elites like Clemente Palma in Lima as well as the work of Brazilian author Euclides da Cunha (and his analysis of banditry) in their turn-of-the-century works. Albújar's celebratory account of bandolerismo reflects an apparent change in popular perceptions of Afro-Peruvian criminality, as newspaper accounts sometimes admitted the "celebrity" status of some bandoleros.

This account and its accompanying image appeared in the weekly magazine *Variedades*, published between 1908 and 1932 in Lima.[40] The brief article reflects the typical ambiguity felt about these feared yet celebrated cultural icons of the era, as it completely elided the subject's ethnoracial identity but noted the many cities in which he had forced the police to work. The article noted that this particular bandolero, Adolfo Rondón, had a long history of crime and misdeeds (*fechorias*) and was "generous with the poor." It went on to list those he had killed, concluding that Rondón's feats will soon be memorialized in folk songs accompanied by guitar, explaining why in the photograph, although deceased, it is as if "he were smiling ironically."[41]

Los Caballeros del Delito is a clear departure from the elite discourses of racial degeneration espoused by Clemente Palma and his professors at the end of the nineteenth century, but the tome's ambiguities bear clear resemblances to Euclides da Cunha's Brazilian epic *Os Sertões*. Albújar defined his regional literature as "*matalachista*," the differing plots unified by the common theme of mestizaje that represented "the position of the Peruvian hybrid with predominance of the black race." He defined *matalachismo* as "an assault of *mulatismo* of those times against the decadent and despotic *godismo*" (an allusion to elite political machinations in Venezuela).[42] Similar to the abolitionist novels of nineteenth-century Cuba, and subsequently the emergence of Brazilian "racial democracy," the Piuran author posits that racial mixing between all ethnic groups and social classes would promote "the most ample democracy."[43] Much like da Cunha, Albújar dedicates the first thirty-six pages of his book to a description of the environmental, geographic, historical, and socioeconomic characteristics of his northern region, the harshness of which has stifled the spiritual "evolution" of its people. The "sensuality" that this land produced among its people, Albújar explained, "the slave maintains even in the misery in which he lives." Positing a continuation of the "misery" of an archetypal condition of enslaved people through the contemporary lives of Afro-Peruvians, he characterizes their condition as "exalted at times, always indolent, unconcerned with communal interests or regional progress, or even with those that relate to their own class interests. Above all the *zambo*—this product of coastal mulatismo—who, at the same time is more spiritually agile, more intuitive, is also more prone to a licentious life."[44] Thus, even while highlighting Afro-Peruvian roles in mestizaje and their contributions to peruanidad, Albújar perpetuated racist stereotypes of race and sexuality that were expressed by protonationalists in the 1790s.[45]

The author repeats and reinforces long-held Peruvian stereotypes of Afro-Peruvian sexuality and immorality, yet his analysis of bandolerismo also rejects the so-called thermal curve of banditry theory, which was widely believed among his criminologist contemporaries. This theory held that regions with warmer temperatures yielded higher rates of delinquent conduct (particularly violent attacks), and regions with lower temperatures yielded more petty crimes, such as theft. The theory was inherently racist without using the language of race, as countries with cooler climates were inhabited by people with lighter skin. Albújar's comparative analysis of crime trends in various regions of the country contradicts the climatically deterministic theory. Even while rejecting climate, the author adds that the causes that determine delinquent conduct must include "the biopsychic, physio-psychic, geographic, economic, social, cultural, moral, etc."[46] The Piuran author's social criminologist analysis thus diverged from Clemente Palma's singular reliance on French racial theory but did not completely reject historic assumptions of racial difference as a determining factor in Peruvian society.

A volume published in 1990 criticized both Varallanos's and Albújar's positivist analyses of Afro-Peruvian banditry. Carlos Aguirre and Charles Walker argue that bandolerismo and popular perceptions of such activity in

Peru reveal social and political relationships. Aguirre argues that although *cimarronaje* (the act of fleeing from slavery) was intimately connected to bandolerismo, the latter "lacked legitimacy" before the popular classes and was more a symptom of social unrest than an action sustained in the support of popular groups against social enemies."[47] Furthermore, Walker traces the growing social and political consciousness of coastal bandits from the first decades of the republic. He points to resistance to slavery as a cause of such criminality and provides evidence that Afro-Peruvian bandoleros formed alliances with liberal political movements against conservative regimes.[48]

Albújar's poems, in contrast with his criminological study, celebrated Piuran culture rather than analyzing and explaining it. Ten years after Albújar first published *Matalaché* in a series of chapters released in a weekly newspaper, he published a collection of poems titled *De la Tierra brava: Poemas Afroyungas*. The poems in the collection share common themes of banditry and Afro-Peruvian culture, though the title reflects a cultural appropriation typical of indigenismo, as *afroyungas* is an Afro-Bolivian community with its own unique "Afro-Hispanic language."[49]

The "brave land" to which the collection's title refers is clearly that of Piura-Tumbes, and Albújar includes a poem about the death of a notorious bandido there. The first line of each stanza of the poem "La Muerte del Bandido" ("The Bandit's Death") exclaims, "They've killed Alama! They've killed Alama!" Thousands of voices from the countryside to the cities celebrate the death of the man who was "a servant of the turbulent and bloody life." Everyday citizens, even priests, celebrate the death of the man who could "break through a police blockade" with "one accurate bullet, one bullet, just one" in the first four stanzas of the poem.[50] The stanzas of the second half of the poem, however, paint a more ambivalent and humanizing portrait of the formidable bandido named Alama. For instance, "all of the beloved women who had kissed his lips" seem to react in a more somber tone. The fourth-to-last stanza tells the reader of the murderous enslaver whom Alama had pursued, suggesting that his banditry began as an act of vengeance and continued as he fled from slavery. Still, the most powerful lines appear in the final two stanzas, which tell of Alama's mother and son hearing the news of his death: "Only in one homestead and in a dark room, / a soul always ignited by one fixed thought, / upon learning the news, a creature cries / and, transfixed, murmurs: / They killed my son! They killed my son! / And upon hearing the wail, tragic before the grandmother, / after giving a kiss, with earnestness, to his grandmother, / a young man, who has brandished his carbine and spur, / solemnly swears:—I will avenge you, father! / I will avenge you, father!"[51]

The poem's final lines suggest a continual cycle of bandolerismo, which began as a enslaved person's act of self-defense and escape. His son will violently avenge his father's death, leading him to a similar life of crime and violence. The poem does not explicitly celebrate the lives of such bandoleros, but it clearly displays a contrast between the many voices celebrating the death of a feared bandolero and his family's reaction. This juxtaposition humanizes the infamous bandolero and implicitly locates the roots of such violence in slavery rather than race per se, thereby providing a counternarrative to the dominant discourse of Black criminality.

The parallel tropes of Blackness in Cuban abolitionist novels and *Matalaché* should serve to remind the reader to act as a witness to rather than a spectator of such work. Such a reading requires the recognition of tropes that used romance as a plot device to view slavery as a necessary step toward a racially inclusive democracy. Conversely, the attentive reader should notice the tropes that placed mulatos in superior positions to "Blacks" in ways that implicitly privileged whiteness. Although Albújar highlighted the inherent violence and racism of slavery, a comparative perspective helps to unravel how such power dynamics persisted in twentieth-century literature that seemed to celebrate mestizaje as the end of racism. The apparent celebratory inclusion of Afro-Peruvians in this literature belies the subtle influences of racial pseudoscience in the rhetorical shaping of peruanidad as mestizaje. The writings served the interests of these Creole intellectuals by supporting their public images as inclusive contributors to national culture and identity, although their visions of mestizaje implied the erasure of Blackness.

"POPULAR" LITERATURE, POLITICS, AND PSEUDOSCIENCE: ALBÚJAR AND THE PALMAS

Enrique López Albújar's writings reflected the popular culture of northern Peru to a greater degree than Ricardo Palma's tradiciones reflected popular culture in Lima. Despite Ricardo Palma's apparent political support among the Lima "masses," his literary audience was limited to the educated elite minority.[52] This ambivalent position prompted him to romanticize the city's colonial past in troubling ways, perhaps to assert his coveted and precarious elite social position. Such tension is clear in an oft-overlooked tradición titled *Los Aguadores de Lima*. This story celebrated the demise of the Afro-Peruvian guild, the members of which he described as "drunk," "quarrelsome," and "blindly obedient."[53] Although his writings were pioneering in their inclusion of Afro-Peruvians in the cultural fabric of Lima, they were not always celebratory or complimentary. Both of these authors can be considered *costumbristas*, a form of literature and art that described and romanticized cultural aspects unique to Peru while providing social commentary through the narratives. Ricardo Palma's criticisms of colonial Peru and the aristocratic society that sought to maintain the same social hierarchies in early republican Peru were subtle yet clear. Albújar criticized the harshness of slavery and its legacies, but his vision of matalechismo suggested that mestizaje would foster cultural cohesion and regional, if not national unity.

Although the Piuran author's writings focused on racial and cultural amalgamation in his home region, he did not ignore the politics and elite discourses emanating from Lima. One of his *poemas afroyungas*, in fact, is dedicated to José Gálvez, the former president and minister of government under Castilla who had appointed Ricardo Palma to the position of consul to Pará, Brazil. Gálvez had previously supported Castilla's Liberal Revolution in 1854–1855, pressuring the caudillo to abolish slavery and Indigenous tribute and counseling the drafting of the liberal constitution of 1856. Gálvez was known for his "highly romanticized vision of Lima's past traditions," so it is no surprise that Albújar dedicated a poem to him that similarly romanticizes northern Peru's past.[54] The brief poem, titled "Los Pitingos," rejoices that the "black pitingos" are coming, "swiftly, vociferously." These "rough horsemen" bring "marble, silver and iron."[55] Unlike his poem about the death of a bandolero, this poem presents only a positive view of such Afro-Peruvian "rough-riders," who will be arriving soon with their precious loot. The poem diverges from the mulatismo of Albújar's other works in its representation of Blackness, and the dedication to a prominent abolitionist politician suggests that such literature was explicitly political in its representations.

The costumbrista literature of Ricardo Palma and Albújar clearly differs from Clemente Palma's theses in terms of representation, genre, and politics. However, the popular representations of Blackness in Peruvian culture appear to have influenced Clemente Palma's writing as his career progressed.

His successful literary career was based on a unique genre of science fiction short stories that generally avoided topics of race or ethnicity. At the age of sixty-six, Clemente Palma wrote the prologue to Albújar's collection of *poemas afroyungas*. Naturally, the prologue praised the Piuran author's writing, but he also pointed to their common literary style, as both belonged to the generation that came of age at the end of the nineteenth century. In Clemente Palma's prologue, he identifies as a writer with the same modernist objectives as Albújar. Palma asserts, "We resolved, as boys of that era with literary affinities, to also represent a reaction against the moth-eaten demands of classical art and against the old melodramatic refrains of romanticism."[56] In this 1938 prologue, Clemente Palma's negative assessment of race and nation in his bachelor's thesis seems a relic of his youthful student days. Rather than lamenting the racial degeneration he theorized in 1897, Palma was now celebrating the mulatismo of his Piuran contemporary. He seems to have recognized that such racial determinism better reflected the "moth-ridden" views of the old aristocracy than the modernizing generation of 1900. In the prologue to Albújar's collection of poetry, Clemente Palma describes the novel *Matalaché* as "a stupendous and valiant study of the aristocracy's racial prejudices and of the infiltration of black elements in colonial sociability and converting a large part of the select matrices emblazoned in the democratic crucibles of the predominant mestizaje in our republican society."[57] Clemente Palma's perspective on Blackness and mestizaje in Peru had changed significantly, at least publicly, permitting him to present himself as a progressive twentieth-century intellectual.

Clemente Palma's change in perspective also reflects a shift in the dominant discourse in race and nation in Peru. Albújar's connections to Lima elites developed from his education at UNMSM and the positive reception of his writings. Clemente Palma points out that Albújar's two most popular novels, *Los Caballeros del Delito* and *Nuevos Cuentos Andinos* (*New Andean Stories*), are "perched at the Supreme Court, that is to say, at the most elevated position of our literature."[58] The popularity of Albújar's writings on Afro-Peruvian history and culture from a regional to a national level corresponds with a shift in the elite discourse of mestizaje. His poem, "La Muerte del Bandido" ("The Death of the Bandit") is dedicated to Roberto MacLean Estenós, considered one of the highest authorities on eugenics in 1930s Peru.

The dedication of a poem meant to humanize and explain the roots of Afro-Peruvian bandolerismo in slavery allows the reader to analyze the poem in a political context. Roberto MacLean Estenós, like Albújar, had earned his law degree at the UNMSM in Lima. Unlike the Piuran author and the Palmas, however, MacLean Estenós independently studied the writings of *negritude* in the French Caribbean and of its proponents in the United States. A member of the Lima elite, MacLean Estenós was married to María Ugarteche y Bebín, of the prominent family that included Mariano Ignacio Prado and Manuel Prado y Ugarteche, one of Clemente Palma's thesis advisors.[59] Both Enrique López Albújar and Roberto MacLean Estenós were degreed lawyers and self-trained sociologists and were equally concerned with Peru's history of racism. Albújar likely saw MacLean Estenós as an important voice in vindicating the Afro-Peruvian historical experience and culture, providing a more global and scientific perspective on the Piuran writer's work, which deserved recognition in the form of a dedication.

MacLean Estenós published a comprehensive sociological study of human evolution in his 1936 book, *Del Salvajismo a la Nación* (*From Savagery to Nation*). The book discusses Charles Darwin's and Jean-Baptiste Lamarck's theories of evolution and natural selection, pointing out that they agreed that all humanity shares a common genetic ancestry. The arc of human evolution outlined by MacLean Estenós emphasizes similar processes of group migrations and identity formations based on shared political and/or religious interests. These processes, he points out, occurred in central Greece just as they did in central Mexico, suggesting a cultural relativism in which civilizations are influenced by their long-term environments. While admitting that over time these distinct locations and endogamy produced some genetic differences, MacLean Estenós insists on using the term "ethnicity" rather than "race" to describe the different civilizations that would lead to distinct national identities.[60] The teleological analysis of human evolution leading to nation-state identities resembles Clemente Palma's equation of race and nation, but MacLean Estenós's implicit cultural relativism is much more similar to his contemporary's at Columbia University. In New York, anthropologist Franz Boas saw value in African cultures and history and called for "racial vindication."[61]

MacLean Estenós went on to serve as the sole Peruvian representative at the First Inter-American Demographic Conference in Mexico City in 1943, where he debated the "racist question" with delegates from twenty countries of the Americas (including the United States). The resolution that the delegates unanimously agreed on is surprising and anomalous in the context of the widespread authority of racial degeneration in eugenics theory in the 1930s.[62] It also demonstrates a general Western shift against the pseudoscience of race in response to the horrors of the Nazi Holocaust. Despite this shift, of course, the United States continued to deny African Americans basic civil rights formally until the Civil Rights Act of 1964.

The "Eugenics Commission" agreed on the following set of objectives for the "improvement of the living conditions of people called Afro-Americans, blacks or people of color":

> 1. Discrimination based on race or color be eliminated in all human relations in general and especially in those situations that refer to conditions of work, of living space, of health, and of the distribution of public services.
>
> 2. The exercise of political rights ensured not only by the law but also by the principles and practices that are essential to the demographic spirit of America.
>
> 3. The stimulation of scientific study of black populations, of their conditions, their potentials, their cultures in general, and *their contributions to national and continental heritage. And that said studies and reports be published in school textbooks or in any other appropriate form* and be diffused with the objective of producing a better compensation between the races.
>
> 4. The effective cooperation between all of the so-called racial groups without distinction with the goal of improving the living conditions for the whole society.[63]

MacLean Estenós's earlier research on human evolution and ethnicity laid the foundation for his antiracist agenda. His 1943 book in which he recalled his participation in the First Inter-American Demographic Conference included a chapter that analyzed the "Great black educators": Booker T. Washington, Otis Samuel O'Neal, and Mary McLeod Bethune. The Lima lawyer-sociologist understood the struggle of African Americans fighting for racial vindication and civil rights in the United States as a model for elites to embrace in Latin America. Thus he saw racism and racial exclusion as the true "black problem," unlike the racially deterministic explanation of Clemente Palma's thesis. Albújar thus dedicated his poem on bandolerismo to MacLean Estenós because he saw his work as being aligned with the same objective of denouncing racism and championing Afro-Peruvian culture.

CONCLUSIONS: A SHIFTING DISCOURSE ON RACE, NATION, AND CULTURE

The roles and culture of Afro-Peruvians in the nation's colonial past were first highlighted in the costumbrista paintings of Pancho Fierro (1807–1879), an Afro-Peruvian artist whose watercolors celebrated and romanticized the nation's history of slavery. The literary and pseudoscientific narrative during the period examined in this chapter (1860s–1940s) suggests a correspondence between popular representations in literature and a "softening" of racial theory in the discourse of eugenics. It also provides further evidence of the "elasticity" of this pseudoscience, as in Brazil the "science of eugenics provided a bridge between racial ideology and popular culture."[64] Ricardo Palma's integration of Afro-Peruvian culture and history in his vision of peruanidad insisted that Peruvians recognize their mixed ethnoracial ancestry. This perspective became popular through his writing, despite his apparent internal tension and distancing from Blackness, inciting Lima's masses to come together in defense of their beloved author of Peruvian national identity. Although he turned away from politics after the 1872 revolt, the African-descended Lima author maintained his popularity among the lower classes.

The ideas that Clemente Palma expressed with such fervor in his thesis, in contrast, were not "popular," and by their very nature precluded the acceptance and the support of working-class Peruvians. And yet his theses earned him bachelor's and doctoral degrees from the UNMSM. Moreover, Clemente Palma's advisor, Javier Prado y Ugarteche, was an influential politician and later served as the rector/chancellor of UNMSM from 1915 to 1921, and his decision to approve these theses shows that these ideas also were consistent with his thinking on race and national identity.

Clemente Palma was named Peruvian consul to Spain in 1902, serving in Barcelona until 1904, when he returned to Lima to continue his writing and political career. In contrast, Ricardo Palma traveled to Madrid in 1899 to petition the Real Academia Española to accept a list of *americanismos* and *peruanismos*—words that had become part of the standard

Spanish vocabulary in the Americas, and many of which reflect Afro-Peruvian inflections—into the official Spanish language.[65] The Royal Academy rejected Ricardo Palma's appeal, but his son launched a successful literary career during his time in Europe. Clemente Palma's apparent change in perspective did not lead him to fully embrace his father's celebratory integrationist approach. Rather, his literary career elided questions of race and nation. Their contrasting perspectives serve to illuminate the contradictory and changing elite constructions of Afro-Peruvians within narratives of peruanidad and mestizaje as national identity. Despite their contrasting interpretations, both Ricardo and Clemente Palma contributed to a hegemonic narrative that denied the relevance of Afro-Peruvians within nineteenth- and twentieth-century constructions of national identity. Their formulations of mestizaje allowed them to both celebrate Afro-Peruvians in the past and deny their existence in the present and future while claiming the cultural contributions of African descendants as national and/or Creole. This narrative process of appropriation and whitening mirrored the construction of racial categories that entailed erasing Blackness in the censuses.

Even as "progressive" authors acknowledged the oppression of African descendants throughout the Americas, they identified racism as a foreign phenomenon that existed only in Peru's colonial past. In spite of Roberto MacLean Estenós's efforts to foster a pan-American program to promote racial equality in 1943, the "progressive" sociologist denied that Afro-Peruvians faced racial discrimination in his own country. Black people in Peru, according to this chair of the sociology department at UNMSM, did not face racial discrimination or lynching. According to MacLean Estenós, "In Peru the sense of equality and human dignity is not limited to men of white skin. We are all equal before the Peruvian law, with the same rights and the same work, in the political, economic, and social realms."[66] His reasoning reveals the power of discourses of mestizaje, like the ideology of racial democracy in Brazil, to create a mythos of Peruvian ethnoracial exceptionalism, which acknowledged national diversity and racial mixing but denied the existence of racism. Of course, the legal system of racial segregation of the United States made such juxtapositions possible, as the United States became a common foil to divert attention away from the question of race and racism in Latin America until at least 1964.

The racial ideology of Peruvian white elites, as well as the collective resistance of Afro-Peruvians to racial exclusion and social inequality, demonstrates more similarities than differences in the histories of race in the Americas. After all, the so-called Tannenbaum thesis of 1946 contrasted Brazil's "racial democracy," a supposedly egalitarian and "raceless" society that celebrated its mixed heritage, with the institutional racism and racial inequality in the United States. This chapter thus contributes to a growing body of literature that reveals more similarities than differences in racial exclusion across the Americas. Afro-Peruvians faced persistent negative stereotypes that sought to deny their presence in the elite vision of the nation, excluding them from the full political participation that they had earned through generations of collective action against slavery and for the ideals of an independent, democratic nation. Clemente Palma's internalization of this racial hierarchy led him to deny his own Blackness and lament his nation's racial identity, and his later writings praising Albújar's work embody the elite contradictory visions of race and nation, especially with the rise of positivism among elites throughout Latin America.

In contrast, Enrique López Albújar became a member of the Lima elite through his education and writing and by marrying into an elite family. His experiences in the Peruvian hinterlands and his childhood in Piura provided him a unique perspective on peruanidad to which he contributed by providing a more realistic account of racial oppression and a unique sociological analysis of the enduring legacies of slavery. For all of its realism, Albújar's vision of mulatismo reflects some of the same problematic solutions envisioned by nineteenth-century Cuban abolitionists. Albújar, like Suárez Romero and Gómez de Avellaneda, chose to present two virtuous protagonists as mulatos, thereby implying that diluting Blackness through mestizaje would resolve ethnoracial antagonism. At the same time, Albújar's vision of peruanidad included Afro-Peruvians in selective ways: as culture bearers and as relics of resistance in the colonial past, suggesting their romanticized sexuality caused their invisibility through mestizaje.

Yet Albújar's analysis of the brutality of slavery and its legacies emphasized the root causes of ethnoracial inequality. This was a clear departure from Clemente Palma's racially deterministic assessment, and Roberto MacLean Estenós echoed this development in his analysis of the "black problem." Of course, the "elite discourse" on race and nation was not monolithic, as evinced by the influential Marxist intellectual José Carlos Mariátegui, analyzed in the following chapter.[67] Such contradictions ultimately reveal that racial determinism remained a part of the ideology of mestizaje as peruanidad. Although racist attitudes and prejudice against Afro-Peruvians certainly remained in twentieth-century Peru, the elite discourse on race and nation came to reflect the popular representations of racial mixing as unification and as a recognition of the cultural contributions of Afro-Peruvians. Put simply, the continuities in the array of writings in this era show that the recognition of cultural contributions in popular literature matters. If the pseudoscience of race and ethnicity in early twentieth-century Latin America was influenced by assumptions and expectations, popular literature likely influenced the shift in elite discourse between the 1860s and 1940s.

López Albújar's perspective developed from his upbringing in Piura, suggesting this northern department was an important source of Afro-Peruvian culture despite the limited research on this region. The following chapter turns to the culmination of elite discourses on race, nation, and mestizaje by focusing on the elite-dominated discourse of indigenismo, which consolidated a false dichotomy of Peruvian "dualism" and rendered the Afro-Peruvian population completely invisible.

Chapter 5

Afro-Peruvian Invisibility in Narratives of *Mestizaje*

Locating African Descendants in National Dualism and *Indigenismo*

The term criollo/a (Creole) tends to be defined in contemporary works on Latin American history as a person of Iberian descent born in the colonial Americas. However, the meaning, understanding, and connotations of the term varied and changed a great deal from the eighteenth through the twentieth centuries in Peru. As the word changed in connotation, it played an important role in shaping a national identity rooted in the coastal population's Iberian heritage and in erasing Afro-Peruvians as a category of historical analysis with distinct cultural contributions to the national identity. The coastal understanding of Creole national identity appropriated Afro-Peruvian culture while focusing on the majority Indigenous population of the interior in the nineteenth century, contributing to a narrative of national dualism that culminated with a social, intellectual, and political movement known as indigenismo in the 1920s. This history reveals the inherent contradictions of the ideology of mestizaje as it reflected the fluctuating political and social anxieties of the white Creole population. Despite the changing discourse, this chapter argues that anti-Black racism remained consistent in the discourses of Creole nationalism, dualism, and indigenismo, consolidating a narrative of Afro-Peruvian disappearance and invisibility. The discursive shift to focus on the Indigenous roots of Peruvian national identity cast aside the question of Blackness, denying the possibility of racism in Peru. This process began with Eurocentric narratives of Peruvian national identity and history in the 1850s and culminated in expressions of national dualism and mestizaje in the indigenismo movement of the 1920s and 1930s. In Trouillot's terms, the 1920s and 1930s were a "moment of fact retrieval (the making of narratives)," when elites wrote a selective account of Peruvian history that silenced the roles and contributions of African descendants.[1]

The rhetorical construction of mestizaje as a narrative of national identity that excluded Afro-Peruvians began in the 1850s with the writings of Sebastián Lorente. The persistence of anti-Blackness in discourses of mestizaje and peruanidad continued in populist political movements between 1895 and 1930, leading intellectual elites and politicians to completely erase Afro-Peruvians as political subjects. Although Creole elites in this period acknowledged a distinct Afro-Peruvian history under slavery, they agreed that mestizaje had eliminated any ethnoracial distinctions for African descendants and integrated this population into the national identity in class-based terms. It appears that some Afro-Peruvians eventually saw a need to break through the inherent silencing of Blackness in the rhetoric of mestizaje and express their unique experiences of racial exclusion in a 1930 "resolution" that proposed an international antiracist program as a central component of global anti-imperialism. Ironically, this anonymous "resolution" was published in the Marxist and *indigenista* journal *El Amauta*, which contributed to Afro-Peruvian invisibility through its consolidation of Peruvian dualism. Indigenismo played a central role in shaping the ideology of mestizaje, reflecting the outward-looking concerns of Peruvian racial demography expressed by Creole elites as well as their romanticization of the Inca past as the foundation of the modern nation.

The roles of Afro-Peruvians in the nation's history went unrecognized in US scholarship until the 1990s. This invisibility results in part from a dichotomy that posited two uniform and oppositional populations in Peru: the criollo (or European-descended) culture of the Pacific coast and the Indigenous populations of the Andean and Amazon interior. The concept of Peruvian "dualism" falsely renders criollo identity homogeneous or monolithic in early twentieth-century historiography and literature. With some notable exceptions, this dualism persists in rendering Afro-Peruvian identity invisible in popular understandings of Peruvian racial geography.[2]

Peruvian Creoles constructed their Iberian-descended identity along the Pacific coast in cultural and racial opposition to the Indigenous identities of the nation's interior. Elite politicians and intellectuals in Lima established this binary racialized vision of the nation in the mid-nineteenth century in conjunction with narratives of mestizaje that excluded African-descended people from the coastal identity of *lo criollo*.

Contested understandings and uses of the term, along with the deployment of mestizaje as a process that would make racial difference irrelevant, played a definitive role in writing Afro-Peruvians out of the history of the nation. The term criollo is most often associated with people of European descent in colonial Spanish America; however, the term initially referred to enslaved Africans born in the Americas. From the late colonial period through the nineteenth century, criollo increasingly gained connotations of patriotism and nationalism as white elites appropriated Afro-Peruvian culture. Patriotic usage of popular cultural forms for political ends was a common phenomenon in Spanish America, but in Peru the process was key to erasing the history of Afro-Peruvians in shaping national culture and identity. Between 1855 and 1931, elites consolidated a hegemonic narrative that celebrated Afro-Peruvian contributions to literature, arts, and music and yet denied the existence of the African-descended population, a narrative embodied in the discourse of mestizaje as national identity.

The elites who defined the parameters of mestizaje articulated differing interpretations of lo criollo as central to Peruvian national identity, but they agreed that African ancestry was not to be celebrated. While expressing racial anxieties about the moral depravity of the African-descended population, they consolidated a hegemonic narrative that racial mixing would render this population invisible. As Marisol de la Cadena has found, education was a central component of Peruvian mestizaje, allowing elites to "think their discriminatory practices are not racist because they do not connote innate biological differences, but cultural ones."[3] This self-exculpatory form of thinking can be traced to the nineteenth century, when coastal elites shaped a national history curriculum with an emphasis on the Indigenous past rather than one that included African descendants.

Nineteenth-century narratives of national identity that focused on the so-called Indian problem culminated with the indigenista movement of the 1920s, while the persistent racial anxieties regarding the Afro-Peruvian population contributed to their invisibility in the narrative process of mestizaje. In nineteenth-century Peru, elite intellectuals and politicians discussed Blackness in terms of race that did not exclude biological difference but used the language of culture to deny such racism. Whereas education might improve the lot of the Indigenous population and by extension the nation, elite intellectuals persistently saw "Black culture" in negative terms. Thus, they argued that mestizaje would resolve the backwardness associated with Blackness, facilitating national modernization through cultural and biological assimilation.

CREOLE NATIONALISM, PERUVIAN DUALISM, AND THE EUROCENTRISM OF SEBASTIÁN LORENTE

The elite construction of "Creole nationalism" in late colonial Peru shaped narratives of national identity in the nineteenth century, which maintained racial hierarchies and contributed to erasing Afro-Peruvians as a distinct category of historical analysis after independence. Elite concerns over the Indigenous population and the prospect of a Peruvian-Bolivian confederation in the 1830s prompted intellectual elites to highlight the division between the "Creole" population of the coast and the Indigenous populations of the interior, further situating Afro-Peruvians in the Hispanic-dominated coastal culture and associating them with slavery rather than a historically glorious civilization.

Historian Cecilia Méndez G.'s analysis of the conservative backlash to Santa Cruz's confederation shows how Creole political interests contributed to racist language that hardened the narrative dichotomy between the "Creole" coast and the Indigenous interior.[4] While drawing attention to the historic origins of Peru in the Inca Empire, elites disregarded Afro-Peruvian history. By default, coastal elites saw Afro-Peruvians as culturally indistinct from Creoles and insignificant to the nation's politics and identity.

Méndez G. concludes that "the anti-Santacrucista discourse originating in Lima . . . consistently invoked the glorious Inca past to spurn and segregate the Indian" of the present.[5] Elites shaped the rhetoric of race and nation to suit their political agendas, and the Peru-Bolivia Confederation further isolated Afro-Peruvians from the narrative. Although the debate between white elites in Lima cast out Blackness from the discourse of dualism, the negative stereotypes associated with Afro-Peruvians remained.

The political and militarized debate between elites in Lima regarding

Santa Cruz's proposed confederation shifted the dominant discourse on race from concern over African descendants to a focus on the perceived problem of the Indian. This focus was codified and institutionalized by Peruvian *patriota* (patriot) and "great schoolteacher" Sebastián Lorente, who sought to construct a history of the nation with a focus on the role of the Indigenous population. Lorente traveled to Lima from his home in Spain in 1843 to begin collaborating on the nationalist project of constructing Peruvian national history with Ramón Castilla's government, serving as an integral member of the commission to write the first law of general instruction.[6] Lorente completely ignored the Afro-Peruvian population in his construction of a national history. Based on the idea of universal history from the Enlightenment and German historical philosophers such as Hegel, Lorente divided history into four phases: ancient, middle, modern, and contemporary. In this schema, ancient history extended from the origin of humanity to the end of the Roman Empire, the middle period ended with the discovery of the Americas, and the modern period ended with the French Revolution. Lorente considered his contemporary period of the mid-nineteenth century an era of revolutions that toppled monarchies and brought free republics to Europe and the Americas.[7]

Despite Lorente's push to end slavery in the name of individual freedom, the broader purpose of his publications was to educate the young nation of its progress toward civilization. Following his early role in support of Castilla, Lorente established the study of the humanities while serving as chair of the *Facultad de Letras* at the Universidad Nacional Mayor de San Marcos. Here he also founded the study of history in Peru, and his pedagogy inspired public education in national history. His influence survived through his successor at San Marcos, Carlos Wiesse, whose text for the course Historia Crítica del Perú was widely distributed and became the official textbook on Peruvian history for use in public schools until at least 1930.[8] Thus, Lorente played a central role in shaping an official and widely accepted narrative of Peruvian history and national identity from a European perspective. He applied this Eurocentric approach to history to his analysis of Peru's ancient and modern past.

Building on his universal framing of human progress, Lorente focused on the two grand phases of the development of ancient civilization in Peru: from primitive patriarchal tribes to the centralized state of the Incas. In comparison with Enlightened interpretations of this process in the Orient, however, Peru transitioned directly from the ancient period to the colonial period under the influence of modern Spain, thereby bypassing the middle period or stage of feudalism.[9] Recognizing that his Eurocentric education in the universal process of history did not perfectly fit the history of Peru, Lorente sought to reinterpret the nation's ancient history to fit the universal frame. This interpretation was agreeable to elites seeking to make Peru appear more European.

In his analysis of the mestizo national chronicler El Inca Garcilaso de la Vega's writings, Lorente exhibited his concern about the origins of Peru's "national character," reflecting a Rankean empiricism in combination with emerging ideas of race. In the writings of eighteenth-century chroniclers, the mythic Manco Capac was portrayed as the first Inca emperor who united disparate tribes into a sedentary, agricultural civilization, fitting the Enlightenment view of the progression of mankind. Eighteenth-century European explorer-intellectuals such as Humboldt and Raynal speculated that Manco Capac was of Asian or even European origin, even positing that he was "whiter" than his descendants in Peru.[10] Lorente dismissed such theories, however, grounding the great Inca past in the Andes to grant legitimacy and permanency to the Peruvian republic. Asserting that Manco Capac doubtlessly was born in Peru, Lorente argued that "his work carries the stamp of the national race, and that of the country."[11] By situating Inca history in the stages of progress toward civilization, Lorente integrated the Indigenous Other into his vision of a national identity and race. This vision implicitly denied the Afro-Peruvian population a legitimate place in the nation's racial identity despite the fact that Lorente had fought alongside Afro-Peruvian men. The presence and contributions of Afro-Peruvians to Lorente's political cause were clearly visible to him, so his decision to omit this population from his analysis must be understood as intentional.

Lorente and other nineteenth-century patriotas did not build up Peru's Indigenous past to glorify their contemporary Indigenous population. In his 1860 book, *Historia Antigua del Perú*, Lorente instructed, "In the greatness of our past we shall find presentiments of the future."[12] Throughout Lorente's writings, patriota appears to replace a tradition of Creole/criollo intellectual production on national identity under a different signifier. Given his role in Peru's national historiography, his choice of words might be expected. However, the choice also reflects the nature of his project: to integrate the Indigenous "masses" into the national culture through education.

He therefore presented mestizaje as a process of Indigenous acculturation to white "Creole" society. As historian Mark Thurner has argued, Lorente's work reflects similar nationalist projects underway at the same time in Mexico and Cuba, and "the expansion of the name of 'American' to include non-Creoles . . . is most notable in nineteenth-century historical discourse."[13] As a first-generation patriota, Lorente built on the historiography of early chroniclers, but his focus on the Indigenous population exhibits a shift from the concerns of the early criollo nationalists in the 1790s and the narrative assimilation of Afro-Peruvians under the broad category of criollo. This apparent inclusion, however, subsumed Afro-Peruvians in a broader category of mestizos associated with peruanidad, appropriating their culture and erasing them as a distinct collective identity.

This shift resulted from a political proposition that would integrate a larger national territory occupied by Indigenous people. Thurner has aptly summarized the challenge these Creole elites faced: "In Peru, the imagined 'us' of national history was more ambivalent. The Creole 'us' was haunted by a domestically distant and sometimes threatening indigenous 'them,' a compatriot subaltern condemned by liberal history to inhabit the nation's prehistorical golden age. But this dead golden age was the future promise of national history [that] would reemerge in the scientific (langu)age of race as the living legacy of indigenous despotism, the Creole burden of 'our indigenous race.'"[14]

However, analyzing the early patriotic discourses of elite Peruvians reveals a more complex Creole "us," especially in its language of origin (i.e., criollo/a). The *Mercurio Peruano*'s advertisement section consistently included announcements of sales of enslaved persons, but these people-for-purchase were often labeled criollo or negro. Livestock could also be categorized as criollo, and their local origins appear to have increased their value.[15] As the term referred both to local-born people and livestock, these meanings further separated it from connotations of race and connected it to genuine peruanidad while erasing its former association with African ancestry. *El Comercio* displayed similar advertisements for the sale of enslaved people, but in the 1840s the newspaper began to use the term culturally to describe the "character" of Cuban music.[16] In the 1840s, criollo was increasingly used to describe a particular form of national character in Peru, which both absorbed Afro-Peruvian culture and eliminated Blackness.

As Deborah Poole's research on nineteenth-century Peru has shown, photographic images helped to define Andean racial and national "types." With the rise of photography in the 1860s, Peruvian intellectuals sought to construct an image of their national character to be consumed by interested Europeans who categorized Peruvians according to emergent notions of race. Poole's analysis of the nineteenth-century "visual economy" demonstrates the racial anxieties of white elite Limeños who whitened the meaning of criollo/a to distance the nation from any association with Blackness. Poole also points out a linguistic shift in census records in her period of study, as "criollo" appears to be synonymous with "white" by the 1790s. Nineteenth-century census records, however, do not include criollo as a racial category, which appears to have been replaced with "white/*blanco/a*."

An anonymous short story published in *El Comercio* in September 1843 reveals further ambiguity in popular perception of criollo identity. The story follows the travels of and debates among Peruvian elite men, who discuss their mercantile and diplomatic connections to France, England, Germany, and the United States. The men express their concern over a *cuarterona*, or mestiza woman, who fled to Paris while traveling with a merchant company. The term cuarterona is more specific than mestiza, as it signified a person who was one-fourth (*cuarta*) African.[17] Expressing their disgust of this "evil creature" who disguised herself as a man to escape her "protectors," the Monsignor replies that this "seductress" and "evil soul" will be returning to Peru for his use in "certain projects." Fearful of her sexuality, one man exclaims, "Sorceress! Sorceress! It would be necessary to have the soulless eye of a *criollo* to discover a *mixture of blood* in the imperceptible brown matrix that lightly colors the crown of that *cuarterona's* pink nails."[18] Their concern over the seductive capacity of the woman is surprising given that she had disguised herself as a man, and the character's description of a perceptively "soulless" criollo suggests the author understood the term to refer to a similarly mixed-race person of Lima. The story emphasizes a mid-nineteenth-century elite concern about African presence in racial mixture as well as the continued associations of Blackness with wickedness and sexual promiscuity. In this context, criollo still signified an African-descended person born in Peru, and the category mestiza/o included those of African descent. Clearly the discursive shift from a concern over Afro-Peruvian immorality to a focus on the Indigenous population was incomplete. Whereas elites expressed anxieties of Afro-Peruvians in gendered and biologically racial terms, others insisted on "uplifting" the nation's Indigenous populations culturally.

Despite evidence that Afro-Peruvians sought to exercise their hard-earned citizenship rights in the decades following abolition,[19] the historical record reflects elite concerns over Indigenous rights and relations with the state. Thurner has studied archival records from the Andean highlands and Lima to analyze state-peasantry relations and patriotic nationalism among Indigenous populations of Huaylas-Ancash in the 1880s.[20] Although these records emphasize the dualist nature of Andean Indigenous populations and their relations with the white and mestizo populations of the coast, relying on these sources alone produces a limited narrative of the complexity of postcolonial and post-abolition Peruvian society in terms of interethnic and interracial relations. Among the Lima elite, a dichotomy between white European Creoles and Afro-Peruvian Creoles remained, punctuated by racist derisions of "black sexuality," which were echoed more subtly in government analyses of nineteenth-century censuses.

Anthropologist Mary Weismantel has also located and challenged the dominant discourse of Peruvian dualism to understand the ways fear and estrangement influenced ideas of sex and race throughout the Andes. Analyzing the work of the famous twentieth-century Peruvian anthropologist and writer José María Arguedas (1911–1969), Weismantel challenges the traditional understanding of Andean racial dynamics as a dichotomy between Indigenous Andeans in the interior and White Creoles of the coast.[21] Just as examining local juxtapositions within the criollo culture of the Peruvian coast does, Weismantel's approach reveals racist attitudes embedded within narratives of mestizaje that have denied the possibility of discrimination.

Most relevant to this book is Weismantel's analysis of the archetypal "Mama Negra" ("Black Mother"), the center of an annual Andean festival in Ecuador in honor of the Virgen de la Merced. In this procession, the "Mama Negra represents the vendors in their happiest self-invention: as big generous mothers, who provide sustenance like mother's milk to the entire populace of the city in which they live . . . the antithesis of the *pishtaco*. . . ." The Mama Negra is a man dressed as a woman with accentuated female parts: breasts and buttocks. Onlookers hope to catch a few drops from her large bottle of milk that she sprays into the crowd "in order to increase their own bodily strength and reproductive powers." For Weismantel, "this lactating woman echoes the imagery of nationalist mestizaje, as when Uriel Garcia declared the chola 'the rejuvenated organic force' whose breasts nurtured the Peruvian nation 'like a mother or a wet nurse.'"[22] This public performance of Blackness in the Andes replicates nationalist narratives of Peru that celebrate mestizaje as a unifying force while poking fun at the sexual and racial anxieties of white elites. At the same time, however, "the effect is not to invert patriarchy but simply to dissipate it into a racial democracy that overturns sex and gender oppression as well as that of race and class."[23] The dominant discourse of mestizaje in Peru came to focus on white Creole and Indigenous mixing, relegating Afro-Peruvians to symbolic roles associated with amoral sexuality, similar to Ecuador's Mama Negra. However, "enlightened" white creoles refused to see Afro-Peruvians as central to the Creole national identity.

Literary and historical representations of Afro-Peruvian women consistently reduced them to stereotypes of hypersexuality. This racist stereotype began in the colonial era and reflected European desire and fascination. As a Spanish immigrant, Lorente had a unique role in representing Peruvian society from the inside with a "European gaze."[24] He institutionalized this perspective of Afro-Peruvian women and of the nation's racial geography as the director of public instruction for Castilla's government. In his 1855 book, *Pensamientos sobre el Perú* (*Thoughts on Peru*), he writes, "The valleys of the coast are the homeland of life and pleasures: forests of ever-leafing trees; gardens that do not cease to enchant by the perfume and by the brilliant shades of the flowers . . . the cabins, the haciendas and the towns reveal the presence of the man who has come to beautify nature, and to enjoy its gifts in the bosom of peace and plenty."[25]

Lorente's romantic descriptions of the Peruvian environments included environmentally deterministic observations of the people who inhabited the different regions of the nation. While most of this book associated different environments with different Indigenous "types," such as the "Yanacona," "Cholito," and "El Indio de la Montaña," Lorente did not see any reason to provide the ethnoracial background of the men or women of the coastal haciendas. Instead, he chose to romanticize and sexualize the women of the coast in raceless terms. His language is that of a European observer of exotic women in a tropical environment, and his descriptions are addressed to European readers: "The sorceress of the coast attracts you with the magic of her movements; her enchanting voice anchors you to her side like music fixes to a serpent; her radiant beauty face makes you forget the universe; and if she gives you a burning look like the sun that saw her rise, she burns you with love. . . . The haughty woman from the coast, loving to shine in the theater or on the promenade, and fixing her passionate eyes on you, will communicate the boldness of her feelings to you alive; neither one nor the other will inspire those disinterested homages to the majesty of the virgins that come so close to adoration; what you feel in the first case is the gentle impulse of peaceful joys that sweeten the bitter cup of life; in the second you experience the need for stormy pleasures that intoxicate and make you delirious."[26]

Lorente's use of the term *hechicera* echoes that of Creole intellectuals concerned with Afro-Peruvian women's sexuality in the 1840s, and the omission of race in this prose stands in contrast with the frequent references to different environmental "types" of indios throughout the book. In this way, Lorente perpetuated the negative stereotypes of Afro-Peruvian women's sexuality and availability to Europeans. However, his decision to elide Blackness in his prose permitted more ambiguity regarding his thinking on Blackness. As a precursor to indigenismo, this omission simultaneously cast out Afro-Peruvian men from modern citizenship after abolition and framed Afro-Peruvian women as conduits to mestizaje. By presenting their desirable sexuality as open and available to white men, Lorente framed mestizaje as a process playing out along the Pacific coast that birthed mestizo "free citizens" without racial distinction, a narrative trope echoed in the analyses of the early twentieth-century censuses examined in chapter 3.

INDIGENISMO, DUALISM, AND AFRO-PERUVIAN INVISIBILITY

The rhetorical construction of Peruvian dualism originated in the colonial legal system that established a "republic of Indians" and a "republic of Spaniards." Following independence, Creole elites from the coast sought to integrate the "formerly oppressed Indians to be gradually 'enlightened' and 'civilized' so that they could 'join the rest of the free citizens' of Peru."[27] Thurner and others have noted the inherent contradictions of this process, reflecting the archival focus on Indigenous citizenship. The notion that coastal Peruvians were "the rest of the free citizens" presumed that Creole elites immediately accepted Afro-Peruvians as equal citizens following Castilla's revolution, and this myopia culminated with the indigenista movement of the 1920s. The singular focus on Indigenous rights in the archives reflects the dominant discourse of citizenship that emerged with Castilla's Liberal Revolution, and the mid-nineteenth-century political and romantic literature on peruanidad laid the foundations of the twentieth-century movement.

Peruvian liberal elites sought to address the dualism that characterized interpretations of the nation's history through a social, intellectual, and political movement known as indigenismo in the 1920s and 1930s. The movement played out in similar ways in Peru and Mexico, as elites appropriated Indigenous cultures and marginalized African descendants in their constructions of national identities. Historian Analisa Taylor has defined indigenismo in Mexico as "a social scientific paradigm wedded to a set of government institutions and policies as well as an aesthetic sensibility that has shaped a great deal of twentieth century Mexican art and literature." She adds that "for the past two hundred years Indians in Mexico have been narrated as the other: represented through ideological constructions that have allowed mestizos to objectify them as cultural icons of national identity on one hand, and marginalize them from political and social spaces on the other."[28] Scholar Juan Carlos Grijalva has also noted the parallels between Peruvian and Mexican indigenismo. Just as in Mexico, Peruvian elites sought to acknowledge and assimilate the Indigenous majority. They did so by constructing "an abstract and homogenous national identity based on the political manipulation of indigenous and folkloric cultural marks," which "was adopted as official State ideology."[29] Gendered and racial stereotypes remained central to indigenismo's consolidation of Peruvian dualism that denied the importance of the African-descended population. The figure of the Mama Negra in the Ecuadorian Andes resembles the portrayal of Afro-Peruvian women in indigenista discourse: as mothers of the nation who have sacrificed a distinct collective identity to help shape a national identity through mestizaje.

Indigenismo codified a new dichotomy between past and present, casting the mestizo as a modern citizen and indigeneity with the past. In Peru, as in Mexico, this dualism "leaves the many Latin Americans of African, Asian, Jewish, and Middle Eastern descent, as well as many other groups, entirely out of the equation of Latin American culture."[30] In Peru, discourses of mestizaje combined with indigenismo to produce contradictory outcomes for Indigenous and Afro-Peruvian populations: while it cast the

Indigenous population as the Other, it absorbed African descendants into a broader mestizo identity and denied their existence.[31]

An example of the contradictory outcomes of indigenismo is visible in the "radical" indigenista project of "populist" President Augusto B. Leguía. Leguía sought the support of indigenistas after being elected in 1919, leading him to officially endorse the "radical" indigenista project called the Comité Pro-Derecho Indígena Tawantinsuyu in 1920.[32] Seven years later, however, a local government delegate in the department of Cajatambo (just north of Lima) asserted the need for inalienable Indigenous property rights. The regional deputy of this department, Arturo E. Delgado, criticized the "insatiable" landed elites who seized lands from "ignorant" Indigenous Andeans. He argued that landowners (*terratenientes* and *gamonales*) who tricked unwitting Indigenous landowners into selling their small plots should prompt action in keeping with the "progressive thinking of The President of the Republic, August B. Leguía, of 'making every Peruvian a landowner.'"[33] While demanding inalienable land rights, Delgado argued that "the accumulation of territorial property in the few hands that grab the riches coming from the rudimentary labor of the debased Indian, produces ignorance, pauperism, depopulation and ruin."[34] Even as "progressive" programs failed to guarantee the basic Indigenous rights to land, a common objective of indigenismo, proponents of such rights lamented Indian ignorance and decline. They simultaneously disregarded the unique challenges that many Afro-Peruvians faced related to land rights, as many remained tied to hacienda lands as a clear legacy of slavery.[35] Like Lorente's decision to elide the question of Blackness in Peru's past and present, this selective analysis of land and labor challenges facing the working class also seems intentional. Afro-Peruvians were visible on and around coastal haciendas but remained invisible in the making of narratives by the indigenismo movement.

EL AMAUTA AND THE ERASURE OF BLACKNESS IN *INDIGENISMO*

Indigenista discourse perpetuated Peruvian dualism, and its Marxist framework highlighting the role of capitalist exploitation facilitated a transition to class-based rhetoric. Between the mid-nineteenth century and the 1920s, the narrative of Peruvian dualism moved from a racial dichotomy to one based on class and ethnicity. This shift is apparent in the Marxist journal named after the Quechua word for "wise one," or teacher: *El Amauta*. Peru's most famous Marxist intellectual and indigenista, Jose Carlos Mariátegui (1894–1930), founded *El Amauta* in 1926. The transition to a class-based rhetoric that emphasized the plight of the Indigenous, however, required an explicit connection to mestizaje that absorbed Afro-Peruvians as coastal Creoles and erased Blackness. In his 1928 essay "Literature on Trial," one of his *Seven Interpretive Essays on Peruvian Reality*, Mariátegui disregarded the contributions of Chinese immigrants and Afro-Peruvians to the nation's culture, writing, "The contribution of the Negro, who came as a slave, almost as merchandise, appears to be even more worthless and negative. The Negro brought his *sensualism*, his superstition, and his primitivism. His condition not only did not permit him to help create culture, but the crude, vivid example of his barbarism was more likely to hamper such creation. Racial prejudice has diminished; but the progress of sociology and history has broadened the idea that there are differences and inequalities in the evolution of people. Although the inferiority of colored races is no longer one of the dogmas that sustain a battered white pride, all the relativism of today does not suffice to abolish cultural inferiority."[36]

This analysis of race in Peru neatly summarizes how the ideology of mestizaje denied racism while insisting on Afro-Peruvian inferiority in cultural terms, allowing racist stereotypes to trap African descendants in the sensual environment of the national culture. It also insisted that Africans and their descendants were inferior in progress toward civilization, using Enlightenment language to justify a narrative of erasure. Mariátegui was a prolific and influential writer. Despite his Communist ideology, which interpreted Peruvian history through the lens of Marxism, his dismissive analysis of Afro-Peruvian history echoed his elite contemporaries'. He attempted to distance himself from the tropes of biological racism but reiterated them by asserting African cultural inferiority in ways that echoed his contemporaries' disdain for Indigenous (or *serrano*) culture. As a consequence of what de la Cadena has called "silent racism" in Peru, indigenismo justified the silencing of Afro-Peruvians as political subjects by declaring their cultural, rather than biological, inferiority. This allowed Mariátegui to deny the existence of racism while simultaneously denying the existence of Afro-Peruvians, showing how indigenismo influenced the ideology of mestizaje by erasing Blackness.

A 1930 edition of *El Amauta* included an article in the section "Panorama

Móvil" titled "Proyecto de Resolución Sobre la Cuestión de la Raza Negra ("Resolution Project on the Question of the Black Race"), which provides a rare window through which to view how Peruvian indigenistas viewed Afro-Peruvians. On the rare occasions that the indigenista journal addressed the African diaspora, it did so in transnational terms, in this case drawing attention to the world's "150 million exploited blacks." The author advocated for the unification of the "black masses" with "the rest of the oppressed peoples" to struggle against "imperialist domination." After providing an overview of the history of the transatlantic trade in enslaved persons as a product of global capitalism, the article highlighted the continuation of the same imperialist systems that had more recently agreed on the repartition of Africa and the complete subjugation of its peoples. Condemning the "imperialist countries of Europe and America," the author wrote, "if it is true that in the Americas slavery has been abolished as an institution, imperialism continues nonetheless under different forms of oppression of the black populations."[37] While infrequent, such analysis of the challenges unique to "black masses" associated anti-Blackness with US and European imperialism, eschewing the question of such racism in Peru. This rhetorical device began in 1860s Lima nationalist discourse, as seen in chapter 2 of this book.

The contributors to *El Amauta* thus displayed another paradox of indigenismo: by locating racism as a foreign-imposed phenomenon, Lima elites presented themselves as progressive antiracists promoting the interests of all oppressed people. The same 1930 issue of the journal republished a 1904 essay by Manuel González Prada titled "Nuestros Indios" ("Our Indians"). The famous anarcho-syndicalist intellectual's analysis of race and the perpetual oppression of the Indigenous populations of Peru embodied the paradox of 1920s indigenismo by challenging some dominant strains of racial science while embracing others.

In contrast with Clemente Palma's 1897 thesis and contemporary interpretations of the 1872 anti-coup uprising in Lima, González Prada's article derides Gustave Le Bon as "an exaggeration of [Herbert] Spencer." Whereas Lorente had celebrated the mid-nineteenth century as an "era of revolutions" that toppled monarchies, Le Bon argued that the Latin American revolutions would cause "a return to primitive barbarism unless the United States do it the great service of conquering it. . . . To debase the richest regions of the Globe to the level of the black republics of Santo Domingo and Haiti, this is what the Latin race has accomplished in less than a century with half of America." González Prada rejected this negative analysis of Latin American independence, arguing that the "heirs" of August Comte had taken his positivism and "converted it into a heap of ramblings without any scientific basis."[38] The anarcho-syndicalist author criticized European racial pseudoscience and solidified a Peruvian identity rooted in its Indigenous past, defending Indigenous Peruvians from Eurocentric racist derisions but not the Afro-Peruvian population.

González Prada's essay is a unique contribution to indigenismo in its critical analysis of the role of education and its explicit antiracist and anti-imperialist rhetoric. Like many 1920s indigenistas, González Prada rejected the notion that education alone would help uplift the Indigenous population, arguing that "the problem of the Indian is economic and social more than educational. . . . To the Indian one should not preach humility and resignation but pride and rebellion. What has he gained by three or four hundred years of conformity and patience? The less he is subject to authority the more injury he escapes. . . . To sum up, the Indian will be redeemed by his own efforts, not the humanization of his oppressors." Despite his argument for improving the material conditions of Indigenous Peruvians, González Prada echoed Sebastián Lorente's Eurocentric interpretation of history. The author accepted that "feudalism" was "a stage in evolution" but rejected Le Bon's notion that "the era of Hispanic American revolutions is . . . an incurable, final state." In an apparent self-contradiction, González Prada suggested that the white Latin Americans would lead the region to a glorious future: "What the Latin Empires can achieve in Europe, may not the nations of similar origin attempt in the New World? Or are there two sociological laws, one for the Latins of America and another for Latins of Europe?"[39] Despite rejecting European racial pseudoscience, González Prada saw hope for Peru's future in its European-descended population, exalting Creole elites while claiming to represent the political interests of the exploited working class.

While calling for Indigenous rebellion and autonomy, he also formulated a counter-hegemonic pseudoscience of race by pointing out the inherent contradictions of white supremacy in terms of humanist morality. González Prada wrote, "How convenient an invention ethnology is in the hands of some men! If one grants the division of humanity into superior and inferior races and recognizes the superiority of the whites and their consequent right to govern the planet, nothing is more natural than the suppression of the Black in Africa, the Redskin in the United States, the Tagalog in the Philippines, or the Indian in Peru." Situating scientific racism in the Anglophone world, González Prada distanced Latin American "whites" from such proclivities. English theorists of race, according to the author, maintained the tendency of "glorifying the Anglo Saxons and depreciating the Latins." Pointing out a contradiction in this theory, he wrote, "Crimes and vices of the English and the North Americans are things inherent in the human species and do not forecast the decline of a people. On the other hand, crimes and vices of the French or Italians are anomalies and indicate racial degeneration."[40] In this way, the author offered hope for Latin America's future predicated on its white, "Latin" roots. He advocated Indigenous rebellion against the same white Creole elites while denying the relevance of Afro-Peruvians from such concerns.

The Peruvian intellectual's defense of Latin American independence did not include a defense of Blackness. In typical indigenista fashion, González Prada emphasized Peru's Indigenous roots while casting aside the question of Blackness. African ancestry remained a corrupting, foreign element in Peruvian national identity that would soon disappear. The author argued that mestizaje produced an intermediary "half-caste, including in this term not only the cholo or mestizo of the sierra (mountains) but also the mulatto and zambo of the coast." Criticizing the cruelty of the *gamonales* (landowning political bosses of haciendas), the author asserted that "the Black seems to decline [in numbers]. . . . But the Indian remains, since three hundred to four hundred years of cruelty have not succeeded in exterminating him. The vile creature obstinately insists on living!" This sardonic exaltation of Indigenous resilience elided Le Bon's racist attacks on Blackness in the Americas by suggesting that Afro-Peruvians were disappearing through mestizaje. Contrasting this population with the Indigenous one, González Prada suggested Afro-Peruvian invisibility was the result of their inferiority and smaller numbers. With Blackness cast aside, the real victims of white exploitation were the "Indians," whose past and present resilience should be celebrated. In both cases, however, racial mixing created ethnic intermediaries who contributed to the exploitation of Blacks and Indians. In criticizing racism in the Anglophone world, González Prada awkwardly locates haciendas in the Peruvian interior rather than on the coast. Despite his criticisms of labor exploitation on haciendas, he replicated the false dichotomy of Peruvian dualism, writing, "While in the coastal region one sees a shadow of protection under a feigned republic, in the interior the violation of all rights under a feudal regime is open."[41] Thus even as antiracist indigenistas rejected elements of Eurocentric racial pseudoscience, they solidified a dualist narrative between coastal mestizos and the Indigenous interior that presumed the disappearance of Afro-Peruvians along the coast.

Peruvian indigenismo was by no means monolithic in its interpretations of race, modernization, and Indigenous identity. While some indigenistas stressed the need for Indigenous Peruvians to assimilate culturally through education, others glorified the Indigenous past in the Andes and sought to become Indigenous themselves. As Deborah Poole notes, indigenistas of the 1920s, such as José Uriel García, believed that Andean culture could be constructed "only by building a united highland identity that would encompass peasant and intellectual alike." In this environmentally deterministic analysis, the Andean highlands provided a leveling and homogenizing function that Uriel Garcia called "syncretic tellurism." This was understood as "the historical process through which all inhabitants of the Andes—intellectual and Indian alike—would eventually acquire a homogenous identity centered on the specific form of 'emotion' that emanated from the Andean landscape."[42] Simultaneously, Uriel Garcia and other indigenistas wrote out the relevance of similar oppression of Afro-Peruvians by gamonales along the coast. Building on González Prada's analysis, such indigenista constructions of racial geographies reinforced Peruvian dualism.

CONCLUSIONS

This chapter has traced the erasure of Blackness from Peruvian national identity to the formative writings of Sebastián Lorente during Castilla's Liberal Revolution and the moment of slavery's abolition. This narrative of invisibility became part of the standard curriculum for Peruvian schoolchildren, erasing Afro-Peruvians in an "official" way through the education system. Despite the high percentage of African descendants in coastal Peru in the colonial era, political and intellectual elites denied the value of their contributions to the national culture, effectively denying their presence in the post-abolition republic. In this context, González Prada can be understood as a proto-indigenista who intentionally ignored Afro-Peruvians, shaping the subsequent discourse of mestizaje as indigenismo. This nineteenth-century narrative of dualism shaped the discourse of indigenismo in the early twentieth century.

In contrast with the Andean Indigenous populations, dominant discourses of race and national identity agreed that Africans had no useful history and would inevitably disappear as mestizos or criollos along the coast. The subtle shifts in racial connotations of the term criollo over the nineteenth century demonstrate white racial anxieties of African "degeneration" in coastal mestizaje. The narrative shift toward the Peruvian interior and its Indigenous peoples appears to be a product of Santa Cruz's Peruvian-Bolivian Confederation, contributing to the discourse of dualism. Even as Sebastián Lorente supported the abolition of slavery and the end of Indigenous tribute, the "great schoolteacher" codified a narrative of dualism that denied the existence of Afro-Peruvians along the Pacific coast. His emphasis on the Inca origins of the modern Peruvian state provided a framework for twentieth-century indigenistas. Even as these Peruvian intellectuals (many of whom were mestizos themselves) rejected Eurocentric understandings of racial hierarchies, they reified Peruvian dualism while avoiding questions of anti-Blackness by denying the existence of Afro-Peruvians. These narratives played a central role in rendering the minority Afro-Peruvian population invisible while permitting elites to deny their own racist assumptions. Creole elites saw no need to address or recognize Afro-Peruvians, effectively erasing them as political subjects. In this way, the making of sources worked together with the making of narratives to erase Blackness, leading to a reduced number of categories indicating African ancestry in census records and, later, to foregone conclusions that explained Afro-Peruvian invisibility. This narrative process cannot be separated from elite constructions of census categories and the government-sponsored analyses that accompanied them, which "officially" erased Afro-Peruvians through mestizaje.

Conclusion

Afro-Peruvian Invisibility in Retrospective Significance

In *Silencing the Past,* Michel-Rolph Trouillot identified the dilemma of constructivist history, which this book echoes. Narrative constructs of Peruvian history actively contributed to silencing the Afro-Peruvian past; yet this analysis "cannot give a full account of the production of any single narrative."[1] However, by assessing the crucial moments of historical production during which silences were created, my analysis demonstrates "that the historical process has some autonomy vis-à-vis the narrative" and that recognizing "the boundary between what happened and that which is said to have happened is necessary."[2]

The process by which Creole intellectuals erased Blackness in the archives and rendered Afro-Peruvians invisible offers insights into Afro-Latin American invisibility more generally. In post-abolition Peru, the silences in the making of sources and the making of archives reverberated in the subsequent making of narratives. The subtle yet insidious erasure of Blackness echoes the invisibility of Blackness in the ideology of mestizaje. As a top-down process, however, the erasure of Blackness was incomplete. Of course, many Peruvians still identified as negro/a, or might have seen themselves as another label that included African ancestry, despite the refusal or inability of those creating the records to include this representation. Not necessarily an act of "active forgetting," the erasure of Blackness in Peru was a subtle omission based on a consensus that ignoring Blackness would eliminate the historic and contemporary problems surrounding the legacies of slavery, racism, and racial inequality. Through omission, white Peruvians maintained the status quo, a racial hierarchy obscured by mestizaje but universally understood as the legitimate "science" in its context. Trouillot reminds us that "any historical narrative is a particular bundle of silences."[3] By reading a variety of archival sources to locate these silences, as well as scrutinizing nation-making narratives of mestizaje, the book has sought to uncover the nuances of erasing Blackness in post-abolition Peru, with implications for other countries in the region in which African descendants continue to struggle for political visibility and representation.

While Haitian revolutionaries began the bloody process of fighting for their freedom from slavery and for an independent republic in the 1790s, their collective action was "unthinkable" to white contemporaries, even as they watched. In Europe, news of the Haitian revolution "had to be false [because]: a) anyone who knew the blacks had to realize that it was simply impossible for fifty thousand of them to get together so fast and act in concert; b) slaves could not conceive of rebellion on their own, and mulattoes and whites were not so insane as to incite them to full-scale violence; c) even in if the slaves had rebelled in such large numbers, the superior French troops would have defeated them."[4] Trouillot shows how racist European assumptions that this was beyond the realm of possibility silenced the event in Western historiography in a process he calls "formulas of erasure." In the case of Peru, Sebastián Lorente's post-abolition writings that became the textbook of Peruvian history produced the initial silencing of Afro-Peruvian agency. Their roles in the Liberal Revolution, civic associations, electoral politics, and sociopolitical movements was beyond the realm of possibility for this influential observer, and the tropes he produced were later echoed by "specialists," the indigenista Creole intellectuals who agreed that Afro-Peruvians had or would disappear through mestizaje.

As Trouillot suggests, "There may be structural similarities in global silences, or at the very least . . . erasure and banalization are not unique to the Haitian Revolution."[5] The silencing of Afro-Peruvian history bears resemblances to the erasure of Blackness in both Mexico and Brazil, in particular. This work has shown that racist assumptions first established during Iberian colonialism both persisted in the pseudoscience of race in the nineteenth century and produced a selective account of Peruvian reality in the archives, which erased Blackness and rendered Afro-Peruvians invisible. As Clemente Palma's writings revealed, Peruvian elites sought to "improve the race" in the late nineteenth century through European immigration. Peru had less success in this endeavor than did Brazil and Argentina, so Creole elites bent their findings toward mestizaje to match their desired results. The most significant outcome of this elite fashioning of mestizaje was the erasure of Blackness, reflecting the common tendency of elites to bend "scientific" and quantitative findings to fit their desired outcome. As with the contemporary European observers of the Haitian Revolution, "worldview wins over facts: white hegemony is natural and taken for granted; any alternative is still in the domain of the unthinkable."[6] Each of these countries maintained implicit racial hierarchies in nation-making narratives of mestizaje (or *mestiçagem*, in Brazil) that aspired to European standards and maintained negative associations with Blackness.

The unwillingness of European observers to recognize African contributions to civilization and culture has a long history rooted in early imperial encounters. Historian Edith Sanders has traced a long history of biblical myths that French anthropologists reshaped in the late eighteenth and early nineteenth centuries to justify their economic exploitation of Africans. The so-called Hamitic hypothesis began in the Babylonian Talmud and claimed that "the descendants of Ham are cursed by being black." When Napoleon encountered advanced civilizations in Africa during his 1798 expedition to Egypt, this hypothesis became "a convenient explanation for all the signs of civilization found in Black Africa."[7] As the Haitian Revolution's success shows, racial ideologies blinded white elites to the realities that they observed firsthand, presuming Africans and their descendants in the Americas were incapable of civilization and enlightened citizenship. Demonstrating the "adaptability" of this convenient narrative, in the Western world the Hamitic hypothesis "implied a self-appointed duty of the 'higher' races to civilize the 'lower' ones."[8] In nineteenth-century Latin America, the rise of scientific racism reified the racist assumptions of those in power, leading them to believe white supremacy was a "natural" fact absent a history of colonialism and slavery. Thus in the eyes of Creole elites, there could be no "useful" history of African descendants beyond their economic value, which ended with abolition.

Afro-Brazilian activist and life-long vocal critic of "racial democracy" Abdias do Nascimento (1914–2011) has drawn attention to "the cult of whiteness" as a cause of the erasure of Blackness in Brazil. Nascimento took this notion of elite-orchestrated whitening through mestiçagem a step further to argue that the whitening that occurred under the ideology of racial democracy constituted a form of "Black genocide."[9] Citing the 1957 work of Brazilian sociologist Guerreiro Ramos, Nascimento defined the "cult of whiteness" as a "morbid desire, harboured by every Brazilian, to be white and European. Economic and political power, as well as social prestige, is granted exclusively to those who adhere to the paragons of whiteness." For Nascimento, "internalising exclusively European concepts of 'culture' and 'aesthetics,' blacks are led to deny their African roots, traditions, and creations." This racial hierarchy could not be separated from the apparent demographic decline in Afro-Brazilians between 1822—when Brazil became an independent monarchy that preserved slavery—and 1950: "In 1822, Brazil had two-and-a-half times more blacks than whites. By 1872, half were Afro-Brazilian, and in 1950 the figure was down to 37%."[10] The elite reference to racial mixing has been central to Brazilian claims of being "nonracist," just as it has in the Peruvian ideology of mestizaje, showing the hemispheric tendency of white elites to occlude Blackness in discourses of national identity while subtly showing the disappearance of African descendants through racial mixing in census records. In order to understand Afro-Latin American invisibility, we must analyze dominant discourses of race and nation alongside statistical records of racial categories in the censuses.

The common language of race and racial science in the early twentieth century that held whiteness as superior led social engineers throughout Latin America to bend their statistical findings to their narratives of mestizaje as whitening. In Peru, this was more of a challenge for elite Creole reformers who had trouble recruiting European immigrants. Their stereotypes of Afro-Peruvian women's sexuality persisted from the late colonial period through to the mid-twentieth century, shaping the "official" analyses of the census records and the census forms themselves. As positivism peaked in its influence of social engineering and shaping national identities in Latin America in the 1890s and early 1900s, Peruvian intellectual elites found that Afro-Peruvian women had high birth rates. In their vision of a mestizo nation, however, these elites interpreted this data in a way that suited their narrative of mestizaje as a process of whitening. Thus, the children of Afro-Peruvian women, in their view, could be categorized only as mestizos, exhibiting their selective reading of the records to erase Blackness by denying the African ancestry of these children in the early twentieth century.

In contrast with Brazilians architects of racial democracy, Peruvian elites were not forced to negotiate the terms of Afro-Peruvian inclusion with a "black press." As Paulina Alberto has shown, this led elites in Brazil's

First Republic to hold up Afro-Brazilian women as "mothers of the nation," whose sexual and cultural openness birthed a mixed-race nation that ended racism, thereby celebrating their perceived sexuality and femininity. This led to imagery and symbolism that purported to represent Afro-Brazilians as central to the nation's history of mestiçagem while proclaiming an end to racial differences, exemplified in the statue of the *Mãe Preta* (*Black Mother*) in São Paolo.

Alberto connects the image of the *Mãe Preta* statue to the history of Afro-Brazilians' roles as wet nurses, a central topic of Gilberto Freyre's 1933 book, *Casa Grande y Senzala* (*The Masters and the Slaves*), which laid the foundations of racial democracy. Supporters of the monument in Rio de Janeiro "made it clear that the Mãe Preta stood for specifically black or African contributions to a hybrid Brazilian identity." Other commentators pointed out that "while celebrating the fraternity between the wet-nurse's black and white sons, [the statue] also spotlighted the remembered grievances if not of the enslaved woman herself, then of the sons that she bore."[11] Poignantly, the Casa Museo Ricardo Palma and the National Afro-Peruvian Museum in Lima display several images of enslaved Afro-Peruvian wet nurses, but these images have a more sinister visual element. The women quite literally fade away in the dark tones, and the lighter-skinned children in bright white garments emerge more clearly, providing an apt metaphor for the disappearance of Afro-Peruvians predicated on the invisibility of Afro-Peruvian women. Whereas Afro-Brazilian intellectuals debated the merits of such imagery and the ideology of racial democracy itself, the erasure of Blackness in nineteenth- and twentieth-century narratives of mestizaje stifled such public debates among Afro-Peruvians. They were denied a voice in the public sphere, and mestizaje maintained negative tropes of Afro-Peruvian women while implicitly celebrating their contributions to a raceless national identity.

Outside these sites that commemorate Afro-Peruvians, imagery that celebrates motherhood is more abstract, bearing resemblances to the archetypal Mamá Negra of the Ecuadorian Andes. One final example sits in the central plaza of the regional public library of Piura. The statue known as the *Monument to the Mother* is racially abstract yet bears clear resemblance to the historic roles of Afro-Peruvian women as wet nurses, and to the breast-feeding *Mãe Preta* statue in Brazil.[12]

Figure C.1. Display at the Museo Nacional Afroperuano. Photograph by Daniel S. Cozart

Figure C.2. Afro-Peruvian *ama de leche* ("wet nurse"). From the collection of Museo Nacional Afroperuano. Photograph by Daniel S. Cozart.

Figure C.3. *Monumento a la Madre* (*Monument to the Mother*) by Víctor Delfín. Photograph by Daniel S. Cozart

The decay of the Piuran statue results from the same neglect that Afro-Peruvians in Piura have experienced since abolition and can thus be understood as a metaphor for the failures and contradictions of mestizaje. The notion that racial mixture would put an end to racial difference and discrimination held widespread appeal in the early twentieth century, especially following the rise of Franz Boas's notion of cultural relativism and his debunking of fixed racial "types" in his 1911 lecture "The Instability of Human Types." As anthropologist Lee Baker has noted, Boas understood "the real race problem" to be the slow pace of racial mixture to completely do away with the notion of fixed racial differences. Baker cites Boas's assertion that "in a race of octaroons, living among whites, the color question would probably disappear."[13] The robust scholarship revealing the myth of racial democracy permits a closer reading of the assumptions that remained in such optimism for what Hooker has called "*mestizo futurisms*" in the early twentieth century. As an influence on Gilberto Freyre's interpretation of Brazilian history and his optimism for the future of race relations, Boas's vision of a "raceless" future was predicated on the erasure, or at least dilution, of Blackness through mestizaje. Thus, even the anthropological debunking of scientific racism maintained whiteness as the standard of modernity toward which mestizaje aspired, and this assumption is visible in the 1940 census categories in Peru, as they combined the category "mestiza" with "blanca."

And yet the 1940 census included the category negro/a, showing that the state did recognize African descendants as a category of analysis. As Nascimento's work demonstrates and as this book has argued, the diminution of categories indicating African ancestry cannot be separated from the narratives of race and mestizaje that held Blackness as inferior. This dominant narrative doubtlessly made negro/a an unappealing category for mestizos with African ancestry. Those who claimed an exclusively African-descended identity of negro/a were so few that the category did not appear on subsequent twentieth-century censuses.

This "official" invisibility was paradoxically a legacy of slavery that denied the possibility that Afro-Peruvians faced unique challenges due to that very history. Even as Afro-Peruvians in Piura continued to struggle for freedom, and as many libertos continued working under the same conditions and expectations in post-abolition Peru, elites erased their Blackness from the historical record. Consequently, Afro-Peruvian demands for social rights would be denied on the grounds that they were legally equal.

Afro-Peruvians have been keenly aware of this contradictory exclusionary narrative of inclusion as a key component of the ideology of mestizaje. If considered a part of a broader process of "black genocide" as Nascimento contended, cultural preservation and performance become key tools of resistance through performative visibility. Shortly after the census of 1940, Afro-Peruvian culture made a "revival" and "rediscovery" in Lima.

The 1950s "rediscovery" analyzed by ethnomusicologist Heidi Carolyn Feldman was also the reclamation of a long history of Afro-Peruvian cultural and the political contributions that had been appropriated by white Creole culture and denied by a hegemonic narrative of mestizaje.[14] Feldman's book built on anthropological research on Afro-Peruvian culture and identities since the 1980s, and together these works inspired subsequent research that began to examine the historical records of Afro-Peruvian communities from Chincha in the south to Piura in the north.[15] More recently, scholars have noted the importance of the rediscovery in inspiring Afro-Peruvian activist movements that empowered women and made transnational connections from the 1980s through the present day.[16] The prominent roles of Afro-Peruvian women activists and scholars such as Mónica Carrillo, Cecilia Ramirez Rivas, Susana Matute, Sharún Gonzáles, Ana Lucía Mosquera, and many others have built on the pioneering work of the sibling duo Nicomedes (1925–1992) and Victoria Santa Cruz (1922–2014). While only a few organizations existed between the 1950s and 2000, as Thomas and Lewis point out, Afro-Peruvian women founded and led at least three of the fifteen independent Afro-Peruvian organizations by 2005.[17] Considering the history of gendered racism that has silenced Afro-Peruvian women throughout the history traced in this book, the prominence of women in twenty-first-century activism is a logical and necessary response to the legacies of slavery and to the ideology of mestizaje.

Despite the rather unique form of gendered racism integral to Peruvian mestizaje, Afro-Peruvian activism in the late twentieth and early twenty-first centuries bears similarities to Afro-Mexican activism in their focus on political recognition and visibility in national censuses. In both of these predominantly Indigenous nations, African descendants have suffered neglect since the abolition of slavery and of casta categories, an act that liberal elites believed "signified equality."[18] In the twenty-first century, Afro-Mexican and Afro-Peruvian activists have pushed for changes in the census categories themselves, and both have succeeded in pushing their respective national governments to include the term *afrodescendiente* (African-descended) as a racial category to increase their visibility in response to narratives of disappearance through mestizaje.[19]

In Peru, the activist pressure to include this more inclusive category to indicate African ancestry coincided with grassroots efforts encouraging Peruvians to recognize and claim their African heritage as afrodescendientes, resulting in 3.6 percent of the nation's population self-identifying as African-descended in the 2017 census. This is certainly progress from the 1940 census, and the increase in self-identification with the African diaspora highlights the inadequacies of the twentieth-century censuses to recognize Afro-Peruvians as part of the national fabric. At the same time, the ongoing work of activists underscores the fact that much work remains to recover Afro-Peruvian history, which will contribute to more positive connotations with Blackness and a more comprehensive understanding of the history of the nation. While this work has shown how Afro-Peruvians were erased from the archives and narratives of national identity, it opens possibilities for much-needed research on Afro-Peruvian agency in the modern era. Through a necessarily creative use of the available historical record, more scholarship is needed on the roles of Afro-Peruvians during the nineteenth-century wars, such as the War of the Pacific and the war with Spain in 1866. Additionally, further research is needed to uncover Afro-Peruvian roles and experiences in in populist politics under Nicolás de Piérola, within Manuel González Prada's anarcho-syndicalist movement, and in the Alianza Popular Revolucionaria Americana (American Popular Revolutionary Alliance) party. Highlighting Afro-Peruvian agency in these movements that have gained a great deal of scholarly attention would contribute to challenging dominant stereotypes of immorality and passive disappearance, thereby providing more positive associations with Blackness. Such scholarship would support the objectives of Afro-Peruvian activists today, and my hope is that this book contributes to their efforts as well.

Notes

Preface

1. Heidi Carolyn Feldman, *Black Rhythms of Peru: Reviving African Musical Heritage in the Black Pacific* (Middletown, CT: Wesleyan University Press, 2006), 17.

2. Laura Alicia Valdiviezo, "Interculturality for Afro-Peruvians: Towards a Racially Inclusive Education in Peru." *International Education Journal* 7, no. 1 (2006): 31.

3. "LUNDÚ Center for Afro-Peruvian Studies and Empowerment (website).

Introduction

Jorge Eduardo Moscol Urbina, *Mangachería Rabiosa* (Piura: Autores Piuranos, 1986), 8–10: "Carlota Ramos de Santalaya cantaba a la Mangacheria en su poema "Sangre Mangache" y cuenta una historia que es tradición en el barrio de casitas de barro, vestidas de blanco de techos paja también cubiertos con barro. Carlota pregunta en sus versos "¿Quién te ha dicho / que no tienes una historia que contarnos? ¿Quién te ha dicho que no tienes / tradiciones que nos hablan / de lo que fueron los hombres / y las mujeres piuranas?"

1. Víctor Andrés Belaúnde, "Conceptos de Nación y Patria," in *Peruanidad* (Lima: Ediciones Mercurio Peruano, 1943), 12–13: "Por eso Renán concebía la Nación como un conjunto de hombres unidos por el recuerdo de los hechos que llevaron a cabo en lo pasado y la voluntad de realizarlos en lo futuro. La patria está así constituida de una comunidad de tradiciones e ideales. . . . La nación . . . es una integración humana animada de un espíritu nutrido de las mismas tradiciones y orientado hacia los mismos destinos."

2. Belaúnde, 14: "La fisonomía cultural resultante de la comunidad de tradiciones debe unirse al factor de una voluntad colectiva orientada hacia los mismos ideales para construir la nacionalidad."

3. Belaúnde, 16: "Repugna a la idea nacional no solo el anarquismo, el jacobinismo individualista y la primacía de lo económico sino también la idea de Imperio cuando supone una uniformidad rígida y el dominio de unos pueblos por otros; y el falso humanitarismo que pretende borrar las diferencias nacionales por el concepto de universalismo o cosmopolitismo utópico e informe."

4. Belaúnde, 16: "En lugar del individuo de Rousseau y de Marx, tenemos la familia que representa precisamente 'el culto de las tumbas y de las cunas': la familia que conserva el recuerdo de los antepasados y tiene la preocupación del porvenir; la familia cuyos derechos no proclamó la revolución del 89 y de la cual prescindió la falsa estructura política. La familia se integra en la comuna; y dentro de la comuna surge la integración económica y cultural de los gremios y de las instituciones: gremios e instituciones que se integran en la Nación cuya estructura les da estabilidad, desarrollo y asegura el porvenir."

5. Antoinette Burton, ed., *Archive Stories: Facts, Fictions, and the Writing of History* (Durham, NC: Duke University Press, 2005); Ann Laura Stoler, *Along the Archival Grain: Epistemic Anxieties and Colonial Common Sense* (Princeton, NJ: Princeton University Press, 2009).

6. Jenny Franchot, *Roads to Rome: The Antebellum Protestant Encounter with Catholicism* (Berkeley: University of California Press, 1994), 48. Franchot cites Reginald Horsman, *Race and Manifest Destiny: The Origins of American Racial Anglo-Saxonism* (Cambridge, MA: Harvard University Press, 1986), 239: Prescott "believed that Aztec heterogeneity is the polluted origin of the contaminated difference of the nineteenth-century Mexican, theorized by one editorial as a 'sickening mixture, consisting of such a conglomeration of Negroes and Rancheros, Mestizoes and Indians, with but a few Castilians.' Such mixtures confirmed not only the racial but also the religious purity of the Anglo-American reader."

7. Frank Tannenbaum, *Slave and Citizen* (New York: Alfred A. Knopf, 1946).

8. For an excellent overview of this historiography and how scholarship in the United States has progressed, see Alejandro de la Fuente, "From Slaves to Citizens? Tannenbaum and the Debates on Slavery, Emancipation, and Race Relations in Latin America," *International and Working-Class History* no. 77 (Spring 2010): 154–73. De la Fuente concludes, "The conflicts that created postemancipation societies were informed by expectations and by cultural and legal norms that had been formed under slavery. But this is not the same as claiming that 'slave systems' constitute 'the source' of modern race relations. On the other hand, citizenship was a contentious political construct subject to negotiation, not a fixed and unproblematic category of inclusion. Even after conquering the formal rights of citizens, a process that in many Latin American countries took decades, the struggles of the former slaves and their descendants were far from over. Citizenship meant little unless those rights could be claimed and exercised."

9. See, for example, Paulina Alberto, *Terms of Inclusion: Black Intellectuals in Twentieth Century Brazil* (Chapel Hill: University of North Carolina Press, 2011).

10. For a strong overview of this historiography, see, for example, John Charles Chasteen, *Born in Blood and Fire: A Concise History of Latin America* (Chapel Hill: University of North Carolina Press, 2006); Tulio Halperin Donghi, trans. John Charles Chasteen, *The Contemporary History of Latin America* (Durham, NC: Duke University Press, 1993).

11. Magnus Mörner, *Race Mixture in the History of Latin America* (Boston, MA: Little, Brown and Company, 1967). Mörner's work was ahead of its time in including African-descended populations in his analysis of mestizaje; James Lockhart, *Spanish Peru, 1532–1560: A Social History* (Madison: University of Wisconsin Press, 1968).

12. Several states stubbornly enforced these laws even after the Civil Rights Act, and they finally ended with the landmark 1967 civil rights case, *Loving v. Virginia*.

13. Magnus Mörner, *Race Mixture in the History of Latin America* (Boston, MA: Little, Brown and Company, 1967), 3.

14. Mörner, *Race Mixture*, 4.

15. See, for example, Patricia Seed, *To Love, Honor, and Obey in Colonial Mexico: Conflicts over Marriage Choice, 1574–1821* (Stanford, CA: Stanford University Press, 1988).

16. Mörner, *Race Mixture*, 39.

17. Mörner, *Race Mixture*, 87–88. Mörner cites a letter from Bolívar to his sister showing his "special affection for the obligatory Negro nanny," Hipólita.

18. Mário C. Vázquez, "Immigration and *Mestizaje* in Nineteenth-Century Peru," in *Race*

and Class in Latin America, ed. Magnus Mörner (New York: Columbia University Press, 1970), 73–95, 92–93.

19. Vázquez, "Immigration and *Mestizaje*," 95.

20. See, for example, Carl Degler, *Neither Black nor White: Slavery and Race Relations in Brazil and the United States* (Madison: University of Wisconsin Press, 1971); Thomas E. Skidmore, *Black into White: Race and Nationality in Brazilian Thought* (Durham, NC: Duke University Press, 1974); Jerry Dávila, *Diploma of Whiteness: Race and Social Policy in Brazil, 1917–1945* (Durham, NC: Duke University Press, 2003).

21. See, for example, Paulino Alberto, *Terms of Inclusion: Black Intellectuals in Twentieth-Century Brazil* (Chapel Hill: University of North Carolina Press, 2011); Kim D. Butler, *Freedoms Given, Freedoms Won: Afro-Brazilians in Post-Abolition São Paolo and Salvador* (New Brunswick, NJ: Rutgers University Press, 1998).

22. For example, see José Antonio del Busto Duthurburu, "El mestizaje en el Perú," in *Sobre el Perú: homenaje a José Agustín de la Puente Candamo*, eds. Margarita Guerra Martiniére, Oswaldo Holguín Callo and César Gutiérrez Muñoz (Lima: Fondo Editorial de la Pontificia Universidad Católica del Perú, 2002), 316: "Entre nosotros no hay discriminación racial (no hay deberes ni derechos diferentes entre las diversas razas diferentes); tampoco hay segregación racial (no existen instituciones paralelas para los grupos raciales distintos); pero sí hay prejuicio racial."

23. Frederick Bowser, *The African Slave in Colonial Peru, 1524–1650* (Stanford, CA: Stanford University Press, 1974), 7.

24. Matthew Restall, ed., *Beyond Black and Red: African-Native Relations in Colonial Latin America* (Albuquerque: University of New Mexico Press, 2005); Rachel Sarah O'Toole, *Bound Lives: Africans, Indians, and the Making of Race in Colonial Peru* (Pittsburgh, PA: University of Pittsburgh Press, 2012). For recent work locating the origins of mestizaje in colonial "castizaje" in Mexico, see Ben Vinson III, *Before Mestizaje: The Frontiers of Race and Caste in Colonial Mexico* (Cambridge: Cambridge University Press, 2017).

25. Frederick Bowser, *African Slave*, 321.

26. James Lockhart, *Spanish Peru, 1532–1560: A Social History* (Madison: University of Wisconsin Press, 1968).

27. Frederick Bowser, "Colonial Spanish America," in *Neither Slave nor Free: The Freedman of African Descent in the Slave Societies of the New World*, eds. David W. Cohen and Jack P. Greene (Baltimore, MD: Johns Hopkins University Press, 1972), 53.

28. Christine Hünefeldt, *Paying the Price of Freedom: Family and Labor among Lima's Slaves, 1800–1854* (Berkeley: University of California Press, 1994), 26.

29. Peter Blanchard, *Slavery and Abolition in Early Republican Peru* (Wilmington, DE: Scholarly Resources, 1992), 221. According to Blanchard, "By 1876 blacks and Asians together comprised only 4 percent of the Peruvian population. In Lima, in 1857, around 11 percent of the population of 90,000 was Black; the figure declined to just under 5 percent of a population in 1908, and to just under 5 percent of a population of 140,884 in 1908, and to 2 percent of 562,885 in 1940."

30. Aguirre, Carlos, *Breve Historia de la Esclavitud en el Perú: Una Herida Que No Deja de Sangrar* (Lima: Fondo Editorial del Congreso del Perú, 2005), 101.

31. See, for example, Ira Berlin, "From Creole to African: Atlantic Creoles and the Origins of African-American Society in Mainland North America," *William and Mary Quarterly* 53, no. 2 (1996): 251–88.

32. See, for example, Florencia Mallon, *The Defense of Community in Peru's Central Highlands: Peasant Struggle and Capitalist Transition, 1860–1940* (Princeton, NJ: Princeton University Press, 1983).

33. Jeffrey Gould, *To Die in This Way: Nicaraguan Indians and the Myth of Mestizaje, 1880–1965* (Durham, NC: Duke University Press, 1998), 10–11.

34. Ben Vinson III, *Before Mestizaje: The Frontiers of Race and Caste in Colonial Mexico* (New York: Cambridge University Press, 2018).

35. Milagros Denis-Rosario, *Drops of Inclusivity: Racial Formations and Meanings in Puerto Rican Society, 1898–1965* (Albany: State University of New York Press, 2022), 59. Denis-Rosario powerfully shows how the "Puerto Rican elite of the 1930s protected their culture against the American colonial apparatus by constructing an 'official' national identity that excluded African and indigenous people."

36. Mary Weismantel, *Cholas and Pishtacos: Stories of Race and Sex in the Andes* (Chicago, IL: University of Chicago Press, 2001), xxxi.

37. Marisol de la Cadena, *Indigenous Mestizos: The Politics of Race and Culture in Cuzco, Peru, 1919–1991.* (Durham, NC: Duke University Press, 2000), 9.

38. Maribel Arrelucea, ed., *La Libertad Inconclusa: Entorno a la Esclavitud, su Abolición y los Derechos Civiles* (Lima: CEDET, 2010). Political scientist Paola Galano Toro of ETH Zürich is conducting promising research on uneven state presence in marginalized communities, which she presented at the Conference on Latin American History in December 2021, titled "Whose State, Whose Nation? Uneven States and Nations in Latin America."

39. Michel-Rolph Trouillot, *Silencing the Past: Power and the Production of History* (Boston, MA: Beacon Press, 1995), 26.

40. Heidi Carolyn Feldman, *Black Rhythms of Peru: Reviving African Musical Heritage in the Black Pacific* (Middletown, CT: Wesleyan University Press, 2006).

41. Marisa J. Fuentes, *Dispossessed Lives: Enslaved Women, Violence, and the Archive* (Philadelphia: University of Pennsylvania Press, 2016), 5.

42. Sadiya V. Hartman, *Scenes of Subjection: Terror, Slavery, and Self-Making in Nineteenth-Century America* (Oxford: Oxford University Press, 1997), 4.

43. Juliet Hooker, *Theorizing Race in the Americas: Douglass, Sarmiento, Du Bois, and Vasconcelos* (Oxford: Oxford University Press, 2017), 156.

44. See, for example, Ada Ferrer, *Insurgent Cuba: Race, Nation, and Revolution, 1868–1898* (Chapel Hill: University of North Carolina Press, 1999); Aline Helg, *Our Rightful Share: The Afro-Cuban Struggle for Equality, 1886–1912* (Chapel Hill: University of North Carolina Press, 1995); Kim D. Butler, *Freedoms Given, Freedoms Won: Afro-Brazilians in Post-Abolition São Paolo and Salvador* (New Brunswick, NJ: Rutgers University Press, 1998); Paulino Alberto, *Terms of Inclusion: Black Intellectuals in Twentieth-Century Brazil* (Chapel Hill: University of North Carolina Press, 2011); Alejandra M. Bronfman, *Measures of Equality: Social Science, Citizenship, and Race in Cuba, 1902–1940* (Chapel Hill: University of North Carolina Press, 2005); Alejandro de la Fuente, *A Nation for All: Race, Inequality, and Politics in Twentieth-Century Cuba* (Chapel Hill: University of North Carolina Press, 2001).

45. George Reid Andrews, *Afro-Latin America, 1800–2000* (Oxford: Oxford University Press, 2004). See also Peter Blanchard, *Under the Flags of Freedom: Slave Soldiers and the Wars of Independence in Spanish South America* (Pittsburgh, PA: University of Pittsburgh Press, 2008).

46. Marixa Lasso, *Myths of Harmony: Race and Republicanism during the Age of Revolution, Colombia, 1795–1831* (Pittsburgh, PA: University of Pittsburgh Press, 2007), 14.

47. Erika Denise Edwards, *Hiding in Plain Sight: Black Women, the Law, and the Making of a White Argentine Republic* (Tuscaloosa: University of Alabama Press, 2020), 2–3.

48. Edwards, *Hiding in Plain Sight.*

49. Heidi Carolyn Feldman, *Black Rhythms of Peru: Reviving African Musical Heritage in the Black Pacific* (Middletown, CT: Wesleyan University Press, 2006).

50. Tanya Golash-Boza, *Yo Soy Negro: Blackness in Peru* (Gainesville: University Press of Florida, 2011).

51. See, for example, Eshe Lewis and John Thomas, "'Me Gritaron Negra': The Emergence and Development of the Afro-descendant Women's Movement in Peru," *Journal of International Women's Studies* 20, no. 8 (October 2019): 18–39.

52. Golash-Boza, *Yo Soy Negro*, 33.

53. Golash-Boza, *Yo Soy Negro*, 3.

54. Humberto Rodríguez Pastor, *Negritud: Afroperuanos: Resistencia y Existencia* (Lima: Centro de Desarrollo Étnico, 2008), 49–51.

55. Jorge Basadre, *Historia de la República de Perú (1822–1933) Tomo IV* (Lima: Editorial Universitaria, 2005), 159.

56. Escribano Público Manuel Rebolledo, *Notarios—Protocolos de 1854–1885*, 7 de marzo de 1884, ARP. All translations by the author unless otherwise noted.

57. Rebolledo, *Notarios*, 17 de marzo de 1884, folios 142 y 148. ARP; Escribano Público Manuel Rebolledo, "Notarios: Protocolos del 1854–1855," leg. 239. exp. 5189 (1855), folio 1, Archivo Regional de Piura (ARP).

58. Maribel Arrelucea, ed., *La Libertad Inconclusa: Entorno a la Esclavitud, Su Abolición y los Derechos Civiles* (Lima: CEDET, 2010).

59. Trouillot, *Silencing the Past*, 26.

60. See, for example, Denys Cuche, *Poder Blanco y Resistencia Negro en el Perú: Un Estudio sobre la Condición Social del Negro en el Peru Después de la Abolición de la Esclavitud* (Lima: Instituto Nacional de Cultura, 1975); Benjamin Vicuña MacKenna, *Historia de la Campaña de Lima, 1880–1881* (Santiago: Ed. Rafael Jover, 1881). In contrast with these accounts, Vincent Peloso has shown the elite narratives that did include Afro-Peruvian roles, which depicted Afro-Peruvian women as blood-thirsty: Vincent C. Peloso, "Racial Conflict and Identity Crisis in Wartime Peru: Revisiting the Cañete Massacre of 1881," *Social Identities* 11, no. 5 (2005).

61. See, for example, Rubén Quiroz Ávila, *La Razón Racial. Clemente Palma y el Racismo a Fines del Siglo XIX* (Lima: Universidad Científica del Sur, 2015).

62. For more on Latin American eugenics, see Nancy Leys Stepan, *The Hour of Eugenics: Race, Gender, and Nation in Latin America* (Ithaca, NY: Cornell University Press, 1991). For more on the "cult of mestizaje" in early twentieth-century Latin America, see Nancy P. Appelbaum, Anne S. Machperson, and Karin Alejandra Rosemblatt, eds., *Race and Nation in Modern Latin America* (Chapel Hill: University of North Carolina Press, 2003).

1. Chapter 1

Quoted in Eduardo Antonio Rodríguez Flores, "El Ritmo del Retraso. La Construcción del Afrodescendiente como Mecanismo Deslegitimador de la Política en *Zamacueca Política* (1859)," (Lima: Universidad Peruana de Ciencias Aplicadas, Juegos Florales, 2015), 2.

2. Antonio Rodríguez Flores, "El Ritmo del Retraso," 4.

3. Cecilia Valenzuela,"Ramón Castilla: Trece Obras Importantes a 147 Años de Su Muerte," May 30, 2014, Peru 21 (website).

4. Carlos Aguirre, *The Criminals of Lima and Their Worlds* (Durham, NC: Duke University Press, 2005), 25.

5. Paul Gootenberg, *Between Silver and Guano: Commercial Policy and the State in Postindependence Peru* (Princeton, NJ: Princeton University Press, 1989), 21.

6. Carlos Aguirre, *The Criminals of Lima*, 3.

7. A similar argument is made in Nancy Appelbaum, Anne MacPherson, and Karin A. Rosemblatt, eds., *Race and Nation in Modern Latin America* (Chapel Hill: University of North Carolina Press, 2003).

8. Benedict Anderson, *Imagined Communities: Reflections on the Origin and Spread of Nationalism* (New York: Verso, 1983).

9. John Charles Chasteen and Sara Castro-Klarén, eds., *Beyond Imagined Communities: Reading and Writing the Nation in Nineteenth-Century Latin America* (Baltimore, MD: Johns Hopkins University Press, 2003), xv.

10. Florencia Mallon, *Peasant and Nation: The Making of Postcolonial Mexico and Peru* (Berkeley: University of California Press, 1995), 90. Mallon defines "the idea of discourse as the product of an open-ended process of cultural, political, and ideological interaction. Particular ideas, concepts, or perceptions can become articulated with each other, as elements, either by emphasizing lines of similarity or by using difference to construct boundaries of antagonism."

11. Etienne Balibar and Immanuel Wallerstein, *Race, Nation, Class: Ambiguous Identities* (New York: Verso, 1991), 214.

12. Jorge Basadre, *Perú Independiente* (Lima: El Comercio, 2010), Biblioteca Nacional del Perú (BNP), sala de investigaciones, 165–66.

13. Maribel Arrelucea Barrantes y Jesús Cosamalón Aguilar, *La Presencia Afrodescendiente en el Perú*, 124.

14. Blanchard, *Slavery and Abolition*, 220.

15. Blanchard, *Slavery and Abolition*, 14.

16. *Ley Orgánica de Elecciones Dada por el Congreso de 1860* (Lima: Imprenta del Gobierno por Eusebio Aranda, 1861), BNP, sala de investigaciones.

17. Barrantes y Aguilar, *La Presencia Afrodescendiente*, 127.

18. El Libertador Ramón Castilla, *Constitución Política del Perú*, 10 de noviembre de 1860, título XVI, articulo 123, Archivo digital de la legislación del Perú (website).

19. *La Sociedad de Fundadores de la Independencia del Perú se da la Siguiente Constitución* (Lima: Impreso por Francisco Solis, 1861), BNP, sala de investigaciones.

20. Christine Hünefeldt, *Paying the Price of Freedom: Family and Labor among Lima's Slaves, 1800–1854* (Berkeley: University of California Press, 1994), 86, 26.

21. *La Sociedad de Fundadores.*

22. *La Sociedad de Fundadores*, titulo III.

23. *La Sociedad de Fundadores*, titulo XVI.

24. Dain Borges, "'Puffy, Ugly, Slothful, and Inert': Degeneration in Brazilian Social Thought, 1880–1940," *Journal of Latin American Studies* 25, no. 2 (May 1993): 23–46.

25. Quoted in Carlos Aguirre, *The Criminals of Lima and Their Worlds*, 25.

26. Denys Cuche, *Poder Blanco y Resistencia Negro en el Perú: Un Estudio sobre la Condición Social del Negro en el Perú después de la Abolición de la Esclavitud* (Lima: Instituto Nacional de Cultura, 1975), 150. Cuche points out that "pierolistas identified themselves so much with Blacks that the nickname 'zambo' was given to any of his followers."

27. *La América,* April 5, 1862, BNP, hemeroteca.

28. *La América,* April 5, 1862, BNP, hemeroteca.

29. See, for example, Roger Alan Kittleson, *The Practice of Politics in Postcolonial Brazil: Porto Alegre, 1845–1895* (Pittsburgh, PA: University of Pittsburgh Press, 2006); Stanley Blake, *The Vigorous Core of Our Nationality: Race and Regional Identity in Northeastern Brazil* (Pittsburgh, PA: University of Pittsburgh Press, 2011). A similar theme appeared in Brazilian newspapers in the decades following its independence, as analyzed in Jeffrey Mosher, "Political Mobilization, Party Ideology, and Lusophobia in Nineteenth-Century Brazil: Pernambuco, 1822–1850," *Hispanic American Historical Review* 80, no. 4 (2000): 881–912.

30. Francisco de P. G. Vigil, "Ojeada Comparativa al Imperio de Brasil," *La América,* June 4, 1862. BNP, Hemeroteca.

31. de P. G. Vigil, "Ojeada Comparativa al Imperio de Brasil."

32. de P. G. Vigil, "Ojeada Comparativa al Imperio de Brasil."

33. de P. G. Vigil, "Ojeada Comparativa al Imperio de Brasil."

34. "The Spanish-Peruvian Difficulty," *New York Times,* March 12, 1865. An account of the Talambó incident appeared in the Peruvian newspaper *El Peruano* on April 17, 1864.

35. "Circular a los Gobiernos de América," *El Peruano,* August 24, 1861, BNP, hemeroteca.

36. "Circular a los Gobiernos de América," *El Peruano,* August 24, 1861, BNP, hemeroteca.

37. "Circular a los Gobiernos de América."

38. *La América,* April 5, 1862.

39. *La América,* April 5, 1862.

40. Hilda Sabato, *Republics of the New World: The Revolutionary Political Experiment in Nineteenth-Century Latin America* (Princeton: Princeton University Press, 2018).

41. Sabato, *Republics of the New World,* 9.

42. *La América,* April 5, 1862: "La raza de nuestros padres no ha degenerado todavía; aún viven los restos de los héroes de Junín y Ayacucho, y la memoria reciente de sus hazañas, templará los ánimos de la presente generación."

43. *La América,* April 5, 1862.

44. *La América,* April 5, 1862.

45. See, for example, Susan Martín-Márquez, *Disorientations: Spanish Colonialism in Africa and the Performance of Identity* (New Haven, CT: Yale University Press, 2008).

46. Carlos Aguirre provides further evidence of this hierarchy in relation to criminology in 1860s Lima in *The Criminals of Lima and Their Worlds.*

47. *La América,* April 5, 1862.

48. Nicolás de Piérola, *Declaración de Principios del Partido Demócrata* (Lima: Tip. La Voce D'Italia, 1912), 8–9.

49. *La América,* April 9, 1862.

50. *La América,* April 9, 1862.

51. *La America,* April 16, 1862.

52. *La América,* April 9, 1862: "A Washington: ¡Jenio de Libertad! En paz y en guerra / Tipo de mas sublime patriotismo / Que el poder recibiste de Dios mismo / De crear un Eden sobre la tierra / . . . Mas ¡Que veo! Tu sombra conturbada / Al rumor de la guerra fratricida / Lanza sobre la patria una mirada / Y con voz poderosa y conmovida: / ¡Union (dice) los hombres son hermanos, / También acá en el cielo hay africanos."

53. *La América,* April 23, 1862.

54. "La Unión de las Repúblicas Americanas," *La America*, May 17, 1862.

55. *La America*, May 10, 1862. The closing lines of the article state, "Por Presidente Lincoln. ¡Por los Estados Unidos de America! ¡Por su pacificación con el triunfo de libertad!"

56. *La América*, May 31, 1862.

57. *La América*, May 31, 1862. "¿Porque razón se toma solamente a la gente de poncho o bluza y no a los que se titulan *decentes*? ¿Por qué? porque los primeros no tienen titulo para ser respetados: al paso que los segundos poseen al señor D. Dinero que los hace sagrados para los reclutadores."

58. *La América*, May 31, 1862.

59. Peter Beattie, *The Tribute of Blood: Army, Honor, Race, and Nation in Brazil, 1864–1945* (Durham, NC: Duke University Press, 2001), 5.

60. Beattie, *The Tribute of Blood*, 13.

61. *La América*, June 4, 1862: "Formando todos los hombres parte de la asociación política, están obligados civil y moralmente a la defensa de su patria: y todos en armonía deben trabajar porque se la tribute el debido respeto: de aqui proviene la contribución llamada 'de sangre' y que no tiene otro objeto que el enunciado."

62. Emilio Castelar, *La America*, June 7, 1862.

63. Emilio Castelar, *La America*, June 7, 1862.

64. *La América*, June 7, 1862.

65. *La América*, June 7, 1862.

66. I have written on this topic in more detail in "The Rise of APRA in Peru: Victor Raúl Haya de la Torre and Inter-American Intellectual Connections, 1918–1935," *Latin Americanist* 58, no.1 (March 2014): 77–88.

67. M. Palma, "Ensayo sobre los Principios de Economía Política en Sus Relaciones con las Riquezas del Peru," *La América*, December 20, 1862.

68. Jorge Basadre, *La Iniciación de la República: Tomo Primero* (Lima: Fondo Editorial de la UNMSM, 2002), 100–101. Basadre includes the newspapers *La Democracia, El Pedestal de la Libertad, La República*, and *El Perú* as publications with similar objectives from this era. The 1860s saw an increase in associations aimed at maintaining "public agitation," such as "la Sociedad Unión Americana, la Sociedad Liberal Central, la Sociedad Defensores de la Independencia, la Sociedad Fundadores de la Independencia."

69. Basadre, *La Iniciación de la República*.

70. Ricardo Rosell, "Canto a la Patria," *La América*, December 13, 1862.

Chapter 2

1. Ida Pfeiffer, *A Lady's Second Journey round the World from London to the Cape of Good Hope, Borneo, Java, Sumatra, Celebes, Ceram, the Moluccas, etc., California, Panama, Peru, Ecuador, and the United States* (New York: Harper and Brothers, 1856), 349–50.

2. See, for example, Deborah Poole, *Vision, Race, and Modernity: A Visual Economy of the Andean Image World* (Princeton, NJ: Princeton University Press, 1997), 149–50. Poole analyzes the writings of elite journalist Manuel Anastasio Fuentes, known as "El Murciélago." As the head of Peru's department of statistics in the 1870s, Fuentes "was concerned on some level to correct European misperceptions of his own country. . . . He needed to prove that Peruvians, despite their different origins and language, spoke the same language of beauty, taste, and distinction as the cultivated French or British citizen."

3. See, for example, Mary Graham, *Journal of a Residence in Chile during the Year 1822*

(Charlottesville: University of Virginia Press, 2003); John Mawe, *Travels in the Interior of Brazil* (London: Longman, Hurst, Rees, Orme, and Brown, 1812).

4. Vincent Peloso and José Ragas, "Estadística y población en el Perú postcolonial: el desconocido censo de Lima de 1860," *Histórica* XXV, no. 2 (2001): 287.

5. Mark Thurner, *From Two Republics to One Divided: Contradictions of Postcolonial Nationmaking in Andean Peru* (Durham, NC: Duke University Press, 2006), 44.

6. Christine Hünefeldt, *Paying the Price of Freedom: Family and Labor among Lima's Slaves, 1800–1854* (Berkeley: University of California Press, 1994), 194.

7. Thurner, *From Two Republics to One Divided.*

8. Rachel Sarah O'Toole, *Bound Lives: Africans, Indians, and the Making of Race in Colonial Peru* (Pittsburgh: University of Pittsburgh Press, 2012), 164–65.

9. Humberto Rodríguez Pastor, *Negritud: Afroperuanos Existencia y Resistencia* (Lima: Centro de Desarrollo Étnico, 2008), 31. Rodríguez Pastor has analyzed similar records to show that in 1857, 11.3 percent of Lima's population identified as negro or "Black." By 1876, the year of Peru's first "modern" national census, this number dropped to 9.4 percent of the city's population.

10. Hünefeldt notes that enslaved Afro-Peruvian women claimed mestizaje ("miscegenation") with white men to obtain the freedom of their children. The embarrassment and financial losses these legal claims caused likely made white men in Lima reluctant to admit that such sexual relations were common.

11. Iñigo L. García-Bryce, *Crafting the Republic: Lima's Artisans and Nation Building in Peru, 1821–1879* (Albuquerque: University of New Mexico Press, 2004), 9.

12. Jesús A. Cosamalón Aguilar, "Mestizaje e Interrelación Social en el Tránsito de la Sociedad de las Castas a la República Liberal. Lima, 1790–1860," in *El Nudo del Imperio: Independencia y Democracia en el Perú*, eds. Carmen McEvoy, Mauricio Novoa, and Elías Palti (Lima: Instituto Francés de Estudios Andinos, 2012), 353.

13. Cosamalón Aguilar, "Mestizaje e Interrelación Social," 390.

14. Humberto Rodríguez Pastor, *Negritud: Afroperuanos Resistencia y Existencia* (Lima: Centro de Desarrollo Étnico, 2008), 31, 40.

15. Carlos Aguirre, "Silencio y Ecos: La Historia y el legado de la abolición de la esclavitud en Haití y el Perú," in *La Libertad Inconclusa: Entorno a la esclavitud, su abolición y los derechos civiles*, ed. Maribel Arrelucea, (Lima: Centro de Desarrollo Étnico, 2010), 39.

16. Vincent Peloso and José Ragas, "Estadística y Población en el Perú Postcolonial: El Desconocido Censo de Lima de 1860," *Histórica* XXV, no. 2 (2001): 281.

17. Jesús A. Cosamalón Aguilar, "Mestizaje e Interrelación Social en el Tránsito de la Sociedad de las Castas a la República Liberal. Lima, 1790–1860," in *El Nudo del Imperio: Independencia y Democracia en el Perú*, eds. Carmen McEvoy, Mauricio Novoa, Elías Palti, (Lima: Instituto Francés de Estudios Andinos, 2012), 343–67.

18. Paul Gootenberg, "Population and Ethnicity in Early Republican Peru: Some Revisions," *Latin American Research Review* 26, no.3 (1991): 109–57, 109.

19. Gootenberg, "Population and Ethnicity in Early Republican Peru."

20. Gootenberg, "Population and Ethnicity." Article 41 of the constitution stated that the exercise of citizenship would be suspended for several reasons including number six: "Por el tráfico de esclavos, cualquiera que sea el lugar donde se haga."

21. Gracia G. Solis, "Reading Spaces: Nation and Popular Learning in Nineteenth-Century Lima" (PhD diss., Florida International University, 2017), 100.

22. Solis, "Reading Spaces," 109.

23. Patricia Seed, "The Social Dimensions of Race: Mexico City 1753," *Hispanic American Historical Review* 62, no. 4 (November 1982): 569–606; R. Douglas Cope, *The Limits of Racial Domination: Plebian Society in Colonial Mexico City, 1660–172* (Madison: University of Wisconsin Press, 1994).

24. Rachel Sarah O'Toole, *Bound Lives: Africans, Indians, and the Making of Race in Colonial Peru* (Pittsburgh, PA: University of Pittsburgh Press, 2012).

25. Christine Hunefeldt, *Liberalism in the Bedroom: Quarreling Spouses in Nineteenth-Century Lima* (University Park: Pennsylvania State University Press, 2000), 51.

26. Prisca Gayles and Diane Ghogomu, "The Social Economy of Afro-Argentines and African Immigrants in Buenos Aires," in *The Black Social Economy in the Americas: Exploring Diverse Community-Based Markets*, ed. Caroline Shenaz Hossein (New York: Palgrave MacMillan, 2018), 119–42.

27. Adam Warren, *Medicine and Politics in Colonial Peru* (Pittsburgh: University of Pittsburgh Press, 2008), 170. These *naciones* included Minas, Cabundan, Cangaes, Congos, and Musanga. Historian Rachel Sarah O'Toole calls these *casta* identities in her 2012 book *Bound Lives: Africans, Indians, and the Making of Race in Colonial Peru* (Pittsburgh: University of Pittsburgh Press, 2012).

28. Denys Cuche, *Poder Blanco y Resistencia Negro en el Perú: Un Estudio sobre la Condición Social del Negro en el Peru después de la Abolición de la Esclavitud* (Lima: Instituto Nacional de Cultura, 1975), 72.

29. Cuche, *Poder Blanco y Resistencia Negra*, 13.

30. Cuche, *Poder Blanco y Resistencia Negra*, 9. This figure combines the four categories that connote African descent: mulato, negro, zambo, and pardo. Thirteen percent of the city's artisans (based on a sampling of shoemakers, carpenters, tailors, and tanners) were categorized as mestizo, 16 percent as indio, 2 percent as chino, 25 percent as blanco, and 1 percent as cholo.

31. More specifically, the painting's survival in the earthquakes of October 1687 led to its veneration as a protector of the city and to an annual procession that was institutionalized by the church and civil society in 1771. For more on this process and the cultural appropriation involved, see Julia Costilla, "Una Práctica Negra Que Ha Ganado a los Blancos: Símbolo, Historia y Devotos en el Culto al Señor de los Milagros de Lima (siglos xix–xxi)," *Anthropologica* xxxiv, no. 36 (2016):149–76.

32. Steve Stein, *Lima Obrera 1900–1930, Tomo I* (Lima: Ediciones El Virrey, 1986), 225: Stein cites an article from the October 16, 1925, issue of *El Mundial*, in which Enrique Acosta Salas explained that "después ya entraron una de gente blanca e hicieron una sociedad para ser hermanos del Señor de los Milagros y decían que [el que] había pintado al Señor de los Milagros era un blanco, una de sociedad, blanca."

33. Peter Blanchard, *The Origins of the Peruvian Labor Movement, 1883–1919* (Pittsburgh, PA: University of Pittsburgh Press, 1982). Blanchard cites an article from an 1889 edition of the Lima newspaper *El Nacional* that makes this claim. However, the brotherhood, as it was initially called, appears to have become a "mutual aid society" for women in 1919, according to government documents accessed by Carlos Forment (below).

34. Carlos A. Forment, *Democracy in Latin America: 1760–1900, Volume I: Civic Selfhood and Public Life in Mexico and Peru* (Chicago: University of Chicago Press, 2003), 163.

35. García-Bryce, *Crafting the Republic*, 59.

36. García-Bryce, *Crafting the Republic*, 59.

37. García-Bryce, *Crafting the Republic*, 315.

38. García-Bryce, *Crafting the Republic*, 316.

39. Carlos Aguirre and Peter Blanchard agree that self-manumission was the most effective weapon in the fight against slavery. Aguirre, *Agentes de Su Propia Libertad: Los Esclavos de Lima y la Desintegración de la Esclavitud, 1821–1854* (Lima: Pontificia Universidad Católica del Perú, 1993), 232–33; Peter Blanchard, *Slavery and Abolition in Early Republican Peru* (Wilmington, NC: SR Books, 1992). Although Aguirre documents cases in which cofradías served as vehicles toward accessing freedom, he adds that slaves trusted individual strategies more.

40. Peter Blanchard, *The Origins of the Peruvian Labor Movement*, 15. Blanchard's primary sources do not reveal ethnoracial concerns among labor agitators, but his complete omission of Afro-Peruvian laborers is surprising given his 1992 book, *Slavery and Abolition in Early Republican Peru.*

41. *Censo General de Lima 1860: Libro 1, Cuartel Primero*, folios 91–97, AHML.

42. *Censo General de Lima 1860: Libro 1, Cuartel Primero*, folio 94, AHML.

43. For more on racial purity and strategic marriage alliances to achieve "casta dominance" in nineteenth-century Peru, see David Nugent, *Modernity at the Edges of Empire: State, Individual, and Nation in the Northern Peruvian Andes, 1885–1935* (Stanford, CA: Stanford University Press, 1997).

44. As defined in O'Toole, *Bound Lives*, 225.

45. O'Toole, *Bound Lives.*

46. Hünefeldt, *Liberalism in the Bedroom*, 51.

47. *Censo General de Lima 1860: Libro 3, Cuartel Tercero. Distrito Quinto: Calle de San Ysidro*, folios 119–32, AHML.

48. Carlos Aguirre, "Silencio y Ecos," 35. I discuss how bandoleros in the northern region of Piura became the protagonists of national folklore in chapter 5.

49. Jesús Cosamalón Aguilar also categorizes chinos as Afro-Peruvians.

50. Rodríguez Pastor, *Negritud*, 198.

51. *Censo General de Lima 1860*, folios 119–32, AHML.

52. *Censo General de Lima 1860*, folio 127, AHML.

53. *Censo General de Lima 1860*, folio 126, AHML.

54. *Censo General de Lima 1860*, folio 126, AHML.

55. *Censo General de Lima 1866: Cuartel Tercero*, folios 26–33, AHML.

56. *Censo General de Lima 1866: Cuartel Tercero*, folio 30, AHML.

57. *Censo General de Lima 1866: Cuartel Tercero*, folio 31, AHML.

58. *Censo General de Lima 1866: Cuartel Tercero*, folio 30, AHML.

59. *Censo General de Lima 1866: Cuartel Tercero*, folios 33, 30, 28, AHML. In the box used to indicate if the person could read, census officials wrote in either "Aprendiendo" or "A," presumably for "Aprendiendo."

60. Both Carlos Aguirre and Rodríguez Pastor emphasize this point.

61. *Censo General de Lima 1860: Libro 3, Cuartel Tercero. Distrito Quinto: Calle de San Ysidro*, folio 130, AHML.

62. *Censo General de Lima 1860*, folio 123, AHML.

63. Thirty-one of the fifty-two people who identified as Black on Calle San Ysidro were Lima natives.

64. *Censo General de Lima 1860: Libro 3, Cuartel Tercero. Distrito Quinto: Calle de San Ysidro*, folios 119–32, AHML.

65. *Censo General de Lima 1866: Cuartel Tercero*, folios 26–33, AHML.

66. Rachel Sarah O'Toole, *Bound Lives: Africans, Indians, and the Making of Race in Colonial Peru* (Pittsburgh, PA: University of Pittsburgh Press, 2012), 224.

67. Maribel Arrelucea Barrantes, *Replanteando la Esclavitud: Estudios de Etnicidad y Género en Lima Borbónica* (Lima: CEDET, 2009); José Ramón Jouve Martín, *Esclavos de la Ciudad Letrada: Esclavitud, Escritura y Colonialismo en Lima (1650–1700)* (Lima: Instituto de Estudios Peruanos, 2005).

68. *Censo General de Lima 1866: Cuartel Tercero*, folios 26–33, AHML.

69. *Censo General de Lima 1866: Cuartel Tercero*, folios 28–29, AHML.

70. *Censo General de Lima 1866: Cuartel Tercero*, folios 26–30, AHML.

71. *Censo General de Lima 1866: Cuartel Tercero*, folio 29, AHML.

72. Jesús Cosamalón Aguilar, "Mestizaje e Interrelación Social en el Tránsito de la Sociedad de las Castas a la República Liberal. Lima, 1790–1860," 355.

73. *Censo General de Lima 1866: Cuartel Tercero*, folios 31–33, AHML.

74. *Censo General de Lima 1866: Cuartel Tercero*, folios 31–33, AHML.

75. *Censo General de Lima 1866: Cuartel Tercero*, folios 31–32, AHML.

76. *Censo General de Lima 1860: Libro* 3, Cuartel Tercero. Distrito Quinto: Calle de San Ysidro, folios 119–32, and *Censo General de Lima 1866: Cuartel Tercero*, folios 26–33, AHML.

77. José Ramón Jouve Martín, *Esclavos de la Ciudad Letrada: Esclavitud, Escritura y Colonialismo en Lima (1650–1700)* (Lima: Instituto de Estudios Peruanos, 2005).

78. O'Toole, *Bound Lives*, 163.

79. Carlos Aguirre, *The Criminals of Lima and Their Worlds* (Durham, NC: Duke University Press, 2005), 33.

80. Jorge Basadre, *Perú Independiente* (Lima: El Comercio, 2010), 151.

81. Cosamalón Aguilar, "Mestizaje e Interrelación Social," 351.

Chapter 3

1. Francisco Rateci, *Al Señor Director de Estadística en el Ministerio del Gobierno*, Julio 15 de 1878, archivo General de la Nación Peruana (AGP). 79681 (H-6-409) (F. 712, F. 781–83): "En Chincha, como en los demás territorios de la costa del Perú, bañados por ríos, se forman fácilmente humedades y pantanos, con especialidad en los lugares bajos e inmediatos al mar, cuyas emanaciones o efluvios esparcidos en el aire atmosférico y puesto en contacto de la economía animal, ocasionan las enfermedades endémicas, conocidas en todas partes con el nombre de fiebres palúdicas. En Chincha, además de esos focos comunes de infección, existen otros no menos insalubres y principalmente en la campiña de Chincha Alta. . . . Para concluir añadiré algo muy útil para el bienestar de los habitantes de Chincha. Si en Chincha se practicara zanjones [*sic*] de desagüe en las inmediaciones del mar, si se limitaran los estanques de líquidos comprimidos en la campiña, si al pueblo se le proporcionase agua limpia que beber, si las condiciones higiénicas pudiesen mejorarse, y por fin si se educasen las masas, desaparecerían un gran número de enfermedades y la mortalidad disminuiría principalmente en los niños."

2. Eduardo Huárag Álvarez, ed., *Los Afrodescendientes en el Perú Republicano* (Lima: Pontificia Universidad Católica del Perú, Instituto Riva-Agüero, 2014), 50–51.

3. Huárag Álvarez, ed., *Los Afrodescendientes*, 54.

4. F. Arancivia, Ingeniero del Estado, "Río de Chincha," *Informes de los Ingenieros* (Lima: 26 de junio de 1899), 442–45, in Sr. Edilberto Castillo, *Anales de las Obras Públicas del Perú, Año 1899* (Lima: Imprenta Torres Aguirre, Union 150), 1900.

5. Heidi Carolyn Feldman, *Black Rhythms of Peru: Reviving African Musical Heritage in the Black Pacific* (Middletown, CT: Wesleyan University Press, 2006), 3: "From 1593 on, Blacks made up half the population of Lima, and they outnumbered Whites nationwide by 1650. However, in the 1940 census (the last to include racial data), Blacks apparently had declined to an estimated 0.47 percent of the country's population. . . . . By the twentieth century, many Black Peruvians demonstrated little sense of belonging to an African diaspora."

6. George Reid Andrews, *The Afro-Argentines of Buenos Aires, 1800–1900* (Madison: University of Wisconsin Press, 1980), 79. Andrews summarizes previous explanations of the demographic decline of Afro-Argentines, which rest on little documentary evidence. He also points out that "North and South American censuses have demonstrated a consistent tendency to underenumerate black people" for a variety of reasons, including Black fear of census takers and the difficulty census officials faced in accessing marginal "black neighborhoods."

7. Theodor W. Cohen, *Finding Afro-Mexico: Race and Nation after the Revolution* (Cambridge: Cambridge University Press, 2020), 5.

8. Eduardo A. Zimmermann, "Racial Ideas and Social Reform: Argentina, 1890–1916," *Hispanic American Historical Review* 72, no. 1 (February 1992), 23–46, 23.

9. Juliet Hooker, *Theorizing Race in the Americas: Douglass, Sarmiento, Du Bois, and Vasconcelos* (Oxford: Oxford University Press, 2017), 5.

10. J. L. Hochschild and B. M. Powell, "Racial Reorganization and the United States Census 1850–1930: Mulattoes, Half-Breeds, Mixed Parentage, Hindoos, and the Mexican Race," *Studies in American Political Development* 22, no.1, (2008): 59–96.

11. Hochschild and Powell, "Racial Reorganization."

12. Quoted in Alida Diaz, *El Censo General de 1876 en el Perú*, Seminario de historia rural andina, (Lima: Universidad Nacional Mayor de San Marcos, 1975) 25–26: "Cinco subdivisiones: blanca, india, negra, mestiza, asiática. Estos datos tenían que obtenerse con la mayor precaución para no herir la susceptibilidad de las personas, especialmente, con la cuarta subdivisión que comprendía todas las mezclas sin distinción."

13. Rómulo Eyzaguirre, Jefe de la Sección de Demografía, *Decretos y Resoluciones Relativos al Censo de la Provincia de Lima 1908, Tomo I* (4 de enero de 1908), Decretado y Levantado durante la Administración del Excmo. Señor don José Pardo (Lima: Imprenta de "La Opinión Nacional" Calle Correo 194, 1915), 12–13, BML.

14. Rómulo Eyzaguirre, *Decretos y Resoluciones Relativos al Censo de la Provincia de Lima 1908*, 19–27.

15. The census of 1908 asked residents to identify as "B. por Blanco, I. por Indio, M. por Mestizo, N. por Negro y A por Amarillo."

16. Eyzaguirre, *Decretos y Resoluciones Relativos*, 90–91.

17. Eyzaguirre, *Decretos y Resoluciones Relativos*, 93.

18. Robert L. Sanchez, "Black Mosaic: The Assimilation and Marginalization of Afro-Peruvians in Post-Abolition Peru, 1854–1930" (PhD diss., University of Illinois at Urbana-Champaign, 2008), 77.

19. Enrique Leon Garcia, "Las Razas en Lima: Estudio Demográfico," (PhD diss., Facultad de Medicina, Universidad Nacional Mayor de San Marcos, 1909), 15.

20. Garcia, "Las Razas en Lima," 124–25.

21. Garcia, "Las Razas en Lima," 127.

22. Garcia, "Las Razas en Lima, 125.

23. Erika Denise Edwards, *Hiding in Plain Sight: Black Women, the Law, and the Making of a White Argentine Republic* (Tuscaloosa: University of Alabama Press, 2020).

24. Garcia, "Las Razas en Lima," 125.

25. George Reid Andrews, *The Afro-Argentines of Buenos Aires*, 73: Andrews points out that this "Black fertility was slightly higher than white, but not enough to overcome the differential between the two races' infant mortality." This does not seem to be the case for Peru, according to the census's accompanying analysis.

26. García, "Las Razas en Lima," 127.

27. Marisol de la Cadena, "Silent Racism and Intellectual Superiority in Peru," *Bulletin of Latin American Research* 17, no. 2, (1998): 156, 151.

28. Humberto Rodríguez Pastor, *Negritud: Afroperuanos: Resistencia y Existencia* (Lima: CEDET 2008), 40. Rodríguez Pastor provides a graph demonstrating census findings that show this decline was surpassed only by that which occurred between the censuses of 1614 and 1790, when the percentage of Blacks decreased from 39.3 percent to 17.1 percent of the city's population.

29. García, "Las Razas en Lima," 15.

30. García, "Las Razas en Lima," 15.

31. Nancy Appelbaum, Anne MacPherson, and Karin A. Rosemblatt, eds., *Race and Nation in Modern Latin America* (Chapel Hill: University of North Carolina Press, 2003), 8–9. This volume's introduction argues that the "cult of the mestizo" coincided with the rise of indigenismo in the 1920s, although Peruvian indigenistas thought maintaining "pure" Indigenous ancestry was preferable to racial mixing.

32. García, "Las Razas en Lima," 16–17.

33. *Registro de Bautizos de 1854*, Catedral de Chulucanas, Parroquia de Frías, legajo 12-B, folios 1–30, registros 1–150.

34. *Registro de Bautizos de 1885–1889*, Catedral de Chulucanas, Parroquia de Frías, legajo 12-B, folios 1–52, registros 1–209.

35. *Registro de Bautizos de 1885–1889*, Catedral de Chulucanas, Parroquia de Frías, legajo 12-B, folios 1–52, folios 222–300, registros 901–1116.

36. According to the brother who administers the cathedral's archive, the priests ascribed the race label to the child being baptized without input from the parents.

37. *Registro de Bautizos de 1897*, Catedral de Chulucanas, Parroquia de Frías, legajo 12-B, folios 1–34, registros 1–108. When I asked the brother helping me access these records why priests had stopped recording the "social condition" of children that year, he simply replied, "That year we decided all were children of God."

38. García, "Las Razas en Lima," 39.

39. Steve Stein, *Lima Obrera 1900–1930, Tomo I* (Lima: Ediciones El Virrey, 1986), 15–16.

40. José Antonio del Busto Duthurburu, *Breve Historia de los Negros del Perú* (Lima: Fondo Editorial del Congreso del Perú, 2000), 14.

41. Stein, *Lima Obrera*, 238.

42. Stein, *Lima Obrera*, 234. For more on race, class, and national identity in Latin American fútbol, see Ilan Stavans, ed., *Fútbol* (Santa Barbara: ABC-CLIO, 2011). For more on

fútbol in twentieth-century Peru, see Carlos Aguirre, *Ese Gol Existe: Una Mirada al Perú a Través del Fútbol* (Lima: Pontificia Universidad Catolica del Peru, 2008).

43. Maribel Arrelucea Barrantes and Jesús Cosamalón Aguilar, *La Presenia Afrodescendienete en el Peru, Siglos XVI- XX* (Lima: Perú Ministerio de Cultura, 2015), 122.

44. de la Cadena, "Silent Racism and Intellectual Superiority in Peru," 156. *Asalariados Rurales* translates to "rural wage-earners."

45. "Notas Explicativas al Censo de 1940," *Censo Nacional de Población—1940, Volumen V: Departamento de Lima*, Ministerio de Hacienda y Comercio, Dirección Nacional de Estadística, Biblioteca del Instituto Nacional de Estadística e Informática (BINEI), 41.

46. Severo Martínez Peláez, "The Ladino," trans. Debeorah T. Levenson, in *The Guatemala Reader: History, Culture, Politics*, eds. Greg Grandin, Deborah T. Levenson, and Elizabeth Oglesby (Durham, NC: Duke University Press, 2011), 129–32.

47. Gould, *To Die in This Way*.

48. Gould, *To Die in This Way*, 5.

49. de la Cadena, "Silent Racism and Intellectual Superiority," 160.

50. *Censo Nacional de Población—1940, Volúmenes V y III: Departamentos de Lima, Lambayeque, Libertad, y Ancash.* (Lima: Ministerio de Hacienda y Comercio, 1940). 141, 14, 34, 39, BINEI.

51. Andrews, *The Afro-Argentines*, 7.

52. *Censo Nacional de Población- 1940, Primer Volumen* (Ministerio de Hacienda y Comercio, 1940), Director: Alberto Arca Parró, Dirección Nacional de Estadística, Biblioteca del Instituto Nacional de Estadística e Informática, 1944, 28–29 (emphasis in original).

53. *Censo Nacional de Población—1940,* Volúmenes V y III: Departamentos de Lima, Lambayeque, Libertad, y Ancash (Ministerio de Hacienda y Comercio, 1940), 29–30, BINEI (emphasis added).

54. Leon Garcia, "Las Razas de Lima," 42–43.

55. Muriel Nazzari, "Vanishing Indians: The Social Construction of Race in Colonial São Paulo," *Americas* 57, no. 4 (April 2001): 499.

56. Nazzari, "Vanishing Indians," 509.

57. Andrews, *The Afro-Argentines*, 4.

58. Andrews, *The Afro-Argentines*, 178.

59. Mario Marcone, "El Perú y la Inmigración Europea en la Segunda Mitad del Siglo XIX," *Histórica* 16, no. 1 (June 1992): 63–88. For more on European immigration to South America in this era, see José C. Moya, *Cousins and Strangers: Spanish Immigrants in Buenos Aires, 1850–1930* (Berkeley: University of California Press, 1998).

60. Andrews, *The Afro-Argentines*, 77.

61. Trouillot, *Silencing the Past*, 26.

Chapter 4

1. See, for example, Luis F. Paredes, "Perú Negro: Choreographing and Performing Afro-Peruvian identity, 1969 to the Present" (PhD diss., State University of New York at Albany, 2015); Robert L. Sanchez, "Black Mosaic: The Assimilation and Marginalization of Afro-Peruvians in Post-Abolition Peru, 1854–1930" (PhD diss., University of Illinois at Urbana-Champaign, 2008).

2. I use the term "ethnoracial" to connote the confluence of perceived differences in the social constructions of both race and ethnicity based on the work of sociologist Edward

Telles. See, for example, *Pigmentocracies: Ethnicity, Race, and Color in Latin America* (Chapel Hill: University of North Carolina Press, 2014). My using this term is a conscious decision to push back against historiographical tendencies to discuss Afro-Latino populations in terms of "race" and Indigenous populations in terms of "ethnicity." See also Diego Von Vacano, *The Color of Citizenship: Race, Modernity, and Latin American/Hispanic Political Thought* (Oxford: Oxford University Press, 2011).

3. Edward Telles, *Pigmentocracies: Ethnicity, Race, and Color in Latin America* (Chapel Hill: University of North Carolina Press, 2014), 130.

4. Marisol de la Cadena, *Indigenous Mestizos: The Politics of Race and Culture in Cuzco, Peru, 1919–1991* (Durham: Duke University Press, 2000); Tonya Golash-Boza, *Yo Soy Negro: Blackness in Peru* (Gainesville: University Press of Florida, 2011).

5. Doris Summer, *Foundational Fictions: The National Romances of Latin America* (Berkeley and Los Angeles: University of California Press, 1991). When Summer briefly mentions such fictions in Peru, she cites Clorinda Matto de Turner's 1889 *Aves sin Nido*, an important work of "racial disencounters . . . between Indians and whites."

6. José Campos and José Respaldiza, eds. *Letras Afroperuanas: Creación e Identidad* (Lima: Fondo Editorial del Congreso del Perú, 2011), 350.

7. Laura Briggs, *Reproducing Empire: Race, Sex, Science, and U.S. Imperialism in Puerto Rico* (Berkeley: University of California Press, 2003); Nancy Leys Stepan, *"The Hour of Eugenics": Race, Gender, and Nation in Latin America* (Ithaca, NY: Cornell University Press, 1991).

8. Merlin D. Compton, *Ricardo Palma* (Boston, MA: Twayne Publishers, 1982).

9. Oswaldo Holguín Callo, "Ricardo Palma y la Cultura Negra," *Fundación Biblioteca Virtual Miguel de Cervantes*, Pontificia Universidad Católica del Perú (website). The song's refrain is "De los coroneles / ¿cuál es el mejor? / El coronel Balta / se lleva la flor."

10. As a result of this effort and as an apparent reward for Afro-Peruvian support, in December 1870 President Balta approved the legal recognition of the "political rights" of the inhabitants of the Afro-Peruvian community of Yapatera in Piura, stipulating that these citizens would repay the "old landowners" the prorated cost of the lands they occupied. Although they had to pay, the yapateranos gained full legal rights to the land they claimed as autonomous territory.

11. Compton, *Ricardo Palma*, 19.

12. Margarita Giesecke, *Masas Urbanas y Rebelión en la Historia. Lima: Golpe de Estado, 1872* (Lima: CDHP, 1978) 54–55.

13. Giesecke, *Masas Urbanas y Rebelión*, 75–78.

14. Oswaldo Holguín Callo, "Ricardo Palma y la Cultura Negra," in *Lo Africano en la Cultura Criolla*, ed. Carolos Aguirre (Lima: Fondo Editorial del Congreso del Perú, 2000), 97–120.

15. Ricardo Palma, *Tradiciones Peruanas* (Lima: Colección Educativa Niñez que Lee, 2007), 91.

16. Larissa Brewer-García, "The Composite Pardo of Seventeenth-Century Lima: Blackness, Whiteness, and Creole Self-Fashioning in the Earliest Portraits of Martín de Porres," *Colonial Latin American Review* 30, no. 2 (June 2021): 273.

17. Rafael Castañeda García, "La Devoción a Santa Ifigenia Entre los Negros y Mulatos de Nueva España. Siglos XVII y XVIII," in *Esclavitud, Mestizaje y Abolicionismo en los Mundos Hispánicos*, ed. Aurelia Martín Casares (Grenada: Editorial Universidad de Granada,

Fundación Dialnet, 2015), 151–72. "En ambos lados del Atlántico la presencia de los santos negros formó parte de un imaginario construido por la Iglesia para cohesionar y establecer lazos de identidad entre la población y sus descendientes, esclavos y libres. En Iberoamérica hubo devoción por San Antonio de Noto, San Benito de Palermo, San Elesbán, Santa Ifigenia, San Baltasar (rey mago negro), y más tardíamente San Martín de Porres."

18. Compton, *Ricardo Palma*, 85.

19. Callo, "Ricardo Palma y la Cultura Negra."

20. Augusto Alcocer Martínez, "Lengua y Sociedad: El Que no Tiene de Inga Tiene de Mandinga," *Letras* 75, no. 107/108 (2004): 33–46.

21. Compton, *Ricardo Palma*, 24.

22. Compton, *Ricardo Palma*, 24. These displays, Compton explains, included a meeting in May to honor Palma, at which "one distinguished speaker after another rose to pay homage to the former director of the library, and wave after wave of applause from the packed house met their remarks."

23. As in Brazil and Mexico at the same time, positivism was at its peak among Peruvian intellectuals in the late nineteenth century. Clemente Palma's positivist contemporaries in Lima included Jorge Polar, Alejandrino Maguiña, Joaquín Capelo, and Carlos Lissón. Clemente's thesis diverged from these positivists, however, in its outright racial determinism. See Ávila, *La Razón Racial*, 23, 30. Quiroz Avila provides more details on Clemente's relationship with Javier Prado, however, who held similarly negative views of Afro-Peruvians.

24. Clemente Palma, *El Porvenir de las Razas en el Perú*, Tesis para optar el grado de bachiller en la Facultad de Letras, Leído por Clemente Palma. Facultad de Letras (Lima: Imp. Torres Aguirre, Unión 150, 1897). Casa Museo Ricardo Palma, viii.

25. Barry Carr, "Radicals, Revolutionaries and Exiles: Mexico City in the 1920s," *Berkeley Review of Latin American Studies* (Fall 2013).

26. Palma, *El Porvenir de las Razas en el Perú*, 4.

27. Ávila, *La Razón Racial*, 30.

28. Palma, *El Porvenir de las Razas en el Perú*, 8.

29. Palma, *El Porvenir de las Razas en el Perú*, 7.

30. Palma, *El Porvenir de las Razas en el Perú*, 23.

31. Palma, *El Porvenir de las Razas en el Perú*, 38.

32. Robert L. Sanchez, "Black Mosaic: The Assimilation and Marginalization of Afro-Peruvians in Post-Abolition Peru, 1854–1930 (PhD diss., University of Illinois at Urbana-Champaign, 2008), 57. Sanchez categorizes J. Francisco Varela, Hildebrando Fuentes, and Clemente Palma as proponents of social Darwinism who advocated for European immigration, especially that of English and German people.

33. José Campos and José Respaldiza, eds., *Letras Afroperuanas: Creación e Identidad*, 348.

34. Enrique López Albújar, *Matalaché* (Lima: Edilipe Joel EIRL, 2007), 5.

35. *El Otro Francisco*. Dir. Sergio Giral, Cuba: ICAIC, 1975.

36. Alison Fraunhar, "*Mulata Cubana*: The Problematics of National Allegory," in *Latin American Cinema: Essays on Modernity, Gender and National Identity*, eds. Lisa Shaw and Stephanie Dennison (Jefferson, NC: McFarland & Company, 2005), 160–78.

37. Gertrudis Gómez de Avellaneda, *Sab* (Madrid: Ediciones Cátedra, 2003), 104.

38. Sadiya Hartman, *Scenes of Subjection: Terror, Slavery, and Self-Making in Nineteenth-Century America* (Oxford: Oxford University Press, 1997), 3–4.

39. Genaro Maza, "Motivaciones de 'Los caballeros del delito'" in *Los Caballeros del Delito*, ed. Enrique López Albújar (Piura: Centro de Investigación y Promoción del Campesinado, CIPCA, 1993), 7–17.

40. "El Fin de un Celebre Bandolero," *Variedades* (Lima: 8 de enero de 1916): 78. Casa Museo Ricardo Palma.

41. "El Fin de un Celebre Bandolero," 78: "En que figure erguido y siniestro, como un héroe de leyenda, este bandolero alevoso que aparece en la foto ya muerto, pero como si sonriera irónicamente."

42. Maza, "Motivaciones de 'Los Caballeros del Delito,'" 8. *Godismo* was a form of political and social conservatism defended by Venezuelan elites in the early nineteenth century.

43. Maza, "Motivaciones de 'Los Caballeros del Delito,'" 8.

44. Enrique López Albújar, *Los Caballeros del Delito* (Piura: CIPCA, 1993), 37: "Es esta sensualidad la que le mantiene esclavo aun de la miseria en que vive, exaltado a ratos, indolente siempre, de espaldas a los intereses comunales, al progreso regional y hasta a lo que se relaciona on sus mismos intereses de clase. Sobre todo el zambo—este producto del mulatismo costeño—quien, por lo mismo que es espiritualmente más ágil, mas intuitivo, es también más propenso a la vida licenciosa."

45. For proto-national formulations of Peruvian nationalism and identity exhibiting racial anxieties of white elites, see Mariselle Meléndez, "Patria, Criollos and Blacks: Imagining the Nation in the Mercurio Peruano, 1791–1795," *Colonial Latin American Review* 15, no. 2 (December 2006): 207–27.

46. Albújar, *Los Caballeros del Delito*, 16.

47. Carlos Aguirre and Charles Walker, *Bandoleros, Abigeos y Montoneros: Criminalidad y Violencia en el Perú, Siglos XVIII–XX* (Lima: Instituto de Apoyo Agrario, 1990), 21.

48. Aguirre and Walker, *Bandoleros, Abigeos y Montoneros*.

49. John M. Limpki, "Afro-Yungueño Speech: The long-lost 'black' Spanish," *Spanish in Context* 4, no. 1 (2007): 1–43.

50. Enrique López Albújar, *De la Tierra Brava: Poemas Afroyngas* (Lima: Imprenta del Estado, 1938), 45, BNP, sala de investigaciones: "¡Ya mataron a Alama! ¡Ya mataron a Alama! / por ciudades y campos van gritando mil voces, / . . . el mozo de la vida turbulenta y sangrienta, / el de la vida corta y de larga fama; / el que en la boca oscura de su oscura pistola / para romper un cerco policial le bastaba / una bala certera, una bala, sola una."

51. Albújar, *De la Tierra Brava*, 47–48: "Sólo en un caserío y en una estancia oscura, / prendida siempre el alma de un pensamiento fijo, / al saber la noticia, llora un criatura, / y, transida, murmura: / --¡Ya mataron a mi hijo! ¡Ya mataron a mi hijo! / Y al oír el lamento, trágico ante la abuela, / después de darle un beso, con unción, a su madre, / un mozo, que ha empuñado carabina y espuela, / jura solemnemente:--¡Yo te vengaré, padre! / ¡Yo te vengaré, padre!"

52. For more on nineteenth-century literacy in Lima, see Elisabeth L. Austin, *Exemplary Ambivalence in Late Nineteenth-Century Spanish America: Narrating Creole Subjectivity* (Lewisburg: Bucknell University Press, 2012).

53. Callo, "Ricardo Palma y la Cultura Negra."

54. Carlos Aguirre, *The Criminals of Lima and Their Worlds: The Prison Experience, 1850–1935*. (Durham, NC: Duke University Press, 2005), 120–21.

55. Albújar, *De la Tierra Brava*, 49.

56. Clemente Palma, "Prologue" to Enrique López Albújar, in *De la Tierra Brava: Poemas Afroyungas*, xii.

57. Clemente Palma, "Prologue" to López Albújar, in *De la Tierra Brava: Poemas Afroyungas* xiv: "Y siguió *Matalaché*, novela trágica, de ambiente colonial, estupendo y valiente estudio sobre los prejuicios raciales de la aristocracia de la infiltración que el elemento negro fue haciendo en la sociabilidad colonial convirtiendo muy buena parte de la selectas matrices blasonadas en crisoles democráticos del mestizaje predominante en nuestra sociedad republicana."

58. Albújar, *De la Tierra Brava*, xv.

59. Ronald Hilton, *Who's Who in Latin America: Part IV, Bolivia, Chile, and Peru* (Stanford, CA: Stanford University Press, 1947), 181.

60. Roberto Mac Lean Estenós, *Del Salvajismo a la Nación: Genesis y Telesis Social* (Lima: Casa Editora Sanmartí y Cía, 1936).

61. For more on Franz Boas, cultural relativism, and "racial vindication," see Lee. D. Baker, *From Savage to Negro: Anthropology and the Construction of Race, 1896–1954* (Berkeley: University of California Press, 1998).

62. See Nancy Leys Stepan, *"The Hour of Eugenics": Race, Gender, and Nation in Latin America* (Ithaca, NY: Cornell University Press, 1991), 177–81. Although Mac Lean Estenós claimed this was the first such conference, there was a pan-American conference on eugenics and homiculture held in Havana in December of 1927. The Peruvian delegate, Carlos Enrique Paz Soldán was "by far the strongest opponent to the code's racist tone and policies," despite his later view that the Japanese "race" should be excluded from Peru in the 1930s.

63. Roberto Mac Lean Estenós, *Negros en el Nuevo Mundo* (Lima: Editorial PTCM, 1948), 108–9 (emphasis added).

64. Jerry Dávila, *Diploma of Whiteness: Race and Social Policy in Brazil, 1917–1945* (Durham, NC: Duke University Press, 2003), 51.

65. Ricardo Sumalavia, *Ricardo Palma: Narrativa Completa* (Lima: PUCP, 2006), 30.

66. Estenós, *Negros en el Nuevo Mundo*, 154.

67. José Carlos Mariátegui, trans. Marjory Urquidi, *Seven Interpretive Essays on Peruvian Reality* (Austin: University of Texas Press, 1971). In this 1928 publication, Mariátegui applied a Marxist analysis to explain the "problem of the Indian," generally disparaged Black people, and suggested that encouraging immigration from Europe was part of the solution to the nation's racial composition.

Chapter 5

1. Trouillot, *Silencing the Past*, 26.

2. For more on this concept and the sixteenth-century writings of Peruvian geography and race, see Benjamin S. Orlove, "Putting Race in Its Place: Order in Colonial and Postcolonial Peruvian Geography," *Social Research* 60, no. 2 (Sumer 1993) 301–36. This book has cited numerous works that overcome dualism to focus on Afro-Peruvian history and experiences. These include the works of Peter Blanchard, Carlos Aguirre, Christine Hünefeldt, Tonya Golash-Boza, and Jean Muteba-Rahier.

3. Marisol de la Cadena, *Indigenous Mestizos: The Politics of Race and Culture in Cuzco, Peru, 1919–1991* (Durham, NC: Duke University Press, 2000), 2.

4. Cecilia Méndez G., "Incas Si, Indios No: Notes on Peruvian Creole Nationalism and Its Contemporary Crisis," *Journal of Latin American Studies* 28, no. 1 (February 1996): 209. See also Natalia Sobrevilla Perea, *The Caudillo of the Andes: Andrés de Santa Cruz* (Cambridge: Cambridge University Press, 2012).

5. Méndez G., "Incas Si, Indios No."

6. Alberto Rubio Fataccioli, *Sebastián Lorente y la Educación en el Perú del Siglo XIX* (Lima: Editorial Allamanda, 1990), 72. According to Fataccioli, the commission began constructing the law in 1846, and it was completed and published on June 14, 1850.

7. Mark Thurner, *Sebastián Lorente: Escritos Fundacionales de Historia Peruana* (Lima: Fondo Editorial Universidad Nacional Mayor de San Marcos, 2005), 41–42.

8. Thurner, *Sebastián Lorente*, 27.

9. Thurner, *Sebastián Lorente*, 42.

10. Thurner, *Sebastián Lorente*, 43.

11. Quoted in Thurner, 44: "Su obra lleva el sello de la raza nacional, y el del país."

12. Quoted in Mark Thurner and Andrés Guerrero, eds., *After Spanish Rule: Postcolonial Predicaments of the Americas* (Durham, NC: Duke University Press, 2003), 143.

13. Thurner and Guerrero, eds., *After Spanish Rule*, 144.

14. Thurner and Guerrero, eds., *After Spanish Rule*, 165.

15. *El Mercurio Peruano, El Amante de la Salud del Público, March 4, 1829:* "En los de diciembre hasta mayo inclusive, en que se mata ganado criollo, cuyo valor es más caro."

16. Jorge Sand, "Las Mujeres de la Habana," *El Comercio*, April 12, 1844. *El Comercio* included advertisements for the sale of "*un negro criollo de 50 años*," on March 17, 18, 20, and 21, 1843.

17. Callo, "Ricardo Palma y la Cultura Negra."

18. *El Comercio*, September 5, 1843: "Hechicera! . . . muy hechicera! . . . Seria menester tener el ojo impío de un criollo para descubrir *mezcla de sangre* en el imperceptible matiz pardo que colora lijeramente la corona de la uñas rosadas de esa cuarterona; nuestras frescas bellezas del Norte no tienen tinte más transparente, cutis más blanco ni pelo de castaño más dorado."

19. For example, Carlos A. Forment, *Democracy in Latin America: 1760–1900, Volume I: Civic Selfhood and Public Life in Mexico and Peru* (Chicago: University of Chicago Press, 2003). Forment documents a dramatic increase in civic institutions in the immediate post-abolition period in Peru, which increased Afro-Peruvian political participation made possible by Castilla's Liberal Revolution.

20. Mark Thurner, *From Two Republics to One Divided: Contradictions of Postcolonial Nationmaking in Andean Peru* (Durham, NC: Duke University Press, 2006).

21. Mary Weismantel, *Cholas and Pishtacos: Stories of Race and Sex in the Andes* (Chicago: University of Chicago Press, 2001), xxiii, xxxi–xxxii.

22. Weismantel, *Cholas and Pishtacos*, 255.

23. Weismantel, *Cholas and Pishtaco*, 258.

24. For more on the persistence of the "European gaze" in Latin American literature and art, see Peter R. Beardsell, *Europe and Latin America: Returning the Gaze* (Manchester: Manchester University Press, 2000).

25. Sebastián Lorente, "Valles de la Costa," in *Sobre el Perú* (Lima: Tipografía de la Voz del Pueblo, 1855) 9–10. "Los valles de la costa son la patria de la vida y de los placeres: bosques de árboles siempre frondosos; jardines que no cesan de encantar por el perfume y por los brillantes matices de las flores . . . las cabañas, las haciendas y los pueblos revelan la presencia del hombre que ha venido a embellecer la naturaleza, y a gozar de sus dones en el seno de la paz y de la abundancia."

26. Lorente, "Valles de la Costa," 11–12: "El clima debilita la organización, encadena sus

fuerzas el ocio al que él condena, gástales el deleite, y tanto del hijo de la costa como el robusto serrano que se fijó en sus valles, nunca conocen al bienestar de una salud: las fiebres, la disentería y la tisis, siegan las generaciones que aun no han acabado su Desarrollo . . . vivimos en aire de muerte, y nos dormimos en una corteza alzada que ni ella misma tiene sólida existencia."

27. Thurner, *From Two Republics to One Divided*, 5.

28. Analisa Taylor, *Indigeneity in the Mexican Cultural Imagination: Thresholds of Belonging* (Tucson: University of Arizona Press, 2013), 1–2.

29. Juan Carlos Grijalva, "Paradoxes of the Inka Utopianism of José Carlos Mariátegui's *Seven Interpretative Essays on Peruvian Reality*," *Journal of Latin American Cultural Studies* 19, no. 3 (December 2010): 320.

30. Grijalva, "Paradoxes of the Inka Utopianism," 3.

31. Grijalva, "Paradoxes of the Inka Utopianism."

32. de la Cadena, *Indigenous Mestizos*, 89.

33. Arturo E. Delgado, Diputado Regional por Cajatambo, "El Hogar Indígena Inalienable," *La Vida Agrícola*, Oyón, 15 de diciembre de 1927, April 1928, 293.

34. Delgado, "El Hogar Indígena," 293: "La acumulación de la propiedad territorial en unas cuantas manos que recogen riquezas provenientes del trabajo rudimentario del indio envilecido, produce ignorancia, pauperismo, despoblación y ruina."

35. Maribel Arrelucea and Jesús Cosamalón Aguilar, *La Presencia Afrodescendiente en el Perú, Siglos XVI–XX* (Lima: Ministerio de Cultura, 2015).

36. José Carlos Mariátegui, *Seven Interpretive Essays on Peruvian Reality*, trans. Marjory Urquidi (Austin: University of Texas Press, 1971), 280 (emphasis added).

37. "Panorama Móvil: Documentos: Proyecto de Resolución sobre la Cuestión de la Raza Negra," *El Amauta*, 29 (Febrero–Marzo 1930): 86–87. Biblioteca Nacional Peruana, Hemeroteca: "Si bien es cierto que en la América la esclavitud ha sido abolida como institución, el imperialismo continua sin embargo bajo otras formas la explotación de los pueblos negros."

38. Manuel González Prada, "Nuestros Indios," *El Amauta* 29 (Febrero–Marzo 1930): 4–7.

39. González Prada, "Nuestros Indios."

40. González Prada, "Nuestros Indios."

41. González Prada, "Nuestros Indios."

42. Deborah Poole, *Vision, Race, and Modernity: A Visual Economy of the Andean Image World* (Princeton, NJ: Princeton University Press, 1997), 186–87.

Conclusion

1. Michel-Rolph Trouillot, *Silencing the Past: Power and the Production of History* (Boston, MA: Beacon Press, 1992), 13 (emphasis in original).

2. Trouillot, *Silencing the Past*, 13.

3. Trouillot, *Silencing the Past*, 27.

4. Trouillot, *Silencing the Past*, 91.

5. Trouillot, *Silencing the Past*, 96

6. Trouillot, *Silencing the Past*, 93.

7. Edith Sanders, "The Hamitic Hypothesis; Its Origin and Functions in Time Perspective," *Journal of African History* X, no. 4 (1969): 532.

8. Sanders, "The Hamitic Hypothesis,"529.

9. Abdias do Nascimento, *O Genocídio do Negro Brasileiro: Processo de um Racismo Mascarado* (Rio de Janeiro: Editoria Paz e Terra, 1978).

10. Abdias do Nascimento, "Brazil: The Cult of Whiteness," *New African* 37, no. 1 (October 2004): 433.

11. Alberto, *Terms of Inclusion*, 70, 97.

12. Notably, an article in the national newspaper *El Correo* in 2022 lamented that this "symbol of maternal love" is in disrepair and has been forgotten. Nilo Valela Monzón, "PIURA: Monumento a la Madre 'un Símbolo del Amor Maternal', en el Olvido," *El Correo* May 7, 2022.

13. Lee Baker, "W. E. B. Du Bois, Franz Boas, and 'the Real Race Problem,'" *History of Anthropology Review* 45 (2021).

14. Heidi Carolyn Feldman, *Black Rhythms of Peru: Reviving African Musical Heritage in the Black Pacific* (Middletown, CT: Wesleyan University Press, 2006).

15. Tanya Golash-Boza, *Yo soy Negro: Blackness in Peru* (Gainesville: University Press of Florida, 2011).

16. See, for example, Eshe Lewis and John Thomas, "'Me Gritaron Negra': The Emergence and Development of the Afro-descendant Women's Movement in Peru," *Journal of International Women's Studies* 20, no. 8 (2019).

17. Lewis and Thomas, "Me Gritaron Negra."

18. Theodore W. Cohen, *Finding Afro-Mexico*, 286.

19. David Agren, "'We Exist. We're Here': Afro-Mexicans Make the Census after Long Struggle for Recognition," *Guardian*, March 19, 2.

Bibliography

Archives

Archivo y Biblioteca Municipal de Lima (ABML)
Archivo Histórico Municipal de Lima (AHML)
Archivo Regional de Piura (ARP)
Biblioteca Nacional Del Perú, Lima (BNP)
Biblioteca del Instituto Nacional de Estadística e Informática, Lima (BINEI)
Casa Museo Miguel Grau, Piura (CMMG)
Casa Museo Ricardo Palma, Lima (CMRP)
Centro de Desarrollo Étnico, Lima (CEDET)
Centro de Investigación y Promoción del Campesinado, Piura (CIPCA)
Museo Nacional Afroperuano (MNA)

Primary Sources

Arancivia, F. Ingeniero del Estado. "Río de Chincha," *Informes de los Ingenieros.* (Lima: 26 de junio de 1899), in Sr. Edilberto Castillo, *Anales de las obras públicas del Perú, año 1899,* 442–45. Lima: Imprenta Torres Aguirre, 1900.

Belaúnde, Víctor Andrés. *Peruanidad.* Lima: Librería Stadium, 1965. Originally published in 1943.

Castelar, Emilio. *La América,* June 7, 1862.

Censo General de Lima 1860. Libro 1, cuartel primero, folios 91–97. Archivo Histórico Municipal de Lima (AHML).

Censo General de Lima 1860. Libro 3, cuartel tercero. Distrito quinto: Calle de San Ysidro, folios 119–32. AHML.

Censo General de Lima 1860. Libro 3, cuartel tercero. Distrito quinto: Calle de San Ysidro, folio 130, AHML.

Censo General de Lima 1860. Libro 3, cuartel tercero. Distrito quinto: Calle de San Ysidro, folios 119–32, AHML.

Censo de la Municipalidad de Lima de 1860. AHML.

Censo General de Lima 1866. Cuartel tercero, folios 26–33, AHML.

Censo General de Lima 1866. Cuartel tercero, folios 26–33, AHML.

Censo Nacional de Población—1940, Volúmenes V y III: Departamentos de Lima, Lambayeque, Libertad, y Ancash. Ministerio de Hacienda y Comercio, 1940. Dirección Nacional de Estadística, Biblioteca del Instituto Nacional de Estadística e Informática (BINEI).

Constitución Política del Perú. 10 de noviembre de 1860. Título XVI, Articulo 123. Archivo Digital de la Legislación del Perú (website).
El Comercio, October 5, 1897.
El Comercio, September 5, 1843.
"El Fin de un Celebre Bandolero." *Variedades*. Lima, 8 de enero de 1916, 78.
Escribano Público Manuel Rebolledo. "Notarios: Protocolos del 1854–1855." Legajo 239, expediente 5189 (1855), folio 1, Archivo Regional de Piura (ARP).
Escribano Público Manuel Rebolledo. "Notarios—Protocolos de 1854–1885," 7 de marzo de 1884, ARP.
Escribano Público Semitagoya. Catálogos: Causas Criminales del 1856–1857, legajo 241, expediente 5341 (1857), Archivo Regional de Piura (ARP).
El Mercurio Peruano. "El Amante de la salud del público," March 4, 1829.
El Peruano. "Circular a los Gobiernos de América," August 24, 1861. BNP, Hemeroteca.
Eyzaguirre, Ramón. *Jefe de la Sección de Demografía, Decretos y Resoluciones Relativos al Censo de la Provincia de Lima 1908, Tomo I (4 de Enero de 1908), Decretado y Levantado durante la Administración del Excmo. Señor don José Pardo*. Lima: Imprenta de "La Opinión Nacional" Calle Correo 194, 1915, 12–13, Biblioteca y Archivo Municipal de Lima (BAML).
Gómez de Avellaneda, Gertrudis. *Sab*. Madrid: Ediciones Cátedra, 2003.
Graham, Mary. *Journal of a Residence in Chile during the Year 1822*. Charlottesville: University of Virginia Press, 2003.
Inscrito en Los Registros Públicos. MNAFC *Pronunciamiento*, 2005. website.
La América, April 5, 1862. BNP, Hemeroteca.
La América, April 23, 1862. BNP, Hemeroteca.
La América, May 10, 1862. BNP, Hemeroteca.
La América, May 17, 1862. BNP, Hemeroteca.
La América, May 31, 1862. BNP, Hemeroteca.
La América, June 4, 1862. BNP, Hemeroteca.
"La Liga Contra el Imperialismo." *El Amauta: Revista Mensual de Doctrina, Literatura, Arte, Polémica*. Año III: Número 13, 88. Lima: BNP, Hemeroteca.
La Sociedad de Fundadores de la Independencia del Perú se da la Siguiente Constitución. Lima: Impreso por Francisco Solis, 1861. BNP, Sala de Investigaciones.
León Garcia, Enrique. "Las razas en Lima: Estudio Demográfico," Tesis para el doctorado, Facultad de Medicina. Universidad Nacional Mayor de San Marcos, 1909.
Ley Orgánica de Elecciones dada por el Congreso de 1860. Lima: Imprenta del Gobierno por Eusebio Aranda, 1861. BNP, Sala de investigaciones.
López Albújar, Enrique. *De la Tierra Brava: Poemas Afroyngas*. Lima: Imprenta del Estado, 1938.
———. *Los Caballeros del Delito*. Piura: Centro de Investigación y Promoción del Campesinado (CIPCA), 1993.
———. *Matalaché*. Lima: Edilipe Joel EIRL, 2007.
Mac Lean Estenós, Roberto. *Del Salvajismo a la Nacion: Genesis y Telesis Social*. Lima: Casa Editora Sanmartí y Cía, 1936.
———. *Negros en el Nuevo Mundo*. Lima: Editorial PTCM, 1948.
Marcone, Mario. "El Peru y la Inmigración Europea en la Segunda Mitad del Siglo XIX." *Histórica* 16, no. 1 (June 1992): 63–88.

Mariátegui, José Carlos. *Seven Interpretive Essays on Peruvian Reality*. Translated by Marjory Urquidi. Austin: University of Texas Press, 1971.

Mawe, John. *Travels in the Interior of Brazil*. London: Longman, Hurst, Rees, Orme, and Brown, 1812.

Moscol Urbina, Jorge Eduardo. *Mangachería Rabiosa*. Piura: Autores Piuranos, 1986.

"Notas Explicativas al Censo de 1940," *Censo Nacional de Población—1940, Volumen V*: Departamento de Lima. Ministerio de Hacienda y Comercio. Dirección Nacional de Estadística. BINEI.

Palma, Clemente. *El Porvenir de las Razas en el Perú, Tesis Para Optar el Grado de Bachiller en la Facultad de Letras, Leído por Clemente Palma*. Facultad de Letras. Lima: Imp. Torres Aguirre, 1897. Casa Museo Ricardo Palma.

Palma, M. "Ensayo sobre los Principios de Economía Política en sus Relaciones con las Riquezas del Peru." *La América*, December 20, 1862. BNP, Hemeroteca.

Palma, Ricardo. *Cartas Inéditas de Don Ricardo Palma*. Lima: February 8, 1881.

———. *Tradiciones Peruanas*. Lima: Editorial Rumi, 2007.

Peru: Resultados Definitivos de los Censos Nacionales 2017. Lima: BINEI.

Pfeiffer, Ida. *A Lady's Second Journey Round the World from London to the Cape of Good Hope, Borneo, Java, Sumatra, Celebes, Ceram, the Moluccas, etc., California, Panama, Peru, Ecuador, and the United States*. New York: Harper and Brothers, 1856.

Rosell, Ricard., "Canto a la Patria." *La América*, December 13, 1862. BNP, Hemeroteca.

Sand, Jorge. "Las mujeres de la Habana." *El Comercio*, April 12, 1844.

Vigil, Francisco de P. G. "Ojeada Comparativa al Imperio de Brasil." *La América*, June 4, 1862. BNP, Hemeroteca.

SECONDARY SOURCES

Agren, David. "'We Exist. We're Here': Afro-Mexicans Make the Census after Long Struggle for Recognition." *Guardian*, March 19, 2020.

Aguirre, Carlos. *Agentes de su Propia Libertad: Los Esclavos de Lima y la Desintegración de la Esclavitud, 1821–1854*. Lima: Pontificia Universidad Católica del Perú, 1995.

———. *Breve Historia de la Esclavitud en el Perú: Una Herida Que no Deja de Sangrar*. Lima: Fondo Editorial del Congreso del Perú, 2005.

———. "Silencio y Ecos: La Historia y el Legado de la Abolición de la Esclavitud en Haití y el Perú." In *La Libertad Inconclusa: Entorno a la Esclavitud, su Abolición y los Derechos Civiles*, edited by Maribel Arrelucea, 23–44. Lima: Centro de Desarrollo Étnico (CEDET), 2010.

———. *The Criminals of Lima and Their Worlds*. Durham: Duke University Press, 2005.

Anderson, Benedict. *Imagined Communities: Reflections on the Origin and Spread of Nationalism*. New York: Verso, 1983.

Andrews, George Reid. *Afro-Latin America: Black Lives, 1600–2000*. Cambridge, MA: Harvard University Press, 2016.

———. *Blackness in a White Nation: A History of Afro-Uruguay*. Chapel Hill: University of North Carolina Press, 2010.

———. *The Afro-Argentines of Buenos Aires, 1800–1900*. Madison: University of Wisconsin Press, 1980.

Appelbaum, Nancy, Anne Macpherson, and Alejandra Rosemblatt, eds. *Race and Nation in Modern Latin America*. Chapel Hill: University of North Carolina Press, 2003.

Arrelucea, Maribel, ed. *La Libertad Inconclusa: Entorno a la Esclavitud, su Abolición y los Derechos Civiles*. Lima: CEDET, 2010.

———. *Replanteando la Esclavitud: Estudios de Etnicidad y Género en Lima Borbónica*. Lima: CEDET, 2009.

Arrelucea, Maribel, and Jesús Cosamalón Aguilar. *La Presencia Afrodescendiente en el Perú, Siglos XVI–XX*. Lima: Ministerio de Cultura, 2015.

Balibar, Etienne, and Immanuel Wallerstein. *Race, Nation, Class: Ambiguous Identities*. New York: Verso, 1991.

Basadre, Jorge. *Historia de la República de Perú (1822–1933) Tomo IV*. Lima: Editorial Universitaria, 2005.

———. *Historia de la República, Tomo IX: Quinto Periodo, 1899–1918*. Lima: La Empresa Editora el Comercio, 2005.

———. *La Iniciación de la República: Tomo Primero*. Lima: Fondo Editorial de la Universidad Nacional Mayor de San Marcos, 2002.

———. *Perú Independiente*. Lima: El Comercio, 2010. Biblioteca Nacional del Perú, Sala de Investigaciones.

Baker, Lee D. *From Savage to Negro: Anthropology and the Construction of Race, 1896–1954*. Berkeley: University of California Press, 1998.

Beattie, Peter. *The Tribute of Blood: Army, Honor, Race, and Nation in Brazil, 1864–1945*. Durham: Duke University Press, 2001.

Berlin, Ira. "From Creole to African: Atlantic Creoles and the Origins of African-American Society in Mainland North America." *William and Mary Quarterly* 53, no. 2 (1996): 251–88.

Blake, Stanley. *The Vigorous Core of Our Nationality: Race and Regional Identity in Northeastern Brazil*. Pittsburgh, PA: University of Pittsburgh Press, 2011.

Blanchard, Peter. *Slavery and Abolition in Early Republican Peru*. Wilmington, DE: SR Books, 1992.

———. *The Origins of the Peruvian Labor Movement, 1883–1919*. Pittsburgh, PA: University of Pittsburgh Press, 1982.

———. *Under the Flags of Freedom: Slave Soldiers and the Wars of Independence in Spanish South America*. Pittsburgh, PA: University of Pittsburgh Press, 2008.

Borges, Dain. "'Puffy, Ugly, Slothful, and Inert': Degeneration in Brazilian Social Thought, 1880–1940." *Journal of Latin American Studies* 25, no. 2 (May 1993): 23–46.

Bowser, Frederick. *The African Slave in Colonial Peru, 1524–1650*. Stanford, CA: Stanford University Press, 1974.

Butler, Kim. *Freedoms Given, Freedoms Won: Afro-Brazilians in Post-Abolition São Paolo and Salvador*. New Brunswick, NJ: Rutgers University Press, 1998.

Burton, Antoinette, ed. *Archive Stories: Facts, Fictions, and the Writing of History*. Durham, NC: Duke University Press, 2005.

Campos, José, and José Respaldiza, eds. *Letras Afroperuanas: Creación e Identidad*. Lima: Fondo Editorial del Congreso del Perú, 2010.

Chasteen, John Charles, and Sara Castro-Klarén, eds. *Beyond Imagined Communities: Reading and Writing the Nation in Nineteenth-Century Latin America*. Baltimore, MD: Johns Hopkins University Press, 2003.

Cohen, Theodore W. *Finding Afro-Mexico: Race and Nation after the Revolution*. Cambridge: Cambridge University Press, 2020.

Cohen, David W., and Jack P. Greene, eds. *Neither Slave nor Free: The Freedman of African Descent in the Slave Societies of the New World.* Baltimore, MD: Johns Hopkins University Press, 1972.

Compton, Merlin D. *Ricardo Palma.* Boston, MA: Twayne Publishers, 1982.

Cope, R. Douglas. *The Limits of Racial Domination: Plebian Society in Colonial Mexico City, 1660–1720.* Madison: University of Wisconsin Press, 1994.

Cosamalón Aguilar, Jesús A. "Mestizaje e Interrelación Social en el Tránsito de la Sociedad de las Castas a la República Liberal. Lima, 1790–1860." In *El Nudo del Imperio: Independencia y Democracia en el Perú,* edited by Carmen McEvoy, Mauricio Novoa, and Elías Palti, 343–67. Lima: Instituto Francés de Estudios Andinos, 2012.

Cuche, Denys. *Poder Blanco y Resistencia Negro en el Perú: Un Estudio sobre la Condición Social del Negro en el Peru después de la Abolición de la Esclavitud.* Lima: Instituto Nacional de Cultura, 1975.

Curtin, Philip D. *The Atlantic Slave Trade: A Census.* Madison: University of Wisconsin Press, 1972.

Dávila, Jerry. *Diploma of Whiteness: Race and Social Policy in Brazil, 1917–1945.* Durham, NC: Duke University Press, 2003.

de la Cadena, Marisol. *Indigenous Mestizos: The Politics of Race and Culture in Cuzco, Peru, 1919–1991.* Durham, NC: Duke University Press, 2000.

———. "Silent Racism and Intellectual Superiority in Peru." *Bulletin of Latin American Research* 17, no. 2 (1998): 143–64.

Degler, Carl. *Neither Black nor White: Slavery and Race Relations in Brazil and the United States.* Madison: University of Wisconsin Press, 1971.

de la Fuente, Alejandro. "From Slaves to Citizens? Tannenbaum and the Debates on Slavery, Emancipation, and Race Relations in Latin America." *International and Working-Class History* no. 77 (Spring 2010): 154–73.

del Busto Duthurburu, José Antonio. *Breve Historia de los Negros del Perú.* Lima: Fondo Editorial del Congreso del Perú, 2000.

Denis-Rosario, Milagros. *Drops of Inclusivity: Racial Formations and Meanings in Puerto Rican Society, 1898–1965.* Albany: State University of New York Press, 2022.

Edwards, Erika Denise. *Hiding in Plain Sight: Black Women, the Law, and the Making of a White Argentine Republic.* Tuscaloosa: University of Alabama Press, 2020.

Fataccioli, Alberto Rubio. *Sebastián Lorente y la Educación en el Perú del Siglo XIX.* Lima: Editorial Allamanda, 1990.

Feldman, Heidi Carolyn. *Black Rhythms of Peru: Reviving African Musical Heritage in the Black Pacific.* Middletown, CT: Wesleyan University Press, 2006.

Forment, Carlos A. *Democracy in Latin America: 1760–1900: Volume I, Civic Selfhood and Public Life in Mexico and Peru.* Chicago: University of Chicago Press, 2003.

Fraunhar, Alison. "Mulata Cubana: The Problematics of National Allegory." In *Latin American Cinema: Essays on Modernity, Gender and National Identity,* edited by Lisa Shaw and Stephanie Dennison, 160–78. Jefferson, NC: McFarland & Company, 2005.

French, Jan H. *Legalizing Identities: Becoming Black or Indian in Brazil's Northeast.* Chapel Hill: University of North Carolina Press, 2009.

Fuentes, Marisa J. *Dispossessed Lives: Enslaved Women, Violence, and the Archive.* Philadelphia: University of Pennsylvania Press, 2016.

García-Bryce, Iñigo L. *Crafting the Republic: Lima's Artisans and Nation Building in Peru, 1821–1879.* Albuquerque: University of New Mexico Press, 2004.

Gayles, Prisca, and Ghogomu, Diane. "The Social Economy of Afro-Argentines and African Immigrants in Buenos Aires." In *The Black Social Economy in the Americas: Exploring Diverse Community-Based Markets*, edited by Caroline Shenaz Hossein, 119–42. New York: Palgrave MacMillan, 2018.

Giesecke, Margarita. *Masas Urbanas y Rebelión en la Historia. Lima: Golpe de Estado, 1872.* Lima: Centro de Divulgación de Historia Popular (CDHP), 1978.

Gómez Acuña, Luis. "Lo *Criollo* en Perú Republicano: Breve Aproximación de un Término Elusivo." *Histórica* 31, no. 2 (2007): 115–66.

Gonzalez, Michael J. *Plantation Agriculture and Social Control in Northern Peru, 1875–1933.* Austin: University of Texas Press, 1985.

Gootenberg, Paul. *Between Silver and Guano: Commercial Policy and the State in Postindependence Peru.* Princeton, NJ: Princeton University Press, 1989.

———. "Population and Ethnicity in Early Republican Peru: Some Revisions." *Latin American Research Review* 26, no. 3 (1991), 109–57.

Gould, Jeffrey. *To Die in This Way: Nicaraguan Indians and the Myth of Mestizaje, 1880–1965.* Durham, NC: Duke University Press, 1998.

Gregory, Steven. *Black Corona: Race and the Politics of Place in an Urban Community.* Princeton, NJ: Princeton University Press, 1998.

Halperín Donghi, Tulio. *The Contemporary History of Latin America.* Translated by John Charles Chasteen. Durham, NC: Duke University Press, 1999.

Hartman, Sadiya V. *Scenes of Subjection: Terror, Slavery, and Self-Making in Nineteenth Century America.* Oxford: Oxford University Press, 1997.

Higgins, James. *Lima: A Cultural History.* Oxford: Oxford University Press, 2005.

Hill, J. D. "Long Term Patterns of Ethnogenesis in Indigenous Amazonia." In *The Archaeology of Hybrid Material Culture*, edited by Jeb J. Card, 165–204. Carbondale: Southern Illinois University Press, 2013.

Hilton, Ronald. *Who's Who in Latin America: Part IV, Bolivia, Chile, and Peru.* Stanford, CA: Stanford University Press, 1947.

Hirsch, Stephen. "Anarchism, the Subaltern, and Repertoires of Resistance in Northern Peru, 1898–1922." In *No Gods, No Masters, No Peripheries: Global Anarchisms*, edited by Barry Maxwell and Raymond Craib, 215–32. Oakland, CA: PM Press, 2015.

Hobsbawm, Eric. *The Age of Empire: 1875–1914.* New York: Pantheon, 1987.

Hochschild, J. L., and B. M. Powell. "Racial Reorganization and the United States Census 1850–1930: Mulattoes, Half-Breeds, Mixed Parentage, Hindoos, and the Mexican Race." *Studies in American Political Development* 22, no.1, (2008): 59–96.

Holguín Callo, Oswaldo. "Ricardo Palma y la Cultura Negra." Pontificia Universidad Católica del Perú, *Cervantes* (website).

Holm, John. *Pidgins and Creoles, Volume I: Theory and Structure.* Cambridge: Cambridge University Press, 1988.

Huárag Álvarez, Eduardo, ed. *Los Afrodescendientes en el Perú Republicano.* Lima: Pontificia Universidad Católica del Perú, Instituto Riva-Agüero, 2014.

Hünefeldt, Christine. *Liberalism in the Bedroom: Quarreling Spouses in Nineteenth Century Lima.* State College: Pennsylvania State University Press, 2000.

———. *Paying the Price of Freedom: Family and Labor among Lima's Slaves. 1800–1854.* Berkeley: University of California Press, 1994.

Jouve Martín, José Ramón. *The Black Doctors of Colonial Lima: Science, Race, and Writing in Colonial and Early Republican Peru.* Montreal: McGill Queens University Press, 2014.

———. *Esclavos de la Cuidad Letrada: Esclavitud, Escritura, y Colonialismo en Lima, 1650–1700.* Lima: Instituto de Estudios Peruanos, 2005.

Kittleson, Roger Alan. *The Practice of Politics in Postcolonial Brazil: Porto Alegre, 1845–1895.* Pittsburgh, PA: University of Pittsburgh Press, 2006.

Larson, Brooke. *Trials of Nation Making: Liberalism, Race, and Ethnicity in the Andes, 1810–1910.* Cabridge: Cambridge University Press, 2004.

Lasso, Marixa. *Myths of Harmony: Race and Republicanism during the Age of Revolution, Colombia, 1795–1831.* Pittsburgh, PA: University of Pittsburgh Press, 2007.

Limpki, John M. "Afro-Yungueño Speech: The Long-Lost 'Black' Spanish." *Spanish in Context* 4, no. 1 (2007): 1–43.

Lockhart, James. *Of Things of the Indies.* Stanford, CA: Stanford University Press, 1999.

———. *Spanish Peru, 1532–1560.* Madison: University of Wisconsin Press, 1968.

Mallon, Florencia E. *Peasant and Nation: The Making of Postcolonial Mexico and Peru.* Berkeley: University of California Press, 1995.

———. *The Defense of Community in Peru's Central Highlands: Peasant Struggle and Capitalist Transition, 1860–1940.* Princeton, NJ: Princeton University Press, 1983.

———. *Peasant and Nation: The Making of Postcolonial Mexico and Peru.* Berkeley: University of California Press, 1995.

Manning, Patrick. *The African Diaspora: A History through Culture.* New York: Columbia University Press, 2010.

Maza, Genaro. "Motivaciones de 'Los caballeros del delito.'" In Enrique López Albújar, *Los Caballeros del Delito,* 7–17. Piura: Centro de Investigación y Promoción del Campesinado, 1993.

Meléndez, Mariselle. "Patria, Criollos and Blacks: Imagining the Nation in the *Mercurio Peruano,* 1791–1795." *Colonial Latin American Review* 15, no. 2 (December 2006), 207–27.

Méndez G., Cecilia. "Incas Si, Indios No: Notes on Peruvian Creole Nationalism and Its Contemporary Crisis." *Journal of Latin American Studies* 28, no.1 (February 1996), 197–225.

———. *The Plebeian Republic: The Huanta Rebellion and the Making of the Peruvian State, 1820–1850.* Durham, NC: Duke University Press, 2005.

Mintz, Sidney, and Richard Price. *The Birth of African American Culture: An Anthropological Perspective.* Boston, MA: Beacon Press, 1992. Originally published as *An Anthropological Approach to the Afro-American Past.* Philadelphia: Institute for the Study of Human Issues, 1976.

Mosher, Jeffrey. "Political Mobilization, Party Ideology, and Lusophobia in Nineteenth-Century Brazil: Pernambuco, 1822–1850." *Hispanic American Historical Review* 80, no. 44 (2000): 881–912.

Moya, José C. *Cousins and Strangers: Spanish Immigrants in Buenos Aires, 1850–1930.* Berkeley: University of California Press, 1998.

Nazzari, Muriel. "Vanishing Indians: The Social Construction of Race in Colonial São Paulo." *Americas* 57, no. 4 (April 2001): 497–524.

Nemtzow, Mary. "Acotaciones al Costumbrismo Peruano." *Revista Iberoamericana* 15, no. 29 (July 1949): 45–62.

Nugent, David. *Modernity at the Edges of Empire: State, Individual, and Nation in the Northern Peruvian Andes, 1885–1935*. Stanford, CA: Stanford University Press, 1997.

Orrego, Juan Luis. *La República Oligárquica (1850–1950)* (website).

O'Toole, Rachel Sarah. *Bound Lives: Africans, Indians, and the Making of Race in Colonial Peru*. Pittsburgh, PA: University of Pittsburgh Press, 2012.

O'Toole, Rachel Sarah, Ben Vinson III, and Sherwin K. Bryant, eds. *Africans to Spanish America: Expanding the Diaspora*. Urbana: University of Illinois Press, 2012.

Paredes, Luis F. "Perú Negro: Choreographing and performing Afro-Peruvian identity, 1969 to the Present." PhD diss., State University of New York at Albany, 2015.

Peloso, Vincent C. "Cotton Planters, the State, and Rural Labor Policy: Ideological Origins of the Peruvian República Aristocrática, 1895–1908." *Americas* 40, no. 2 (October 1983): 209–28.

———. "Racial Conflict and Identity Crisis in Wartime Peru: Revisiting the Cañete Massacre of 1881." *Social Identities* 11, no. 5 (August 2006): 467–88.

Peloso, Vincent C., and José Ragas. "Estadística y Población en el Perú Postcolonial: El Desconocido Censo de Lima de 1860." *Histórica* XXV, no. 2 (2001): 275–93.

Pérez Cantó, Pilar. "La Población de Lima en el Siglo XVIII." Universidad Autónoma de Madrid, *Boletín americanista* (1982), 383–407, 389–90. "Dialnet."

Pike, Frederick. *The Modern History of Peru*. New York: Frederick A. Praeger, 1967.

Poole, Deborah. *Vision, Race, and Modernity: A Visual Economy of the Andean Image World*. Princeton, NJ: Princeton University Press, 1997.

Quiroz Ávila, Rubén. *La Razón Racial: Clemente Palma y el Racismo a Fines del Siglo XIX*. Lima: Universidad Científica del Sur, 2010.

Restall, Matthew, ed. *Beyond Black and Red: African-Native Relations in Colonial Latin America*. Albuquerque: University of New Mexico Press, 2005.

Rodríguez Flores, Eduar Antonio. "El Ritmo del Retraso. La Construcción del Afrodescendiente como Mecanismo Deslegitimador de la Política en Zamacueca Política (1859)." Lima: Universidad Peruana de Ciencias Aplicadas. *Repositorio Académico* UPC, Juegos Florales, 2015.

Rodríguez Pastor, Humberto. *Negritud: Afroperuanos: Resistencia y Existencia*. Lima: Centro de Desarrollo Étnico, 2008.

Sabato, Hilda. *Republics of the New World: The Revolutionary Political Experiment in 19th Century Latin America*. Princeton, NJ: Princeton University Press, 2018.

Sanchez, Robert L. "Black Mosaic: The Assimilation and Marginalization of Afro-Peruvians in Post-Abolition Peru, 1854–1930." PhD diss., University of Illinois at Urbana-Champaign, 2008.

Sanders, Edith. "The Hamitic Hypothesis; Its Origin and Functions in Time Perspective." *Journal of African History* 10, no. 4 (1969): 521–32.

Seed, Patricia. "The Social Dimensions of Race: Mexico City 1753." *Hispanic American Historical Review* 62, no. 4 (November 1982): 569–606.

Skidmore, Thomas. *Black into White: Race and Nationality in Brazilian Thought*. Durham, NC: Duke University Press, 1974.

Skidmore, Thomas, and Peter H. Smith. *Modern Latin America*. 3rd ed. New York: Oxford University Press, 1992.

Sobrevilla Perea, Natalia. *The Caudillo of the Andes: Andrés de Santa Cruz*. Cambridge: Cambridge University Press, 2011.

Stein, Steve. *Populism in Peru: The Emergence of the Masses and the Politics of Social Control*. Madison: University of Wisconsin Press, 1980.

Stepan, Nancy Leys. *The Hour of Eugenics: Race, Gender, and Nation in Latin America*. Ithaca, NY: Cornell University Press, 1991.

Stern, Steve J., ed. *Resistance, Rebellion, and Consciousness in the Andean Peasant World, 18th to 20th Centuries*. Madison: University of Wisconsin Press, 1987.

Stern, Steve J. *Shining and Other Paths: War and Society in Peru, 1980–1995*. Durham, NC: Duke University Press, 1998.

Sumalavia, Ricardo. *Ricardo Palma: Narrativa Completa*. Lima: Pontificia Universidad Católica del Perú, 2006.

Summer, Doris. *Foundational Fictions: The National Romances of Latin America*. Berkeley: University of California Press, 1991.

Telles, Edward. *Pigmentocracies: Ethnicity, Race, and Color in Latin America*. Chapel Hill: University of North Carolina Press, 2014.

Tannenbaum, Frank. *Slave and Citizen: The Classic Comparative Study of Race Relations in the Americas*. Boston, MA: Beacon Press, 1992. Originally published in 1946.

Thurner, Mark. *From Two Republics to One Divided: Contradictions of Postcolonial Nationmaking in Andean Peru*. Durham, NC: Duke University Press, 1997.

———. *Sebastián Lorente: Escritos Fundacionales de Historia Peruana*. Lima: Fondo Editorial Universidad Nacional Mayor de San Marcos, 2005.

Thurner, Mark, and Andrés Guerrero, eds. *After Spanish Rule: Postcolonial Predicaments of the Americas*. Durham, NC: Duke University Press, 2003.

Trouillot, Michel-Rolph. *Silencing the Past: Power and the Production of History*. Boston, MA: Beacon Press, 1992.

Valcarcél, Luis Eduardo. *Ruta Cultural del Perú*. Lima: Editorial Universal, 1945. Biblioteca Municipal de Piura.

Valdiviezo, Laura Alicia. "Interculturality for Afro-Peruvians: Towards a Racially Inclusive Education in Peru." *International Education Journal* 7, no. 1 (2006): 26–35.

Vicuña MacKenna, Benjamin. *Historia de la Campaña de Lima, 1880–1881*. Santiago: Ed. Rafael Jover, 1881.

Vinson, Ben, III. *Before Mestizaje: The Frontiers of Race and Caste in Colonial Mexico*. Cambridge: Cambridge University Press, 2017.

Wade, Peter. *Blackness and Race Mixture: The Dynamics of Racial Identity in Colombia*. Baltimore, MD: Johns Hopkins University Press, 1993.

Warren, Adam. *Medicine and Politics in Colonial Peru: Population Growth and the Bourbon Reforms*. Pittsburgh, PA: University of Pittsburgh Press, 2010.

Weismantel, Mary. *Cholas and Pishtacos: Stories of Race and Sex in the Andes*. Chicago, IL: University of Chicago Press, 2001.

Zimmerman, Eduardo A. "Racial Ideas and Social Reform: Argentina, 1890–1916." *Hispanic American Historical Review* 72, no.1 (February 1992): 23–46.

Index